$57.50

THE ECONOMIC DEVELOPMENT OF IRELAND IN THE TWENTIETH CENTURY

CONTEMPORARY ECONOMIC HISTORY OF EUROPE
SERIES

Edited by Derek Aldcroft

THE ECONOMIC DEVELOPMENT OF IRELAND IN THE TWENTIETH CENTURY

KIERAN A. KENNEDY, THOMAS GIBLIN
and DEIRDRE McHUGH

ROUTLEDGE
London and New York

First published in 1988 by
Routledge
11 New Fetter Lane, London EC4P 4EE

Published in the USA by
Routledge
in association with Routledge, Chapman & Hall, Inc.
29 West 35th Street, New York, NY 10001

Printed and bound in Great Britain by
Mackays of Chatham PLC, Chatham, Kent

British Library Cataloguing in Publication Data

Kennedy, Kieran A. (Kieran Anthony)
    The economic development of Ireland in
    the twentieth century
    1. Ireland. Economic development.
    1900–1987
    I. Title II. Giblin, Thomas
    III. McHugh, Deirdre
    330.9415′082

    ISBN 0–415–00621–X (Hbk)
        0–415–02651–2 (Pbk)

Contents

Part Three: Key Issues in Irish Economic Development

Tables

Figures

Acknowledgements

We would like to thank the following for helpful comments on earlier drafts of some or all of this study: Professor D.H. Aldcroft, University of Leicester; Professor L.M. Cullen, Dr P.J. Drudy, Mr A. Matthews and Professor D. McAleese of Trinity College, Dublin; Professor J. Lee of University College, Cork; Dr C. Ó Gráda of University College, Dublin; Professor N. Gibson of the University of Ulster at Coleraine; Mr D.S. Johnson of Queen's University of Belfast; Dr J. Bradley, Dr R. Breen, Mr J. FitzGerald, Professor D. Hannan, Professor R. O'Connor and Dr E. O'Malley of The Economic and Social Research Institute; Professor P. Lynch, Professor T. Wilson and Dr F. Kennedy.

Abbreviations

ACOT	An Chomhairle Oiliúna Talmhaíochta (Council for Development in Agriculture)
AFT	An Foras Talúntais (Agricultural Institute)
AIFTAA	Anglo-Irish Free Trade Area Agreement
CAP	Common Agricultural Policy
CIO	Committee on Industrial Organisation
CIP	Census of Industrial Production
EFTA	European Free Trade Association
EMS	European Monetary System
ESRI	The Economic and Social Research Institute (Dublin)
GDP	Gross domestic product
GICOR	Gross incremental capital/output ratio
GIPR	Gross investment/productivity ratio
GNDI	Gross national disposable income
GNP	Gross national product
IDA	Industrial Development Authority
NESC	National Economic and Social Council
NIEC	National Industrial and Economic Council
PPP	Purchasing power parity
R & D	Research and development
SIP	Small Industry Programme

For convenience, 'EEC' has been used throughout to designate the European Community, although in recent years 'EC' is the preferred official designation.

Editor's Introduction

Derek Aldcroft†

By comparison with the nineteenth century, the twentieth has been very much more turbulent, both economically and politically. Two world wars and a great depression are sufficient to substantiate this claim without invoking the problems of more recent times. Yet despite these setbacks Europe's economic performance in the present century has been very much better than anything recorded in the historical past, thanks largely to the super-boom conditions following the post-Second World War reconstruction period. Thus, in the period 1946–75, or 1950–73, the annual increase in total European GNP *per capita* was 4.8 and 4.5 per cent respectively, as against a compound rate of just under 1 per cent in the nineteenth century (1800–1913) and the same during the troubled years between 1913 and 1950. As Bairoch points out, within a generation or so European *per capita* income rose slightly more than in the previous 150 years (between 1947 and 1975 by 250 per cent, and between 1800 and 1948 by 225 per cent) and, on rough estimates for the half century before 1800, by about as much as in the preceding two centuries.[1]

The dynamic growth and relative stability of the 1950s and 1960s may, however, belie the natural order of things, as the events of the later 1970s and early 1980s demonstrate. It would certainly seem unlikely that the European economy — or the world economy for that matter — will see a lasting return to the relatively stable conditions of the nineteenth century. No doubt the experience of the present century can easily lead to an exaggerated idea regarding the stability of the previous one. Nevertheless, one may justifiably claim that for much of the nineteenth century there was a degree of harmony in the economic development of the major powers and between the metropolitan economies and the periphery which has been noticeably absent since 1914. Indeed, one of the reasons for the

---

† Head of the Department of Economic and Social History, University of Leicester

apparent success of the gold standard post 1870, despite the aura of stability it allegedly shed, was the absence of serious external disturbances and imbalance in development among the major participating powers. As Triffin writes,

> the residual harmonization of national monetary and credit policies depended far less on *ex post* corrective action, requiring an extreme flexibility, downward as well as upward, of national price and wage levels, than on an *ex ante* avoidance of substantial disparities in cost competitiveness and the monetary policies that would allow them to develop.[2]

Whatever the reasons for the absence of serious economic and political conflict, the fact remains that through to 1914 international development and political relations, though subject to strains of a minor nature from time to time, were never exposed to internal and external shocks of the magnitude experienced in the twentieth century. Not surprisingly, therefore, the First World War rudely shattered the liberal tranquillity of the later nineteenth and early twentieth centuries. At the time few people realised that it was going to be a lengthy war and, even more importantly, fewer still had any conception of the enormous impact it would have on economic and social relationships. Moreover, there was a general feeling, readily accepted in establishment circles, that following the period of hostilities it would be possible to resume where one had left off — in short, to recreate the conditions of the pre-war era.

For obvious reasons this was clearly an impossible task, though for nearly a decade statesmen strove to get back to what they regarded as 'normalcy', or the natural order of things. In itself this was one of the profound mistakes of the first post-war decade since it should have been clear, even at that time, that the war and post-war clearing-up operations had undermined Europe's former equipoise and sapped her strength to a point where the economic system had become very sensitive to external shocks. The map of Europe had been rewritten under the political settlements following the war and this further weakened the economic viability of the continent and left a dangerous political vacuum in its wake. Moreover, it was not only in the economic sphere that Europe's strength had been reduced: in political and social terms the European continent was seriously weakened and many countries in the early post-war years were in a state of social ferment and upheaval.[3]

Generally speaking, Europe's economic and political fragility was ignored in the 1920s, probably more out of ignorance than intent. In their efforts to resurrect the pre-war system, statesmen believed they were providing a viable solution to the problems of the day, and the fact that Europe shared in the prosperity of the later 1920s seemed to vindicate their judgement. However, the post-war problems — war debts, external imbalances, currency issues, structural distortions and the like — defied solutions along traditional lines. The most notable of these was the attempt to restore a semblance of the gold standard in the belief that it had been responsible for the former stability. The upshot was a set of haphazard and inconsistent currency stabilisation policies which took no account of the changes in relative costs and prices among countries since 1914. Consequently, despite the apparent prosperity of the latter half of the decade, Europe remained in a state of unstable equilibrium, and therefore vulnerable to any external shocks. The collapse of US foreign lending from the middle of 1928 and the subsequent downturn of the American economy a year later exposed the weaknesses of the European economy. The structural supports were too weak to withstand violent shocks and so the edifice disintegrated.

That the years 1929–1932/3 experienced one of the worst depressions and financial crises in history is not altogether surprising given the convergence of many unfavourable forces at that point in time. Moreover, the fact that a cyclical downturn occurred against the backdrop of structural disequilibrium only served to exacerbate the problem, while the inherent weakness of certain financial institutions in Europe and the United States led to extreme instability. The intensity of the crisis varied a great deal but few countries, apart from the USSR, were unaffected. The action of governments tended to aggravate rather than ease the situation. Such policies included expenditure cuts, monetary contraction, the abandonment of the gold standard, and protective measures designed to insulate domestic economies from external events. In effect these policies, while sometimes affording temporary relief to hard-pressed countries, in the end led to income destruction rather than income creation. When recovery finally set in in the winter of 1932–3 it owed little to policy contributions, though subsequently some Western governments did attempt more ambitious programmes of stimulation, while many of the poorer Eastern European countries adopted autarchic policies in an effort to push forward industrialisation. Apart from some notable exceptions, in particular Germany and Sweden, recovery from the slump, especially in terms of employment generation, was slow and patchy and even at the peak of the upswing in 1937 many countries were still operating below their full resource capacity. A combination of weak real growth forces and structural imbalances in development would no doubt have ensured a continuation of resource under-utilisation had not rearmament and the outbreak of war served to close the gap.

Thus, by the eve of the Second World War Europe as a whole was in a much weaker state economically than it had been in 1914, with her shares of world income and trade notably reduced. Worse still, she emerged from the Second World War in 1945 in a more prostrate condition than in 1918, with output levels well down on those of pre-war. In terms of the loss of life, physical destruction and decline in living standards, Europe's position was much worse than after the First World War. On the other hand, recovery from wartime destruction was stronger and more secure than in the previous case. This can in part be attributed to the fact that in the reconstruction phase of the later 1940s some of the mistakes and blunders of the earlier experience were avoided. Inflation, for example, was contained more readily between 1939 and 1945 and the violent inflations of the early 1920s were not for the most part perpetuated after the Second World War.

With the exception of Berlin, the map of Europe was divided much more cleanly and neatly than after 1918. Though it resulted in two ideological power blocs, the East and the West, it did nevertheless dispose of the power vacuum in Central/East Europe which had been a source of friction and contention in the inter-war years. Moreover, the fact that each bloc was dominated or backed by a wealthy and rival superpower meant that support was forthcoming for the satellite countries. With the exception of East Germany, the vanquished powers were not burdened by unreasonable exactions, which had been the cause of so much bitterness and squabbling during the 1920s. Finally, governments no longer hankered after the 'halcyon' pre-war days — not surprisingly, given the rugged conditions of the 1930s. This time it was to be planning for the future which occupied their attention, and which found expression in the commitment to maintain full employment and all that that entailed in terms of growth and stability, together with a conscious desire to build upon the earlier social welfare foundations. In wider perspective, the new initiatives found positive expression in terms of a readiness to co-operate internationally, particularly in trade and monetary matters. The liberal American aid programme for the West in the later 1940s was a concrete manifestation of this new approach.

Thus, despite the enormity of the reconstruction task facing Europe at the end of the war, the recovery effort, after some initial difficulties, was both strong and sustained, and by the early 1950s Europe had reached a point from which she could look to the future with some confidence. During the next two decades or so, virtually every European country, in keeping with the buoyant conditions in the world economy as a whole, expanded very much more rapidly than in the past. This was the super-growth phase during which Europe regained a large part of the relative losses which had been incurred between 1914 and 1945. The Eastern Bloc countries forged ahead the most rapidly under their planned regimes, while the Western democracies achieved their success under mixed enterprise systems with varying degrees of market freedom. In both cases the state played a far more important role than hitherto, and neither system could be said to be without its problems. The planning mechanism in Eastern Europe never functioned as smoothly as originally anticipated by its proponents, and in due course most of the socialist countries were forced to make modifications to their systems of control. Similarly, the semi-market systems of the West did not always produce the right results so that governments were obliged to intervene to an increasing extent. One of the major problems encountered by the demand-managed economies of the West was that of trying to achieve a series of basically incompatible objectives simultaneously — namely, full employment, price stability, growth and stability, and external equilibrium. Given the limited policy weapons available to governments, this proved to be an impossible task to accomplish in most cases, though West Germany managed to achieve the seemingly impossible for much of the period.

Although these incompatible objectives proved elusive *in toto*, throughout most of the period to the early 1970s there was little cause for serious alarm. It is true that there were minor lapses from full employment; fluctuations still occurred but they were very moderate and took the form of growth cycles; some countries experienced periodic balance of payments problems; while prices generally rose continuously though at fairly modest annual rates. Such lapses could readily be accommodated, however, even with the limited policy choices, within an economic system that was growing rapidly. Furthermore, there was some consolation from the fact that the planned socialist economies were not immune from some of these problems, especially later on in the period. By the later 1960s, despite some warning signs that conditions might be deteriorating, it seemed that Europe had entered a phase of perpetual prosperity not dissimilar to the one the Americans had conceived in the 1920s.

Unfortunately, as in the earlier case, this illusion was to be rudely shattered in the first half of the 1970s. The super-growth phase of the post-war period culminated in the somewhat feverish and speculative boom of 1972–3. By the following year the growth trend had been reversed, the old business cycle had reappeared and most countries were experiencing inflation at higher rates than at any time in the past half century. From that time onwards, according to Samuel Brittan, 'everything seems to have gone sour and we have had slower growth, rising unemployment, faster inflation, creeping trade restrictions and all the symptoms of stagflation.'[4] In fact, compared with the relatively placid and successful decades of the 1950s and 1960s, the later 1970s and early 1980s have been extremely turbulent, reminiscent in some respects of the inter-war years.

It should of course be stressed that by comparison with the inter-war years, or even with the nineteenth century, economic growth has been quite respectable since the sharp boom and contraction in the first half of the 1970s. It only appears poor in relation to the rapid growth between 1950 and 1973 and the question arises as to whether this period should be regarded as somewhat abnormal, with the shift to a lower growth profile in the 1970s being the inevitable consequence of long-term forces involving some reversal of the special growth-promoting factors of the previous decades. In effect, this would imply some weakening of real growth forces in the 1970s, being aggravated by specific factors — for example, energy crises and policy variables.

The most disturbing feature of this later period was not

simply that growth slowed down but that it became more erratic, with longer recessionary periods involving absolute contractions in output, and that it was accompanied by mounting unemployment and high inflation. Traditional Keynesian demand-management policies were unable to cope with these problems and, in an effort to deal with them, particularly inflation, governments resorted to ultra-defensive policies and monetary control. These strategies were not very successful either, since the need for social and political compromise in policy-making meant that they were not applied rigorously enough to eradicate inflation, yet at the same time their influence was sufficiently strong to dampen the rate of growth, thereby exacerbating unemployment. In other words, economic management is faced with an awkward policy dilemma in the prevailing situation of high unemployment and rapid inflation: policy action to deal with either one tends to make the other worse, while the constraint of the political consensus produces an uneasy compromise in an effort to 'minimise macroeconomic misery'.[5] Rostow has neatly summarised the constraints involved in this context:

> Taxes, public expenditure, interest rates, and the supply of money are not determined antiseptically by men free to move economies along a Phillips curve to an optimum trade-off between the rate of unemployment and the rate of inflation. Fiscal and monetary policy are, inevitably, living parts of the democratic political process.[6]

Whether the current problems of contemporary Western capitalism or the difficulties associated with the planning mechanisms of the socialist countries of Eastern Europe are amenable to solutions remains to be seen. It is not, for the most part, the purpose of the volumes in this series to speculate about the future. Rather, the series is designed to provide clear and balanced surveys of the economic development and problems of individual European countries from the end of the First World War through to the present, against the background of the general economic and political trends of the time. Though most European countries have shared a common experience for much of the period, it is nonetheless true that there has been considerable variation among countries in the rate of development and the manner in which they have sought to regulate and control their economies. The problems encountered have also varied widely, in part reflecting disparities in levels of development.

While most European countries had, by the end of the First World War, achieved some industrialisation and made the initial breakthrough into modern economic growth, there nevertheless existed a wide gulf between the richer and poorer nations. At the beginning of the period the most advanced region was north-west Europe including Scandinavia and as one moved east and south so the level of *per capita* income relative to the European average declined. In some cases, notably Bulgaria, Yugoslavia and Portugal, income levels were barely half the European average. The gap has narrowed over time but the general pattern remains basically the same. Between 1913 and 1973 most of the poorer countries in the east and south (apart from Spain) raised their real *per capita* income levels relative to the European average, with most of the improvement taking place after 1950. Even so, by 1973 most of them, with the exception of Czechoslovakia, still fell below the European average, ranging from 9–15 per cent in the case of the USSR, Hungary, Greece, Bulgaria and Poland, to as much as 35–45 per cent for Spain, Portugal, Romania and Yugoslavia. Italy and Ireland also recorded *per capita* income levels some way below the European average.[7]

In their study of the Irish economy, Kennedy, Giblin, and McHugh draw particular attention to the problems of structural transformation and their influence on the rate of economic progress in the twentieth century. In 1913 Ireland was not an especially poor country by European standards since its ranking in terms of the level of income *per capita* was somewhat above the European average. However, much of the improvement since the Famine had arisen by virtue of the population decline and specialisation in favourably priced livestock production. On the other hand, the structural characteristics of the economy were probably closer to those of East-central European countries rather than to those of the West. Low-income agriculture formed the main base of the economy with a heavy dependence on the British market, while the small manufacturing-sector was dominated by the food processing and drink industries.

The transition to a more viable structure was a slow and painful process since the shift away from agriculture posed employment problems for an economy whose productivity growth tended to match or exceed that of output. In any case, until the growth boom of the post-war years the international economic environment was scarcely conducive to rapid transformation. Initially, therefore, the Irish economy was structurally unready to take advantage of the situation and it was not until the decade and a half prior to the entry to the EEC that Ireland achieved fast growth and shifted from an agricultural to an industrial economy. Even this burst of activity did not prevent a slippage in the European league table over the long term (1913–85) though with some modest relative improvement *vis-à-vis* Britain. Moreover, structural problems still remained and became all too evident in the more unstable international climate of the later 1970s and early 1980s.

Legacies of the past and external events may have been important determinants of Irish economic progress, but additionally economic policy has not always been a propitious factor. In fact in many respects Irish economic policy all too closely reiterated some of the mistakes of British policy. As the authors note, it lacked long-term perspective, the different policy measures did not always fit together 'so that the instruments have often been implemented on a piecemeal basis, sometimes even working against each other', while the education system 'went its own way without much serious examination of the purposes of education, and which for long had little connection with the world of work'. Such criticisms have a familiar ring to them.

On the other hand, viewed in the context of the British economy, Ireland put up a creditable performance in the twentieth century. Given the respective resource stocks and characteristics of the two economies in 1913, it would have been difficult then to predict that in the next half century or so Ireland would have matched the British rate of growth and exceeded it in *per capita* terms. It is true of course that Britain was a growth laggard in this period and that perhaps Ireland should have done better, but in view of the many impediments that country faced, the performance should not be judged too harshly.

This study covers many issues relating to problems of growth and development which are germane to other economies and as such it will provide a wide range of reference for students of the subject.

NOTES

1. P. Bairoch, 'Europe's Gross National Product: 1800–1975', *The Journal of European Economic History*, 5 (Fall 1976), pp. 298–99.

2. R. Triffin, *Our International Monetary System: Yesterday, Today and Tomorrow* (1968, New York), p. 14; see also D.H. Aldcroft, *From Versailles to Wall Street, 1919–1929* (1977), pp. 162–4. Some of the costs of the gold standard system may however have been borne by the countries of the periphery, for example the Latin American.

3. See P.N. Stearns, *European Society in Upheaval* (1967).

4. *Financial Times*, 14 February 1980.

5. J.O.N. Perkins, *The Macroeconomic Mix to Stop Stagflation* (1980).

6. W.W. Rostow, *Getting From Here to There* (1979).

7. See Bairoch, 'Europe's Gross National Product', pp. 297, 307.

Part One

Introduction

1

The State of the Economy at Independence

Like many other features of Irish history, the economic development of Ireland has been profoundly affected by the neighbour-
ing and larger island of Great Britain. British involvement in
Ireland began as early as the twelfth century, with the Norman
invasion of 1169, but it was not until the seventeenth century
that the conquest was complete. With the termination in 1800 of
its largely subordinate parliament, Ireland became an integral
part of the United Kingdom under the Act of Union. Independence was achieved under a Treaty signed in London on 6
December 1921, which accorded dominion status to the Irish
Free State comprising 26 of the 32 counties of Ireland. The
other six counties, known as Northern Ireland, remained part
of the United Kingdom, with limited devolved government.

Our study is primarily concerned with the period since
independence, and with the part of Ireland that became
independent. In this introductory chapter, however, we
examine the state of the economy in the country as a whole on
the eve of independence, and how that state was reached.
Section 1.1 describes the economic process leading up to that
point in terms of three key elements: population, land, and
industry. Section 1.2 compares the level and rate of economic
progress achieved prior to independence with those of other
European countries. The chapter concludes with an outline of
the remainder of the study.

1.1 POPULATION, LAND, AND INDUSTRY

The population of all Ireland in 1921 was 4,354,000, of which

3

3,096,000 (or 71 per cent) were located in the 26 counties. With a total land area of 32,000 square miles, the population density, 137 per square mile, was low compared with the figure of almost 500 for Great Britain. The most striking feature about the population in 1921, however, was that it was little more than half the level of 80 years earlier. The singularity of this position is readily illustrated by comparison with the rest of the United Kingdom. In 1841, the population of Ireland was over three times that of Scotland and more than one-half that of England and Wales. By 1921, the population of Ireland was 10 per cent less than that of Scotland and only one-ninth that of England and Wales.

The decline in population dated from the Great Famine of 1845–7, when the potato, the staple diet of the cottiers and farm labourers, failed. In the course of the Famine itself, it is estimated that between one-half and one million people died — largely from fever due to malnutrition rather than outright starvation — and distress continued to 1850. In the six years from 1847 to 1852, over one and a quarter million persons emigrated to North America, and there was also substantial emigration to Britain. Apart from the immediate population loss, however, the Famine also marks a fundamental break in Ireland's long-term demographic history. In the century preceding the Famine the total population rose at least three-fold and possibly even four-fold, whereas in the following century it halved in size.

The exceptionally rapid Irish population growth in the century preceding the Famine reflected a very high birth-rate. In turn, this was due to high marital fertility and perhaps also to somewhat earlier marriage than was common in the rest of Europe. In the two decades immediately prior to the Famine, birth and marriage rates were probably falling. Certainly there was substantial emigration: in the 30 years preceding the Famine, emigration totalled about one and a half million, predominantly to North America and Great Britain. Consequently, the population data indicate a pronounced deceleration in the rate of growth after 1821 and well before the Famine. Recent scholarship has come to regard the Famine as serving to accelerate trends already in train, rather than as a fundamental watershed.

Nevertheless, population decline began with the Famine and continued for over a century. The previous rate of emigration was dwarfed by the post-Famine experience, when over 5 million persons emigrated in the period up to 1921, most of them young single adults rather than families. Attitudes towards marriage also changed drastically. This was not due solely to the Famine but also to changes in the land tenure system, discussed below, which had started before the Famine. The crude marriage rate per thousand population had fallen from 7 to 5 by 1880, the average age of brides had risen from 21 to 28 by 1914, while the proportion of females never married in the age-group 45–54 had increased from 12 per cent to 26 per cent by 1911.[1] On the other hand, the fertility of marriage remained high, and the net outcome was a birth-rate somewhat above 20 — not abnormal in comparison with other countries.

This period, of course, was one of great migration in Europe generally. What was different about Irish migration was its scale and the fact that relatively little of it was internal migration. Although all areas suffered a substantial fall in population up to 1921, the decline was not evenly spread: it was largest in the provinces of Connacht and Munster (roughly, the west and south of the country), a little below average in Leinster (the east) and well below average in Ulster (the north). In the decade 1901–11 the decline had almost ceased in the provinces of Ulster and Leinster, but continued apace in the other two provinces.

1.1.1 Land and agriculture

Ireland's demographic experience was intrinsically bound up with the land tenure and agriculture systems. The seventeenth century plantations resulted in much of the land being owned by landlords who differed in religion and national allegiance from their tenants. Probably between one-quarter and one-third of the land was owned by absentees. The bulk of the land was operated by tenant farmers. At the bottom of the social hierarchy were the labouring classes, the cottiers and farm labourers. These were the classes which expanded most prolifically in the late eighteenth and early nineteenth centuries, and which were the chief victims of the Famine.

The ease of marriage and its high fertility in pre-Famine Ireland are generally associated with ready access to a plot of land and reliance on the potato as the staple diet of the cottiers and labourers — though other factors were also involved. The doubling of the price of corn between 1760 and 1810 stimulated the process of subdivision by encouraging labour-intensive tillage. Tenant farmers did not have enough working capital to pay wages for the increased labour needed to produce corn, and were willing to dole out strips of ground for potato growing in return for labour. There were grave risks in such heavy dependence by so many on a single foodstuff, which was liable to several diseases, which could be damaged by extremes of wet or frost, which was bulky and expensive to transport, and which could not be stored for more than twelve months at the outside. However, the more fundamental problem was not shortage of food but poverty arising from extreme inequality. The poor did not have money or other resources to buy corn or meat, much of which were exported.

Following the slump in agricultural prices after the Napoleonic wars, there was a tendency for landowners to try to consolidate holdings and to extend pasture, but the degree of consolidation was limited prior to the Famine. Consolidation proceeded more rapidly after the Famine and the agricultural labour force declined substantially. The number of rural labourers fell from 700,000 in 1845 to 300,000 in 1910; the number of cottiers with less than 5 acres fell even more, relatively, from 300,000 to 62,000; and there was also a big decline in the number of farmers with between 5 and 15 acres from 310,000 to 154,000. On the other hand, the number of farmers with more than 15 acres rose slightly from 277,000 to 304,000.[2]

Evictions, though psychologically important in the agitation for a new system of land tenure, were not the main agency of consolidation of holdings. It was in fact the tenant farmer, more than the landlord, who effected the change by his response to the economic conditions facing him. Livestock became more profitable than grain not only because of relative output price changes but also because its production cost rose more slowly. Labour was less plentiful due to Famine deaths and emigration, and wages rose. As the influx of North American grain increased, it became clearer that the Irish climate was never ideal for the harvesting of grain because of the frequency of rainfall. Even in the case of livestock, Irish climatic conditions favoured land-extensive production, especially beef, since they are exceptionally suitable to the growth of grass but less suitable to the harvesting of grass for winter feed. These conditions encouraged a low input/low output system of livestock production with a high degree of seasonality, which was somewhat less acute in beef than in dairying since, due to the mild winter, beef cattle could be left out on grass much longer with less reduction in yield. As pasture gained at the expense of tillage, the demand for the labour of assisting relatives, cottiers and farm labourers declined, and they were forced either to emigrate or to adopt an entirely different perspective on marriage. At the same time, agitation for changes in the relations between landlord and tenant farmer intensified, culminating in a series of land acts, the most important of which was the Wyndham Act of 1903. The eventual outcome was that most tenants bought out their farms with the aid of long-term government loans.

Thus, the 70 years or so leading up to independence witnessed the transformation of the land tenure system to one of peasant proprietorship. Whatever the merits of this change on social grounds, it did not necessarily make for a more dynamic agricultural sector in terms of economic production. Access to technical, marketing and other relevant information by the peasant proprietors was limited. As the age of inheritance increased, receptivity to technical progress declined. The changed practice in regard to marriage made for a cautious and conservative environment as a sizeable fraction of the land came to be held by ageing single farmers. In some cases there was scarcity of capital for development, but investment was also restricted by the unwillingness to take risks, engendered by the insecurity and instability of farm incomes.

1.1.2 Industry

Given that developments in agriculture were exacerbating the problem of rural surplus labour, the question arises as to why more of this was not absorbed into industry through internal migration. Despite the great rural exodus, however, the population of Ireland in the early 1920s remained largely a rural one with only one-third of the people living in towns. Why did Ireland not succeed in developing a larger industrial base? It may be pointed out, of course, that if Ireland is viewed not as a separate country, but merely as a region within the United Kingdom — as it was in fact up to 1921 — then the failure to develop a stronger industrial base appears less unusual. Among the larger European countries, regions as big as Ireland remained industrially undeveloped. Few, if any, however, experienced population decline comparable with that of Ireland. Moreover, the population outflow from Ireland did not mainly take the form of internal migration to other regions of the United Kingdom: the greater part represented overseas emigration unmatched in relative terms by any other European country or region.

It has also been pointed out that, even viewing Ireland as a separate country, the level of industrial development in the country as a whole was not uniquely low at the beginning of the twentieth century. While the share of the labour force engaged in industry in Ireland in 1911, at about one-fifth, was only half the share in Britain, it was of the same order as in some other European countries at the time, such as Italy, Spain and Portugal. True, industrial activity was highly concentrated within Ireland, but such concentration within countries was not unusual. In the six counties that became Northern Ireland, the share of the labour force in industry, at about 35 per cent, approached the British level, and even within Northern Ireland, industrial activity centred largely in and around Belfast. In the remainder of the country, which was to become the Irish Free State, the industrial labour force was only 13 per cent of the total, a low figure in comparison with any other West European nation.

While the foregoing considerations place Ireland's failure to industrialise in a wider context, they do not explain that failure. The question remains an important one not only because of its implications for the new independent state, but also because the nineteenth-century Irish experience was actually one of industrial decline outside the north-east — even though many of the conditions required for industrial development were favourable. In the second half of the century the country had a highly developed rail network. Its plentiful supply of labour was reasonably well-educated by the standards of the time. Capital in the aggregate was not scarce: indeed, Ireland had become a net exporter of capital. As regards export markets, it was adjacent, and had free access, to the richest industrial country in the world — though this could also constitute a negative factor as a strong competitor with Irish industry.

In fact, a minor industrial revolution took place in the last 20 years of the eighteenth century. Prior to this, restraints on Irish trade had been imposed by the British Parliament under the influence of mercantilist ideas, which impeded the development of some Irish industries. The pre-1800 Irish Parliament encouraged the development of industry through tariffs, subsidies or grants. The period was also one of general prosperity and many new industries sprang up. Under the Act of Union, however, which became effective from 1 January 1801, the Irish Parliament was abolished and provision was made for the elimination by 1824 of all tariffs between Great Britain and Ireland. The subsequent decline of Irish industry in the nineteenth century gave rise to the nationalist interpretation that Ireland's incipient industrial revolution was thwarted by the premature elimination of tariffs before indigenous industries were strong enough to withstand foreign competition.

The true position was more complex. Even as late as 1841, there were 696,000 persons who described themselves as textile workers, the majority engaged in domestic industry; by 1907 the number was down to 92,000 of whom 72,000 were employed in linen factories. While the decline in textiles dates from the first half of the nineteenth century, several other industries — such as iron-founding, milling, paper and tanning — continued to grow until the depression in Britain in the mid-1870s. Even granted that the removal of tariff protection was inimical to many industries, it must also be taken into the reckoning that free trade was favourable to other major industries which prospered — notably, brewing in Dublin and shipbuilding and related activities in Belfast. These were large export-orientated industries which profited from being able to import materials duty free and to export to larger markets.

Clearly there were other influences at work besides tariff reductions. The spread of the factory system and the substitution of machines for certain types of labour would have meant the demise of many traditional activities anyway even had tariffs been retained. Ireland lacked significant coal and iron resources which were closely linked to the new technologies. Cheaper transport increasingly opened up the Irish market to competition from British goods. While there was no national scarcity of capital, it is arguable that risk capital was hard to come by. Nor was access to capital the only constraint on investment. Among the developing middle class there was a great quest for the superior security of the professions and of trade, compared with industry — by no means an irrational response in a country that had suffered so many upheavals. The declining population, and the economic trends in agriculture favouring a low input/low output form of production, limited the growth of the domestic market. These disadvantages were reinforced by the strong tendencies already noted for industry to become concentrated in particular geographic regions. Such regions usually enjoyed an initial competitive advantage, in the form of, for example, close access to raw materials and fuel or proximity to markets. However, the initial advantages became greatly enhanced by internal and external economies of scale, enabling some locations to establish dominance at the expense of other locations.[3]

The focus of the nationalist interpretation was therefore too narrow. It laid undue stress on the role of a single instrument, tariff protection, without adequate recognition of the more pervasive market failures involved in the Irish industrial decline. It is possible that these forces might have been countered, at least in part, had there been an independent government which was prepared to play a much more active role in overcoming barriers to entry and expansion. In the prevailing *laissez-faire* environment, however, manufacturing in southern Ireland became more concentrated in food processing and drink, which by the 1920s accounted for two-thirds of total manufacturing net output. Most of the other industries that survived were those with a sheltered home market, protected by transport costs or other logistic factors such as access to local raw materials.

The north-east of the country, however, had an entirely different experience and the question arises as to why Belfast was so different from the rest of the country. Ulster had a considerable linen export industry even in the eighteenth century, organised on a domestic basis and extending into adjacent areas of the south. In the early nineteenth century the value of linen exports from Ireland (mainly from Ulster) exceeded exports of the other two major commodities, cattle and corn. The role of Belfast then was as an organising and trading centre and two-thirds of linen exports went through Belfast. The cotton industry was introduced in 1777 and expanded considerably in the next 40 years. It was aimed mainly at the home market and enjoyed protection from the Irish Parliament and preferential treatment under the Act of Union.

The removal of protection from cotton in 1824 threatened the future of textile production in Belfast, but this was offset by technological developments in linen. The technology for the power spinning of flax improved greatly in 1825, ensuring the concentration of spinning in Belfast, while rural industry was badly hit as a result. By 1841 the population of Belfast, at just over 70,000, had more than doubled since 1815, though it was still very much less than that of Dublin city, at 233,000. Yet even at this stage Belfast was more export-orientated than Dublin, as indicated by the fact that its trade of £7.9 million, half of which was linen, exceeded that of Dublin at £6.9 million.[4] Linen weaving was mechanised in the 1850s, and by reason of its strong competitive position, Belfast linen rapidly captured markets from British linen centres.

The labour force engaged in linen production was predominantly female at about 70 per cent. The next major industry to develop in Belfast, shipbuilding, offset this imbalance. More importantly, it ensured the continued industrial development of Belfast in the last quarter of the nineteenth century at a time when the growth of linen spinning tapered off as cotton regained lost markets following the ending of the American Civil War in 1865. There was already a tradition of shipbuilding in Belfast, the first firm of consequence being that of William Ritchie who came from Ayrshire in 1791. In addition, the textile industry in Belfast had stimulated significant engineering activities, including steam engines, and the local boilermaking industry created favourable conditions for the building of iron ships. It was the advent of Edward Harland from Tyneside in 1854, however, which gave the decisive impetus to the process of building the Belfast shipyards into the largest in the world. Four years later, in 1858, when he was still only 27 years of age, he bought out the ailing shipyard of Hickson, in which he was employed. Together with his partner, G.W. Wolff, who joined him in the early 1860s, they built the firm of Harland and Wolff from one employing 500 in 1861 to 9,000 by the end of the century.

Further developments grew out of these pioneering initiatives. The shipyard of Workman and Clark was formed in 1879 by Frank Workman, who had served his apprenticeship in Harland and Wolff. Sub-supply industries developed to meet the requirements of the basic industries: the largest rope-works in the United Kingdom and a thriving engineering industry for the manufacture and repair of textile machinery. By 1900, the population of Belfast had grown to 350,000, not far short of the population of Dublin and its suburbs. The contrast with Cork, the largest city in Munster and the port adjacent to some of the most fertile lands of Ireland, was even more striking. In 1821, the population of Cork was nearly three times that of Belfast, but by 1901 it had fallen by one-quarter and only amounted to one-fifth of the population of Belfast.

Lee's conclusion that Belfast's progress after 1848 was increasingly due to 'immigrant businessmen'[5] begs the question as to why Dublin or Cork did not attract more of the 'immigrant businessmen'. The immigrant businessmen were presumably attracted to Belfast, and flourished there, because of the more favourable industrial milieu. Whatever initial advantages the Belfast area possessed in the way of a more settled agricultural system, a more extensive domestic textile industry, and a key trading centre, were greatly magnified over time as industrial skills were acquired, venture capital accumulated and success in one activity opened up other possibilities. The disparate industrial performance of Belfast must be viewed pre-eminently as a virtuous cycle of cumulative causation, which, once in train, reinforced itself strongly.

1.2 COMPARATIVE INCOME LEVELS IN IRELAND AND EUROPE

We now turn to the quantification of the outcome of the developments described above in terms of total and *per capita* national product. There are several estimates of Ireland's total product around the time of independence which all suggest that average income *per capita* was about 60 per cent of the British level. An estimate by Cullen puts the gross national product (GNP) for all Ireland in 1911 at £150 million.[6] Dividing by the total Irish population in that year, the average GNP *per capita* would be £34. The latter figure represents 62 per cent of the UK level (including all Ireland) in 1911, as derived from Feinstein,[7] or just under 60 per cent of the average level in Great Britain. Cullen's estimate accords reasonably well with the level of Irish national product at about this time suggested by Feinstein himself, who states that Irish gross domestic product (GDP) accounted for about 6 per cent of the United Kingdom total in

1907.[8] If we assume that the 6 per cent figure held also in 1911, and if we apply it to Feinstein's estimate of £2,493 million for UK GNP at market prices in that year, then the Irish GNP figure would be £149·6 million — almost identical with Cullen's estimate. Later in this section we shall consider the relative position in the north and south of Ireland. Suffice it to say here that the available evidence indicates that the difference between the two areas was not so great as to invalidate treating all of Ireland as a single unit in this context.

These figures suggest that Ireland was substantially poorer than Britain; but given that Britain was economically one of the richest and most advanced countries in the world at the time, they also raise the possibility that Irish living standards may have compared favourably with much of the rest of Europe. This is confirmed by the figures in Table 1.1 showing GNP/GDP *per capita* in European and other countries in 1913 relative to the United Kingdom. Two sets of figures are shown for 1913. The first set in column (2) is based on Bairoch's estimates[9] and relates to GNP *per capita* valued at 1960 US relative prices. These figures show the UK as having the highest level of income *per capita* in Europe, with the Irish figure (relating to the south only here) as being about three-fifths of that of the UK. However, the Irish figure was only a little below the average for Western Europe as a whole and was almost 60 per cent higher than the level for Eastern Europe as a whole. In fact Ireland ranked tenth among the 23 European countries shown in the table, with an average income level greater than in Norway, Finland or Italy, for example, and only a little behind that of France, Austria and Sweden.

The second set of figures for 1913 in Table 1.1 relates to GDP *per capita* and was derived by ourselves in a manner similar to Bairoch but using largely different sources as outlined in the notes to the table. These figures put Ireland in a slightly less favourable light relative to the UK and several other European countries, and Ireland's ranking falls from tenth to twelfth among the 23 European countries. Whereas Bairoch's figures put Ireland's product *per capita* about 15 per cent above the mean of the European countries, the alternative figures suggest that it was marginally below the mean level. Given the uncertainties inevitably attaching to such estimates, both sets of figures are consistent with the broad conclusion that average income *per capita* in Ireland was not widely different from the

Table 1.1: Real product *per capita* in Europe and other countries relative to the UK, 1830, 1913 and 1985

	(1)	(2)	(3) alternative	(4)
	1830 UK=100	1913 UK=100	1913 UK=100	1985 UK=100
European countries (ranked in descending order of GNP *per capita* in 1913 in column 2)				
1. United Kingdom	100	100	100	100
2. Switzerland	65	84	91	123
3. Denmark	61	83	72	113
4. Belgium	65	76	78	98
5. West Germany	65	72	67	111
6. Netherlands	73	69	78	104
7. Sweden	64	66	59	116
8. Austria	65[a]	65	64	99
9. France	74	63	65	107
10. Ireland	40[b]	61	55	62
11. Norway	61	57	52	128
12. Finland	51	49	46	105
13. Czechoslovakia	–	47	63	86
14. Italy	65	43	56	99
15. Spain	54[a]	37	49	70
16. Poland	–	36[c]	51[c]	57
17. Hungary	–	35	53	67
18. Romania	36[a]	35	36	49
19. Soviet Union	49	32	37	72
20. Greece	39[a]	31	28	55
21. Portugal	68	31	26	51
22. Yugoslavia	38[a]	28	30	58
23. Bulgaria	36[a]	23	29	59
Other Countries				
United States	65	126	122	152
Canada	76	104	96	141
Australia	97[a]	102	107	108
New Zealand	70[a]	75	70	93
Japan	49	29	30	108

Notes: [a] 1860; [b] 1841; [c] 1929.
Sources: Cols (1) and (2): P. Bairoch, 'The main trends in national economic disparities since the industrial revolution' in P. Bairoch and M. Levy-Leboyer (eds), *Disparities in economic development since the industrial revolution* (St. Martin's Press, New York, 1981), Tables 1.4 and

1.6. The figures are based on estimates of GNP *per capita* at 1960 US dollars and prices. The country boundaries are those of 1970: hence the UK figures include Northern Ireland and exclude the south, while the 1913 figure for Ireland relates to the south only. The figure for Ireland in column (1) headed 1830 is derived as described in the text.

Cols (3) and (4): The 1985 figures for all the OECD countries (except Switzerland) are taken from OECD, *National accounts, main aggregates vol. 1, 1960–1986*. The data relate to GDP per head using purchasing power parities based on OECD relative prices in 1985. Figures for Switzerland and the East European countries are from R. Summers and A. Heston, 'A new set of international comparisons of real product and prices: estimates for 130 countries, 1950–1985', *Review of Income and Wealth*, series 34, no. 1 (March 1988). The data relate to GDP per head in 1980 international prices. The 1913 figures in col. (3) for all of the OECD countries were derived by taking the 1985 figures back to 1913 using the growth of real GDP *per capita*. These growth rates were calculated from A. Maddison, *Phases of capitalist development* (Oxford University Press, Oxford, 1982) up to 1960, and thereafter from OECD, *National accounts main aggregates, vol. 1, 1960–86*. For the OECD countries not covered in Maddison (except Ireland), the sources used were Bairoch, 'The main trends in national economic disparities' and Summer and Heston, 'A new set of international comparisons'. The Irish figure relating to real GDP *per capita* at factor cost at 1985 OECD purchasing power parities was taken back to 1926 using the sources given later in Table 6.1. It is assumed here that the level relative to the UK was the same in 1913 as in 1926. This assumption seems reasonable enough: while Ireland probably gained relative to the UK during the First World War, this gain was probably lost by the mid-1920s due to a series of bad harvests, the severe fall in agricultural prices and the disruption caused by the war of independence and the civil war. For the East European countries the 1950 estimates of real GDP *per capita* at 1975 international prices in Summers and Heston, 'A new set of international comparisons', were taken back to 1913 using the growth of real product *per capita* from Bairoch, 'The main trends in national economic disparities'. The ratios to the UK were calculated by reference to the UK figure derived on the same basis. Data have been adjusted in the sources cited to take account of frontier changes. Discussion of the implications of the 1985 figures is postponed until Chapter 6.

European average in 1913. Thus, while it would be going too far to imply, as Lee[10] does, that Ireland in 1913 was in the first division among European countries in terms of *per capita* income, nevertheless its relative standing was surprisingly high for a country commonly thought of as very poor and undeveloped.[11]

The obvious question arises as to how Ireland came to enjoy such a relatively favourable position in the early years of the twentieth century, given that only two generations earlier contemporary visitors to pre-Famine Ireland 'clearly believed that the material condition in Ireland was vastly inferior to that in their own countries.'[12] If this is so, did Ireland have a particularly rapid growth of income *per capita* in the second half of the nineteenth century? Or were the claims of exceptionally low living standards in pre-Famine Ireland exaggerated? Although these questions lie outside our period of analysis, and cannot be pursued in depth here, it is nevertheless imperative to say something about them — if only to check the validity of the picture given for conditions prevailing at the start of our own period.

1.2.1 Pre-Famine incomes and subsequent growth

A variety of figures has been given in different sources for Ireland's national income at or about the time of the Great Famine.[13] Several of the estimates can be dismissed as implausible or based on flimsy and unconvincing sources: indeed, there is no estimate that can be regarded as well documented. Probably the best estimate is also one of the most recent, namely, the figure of £75–85 million for all Ireland given in Mokyr for the first half of the 1840s.[14] It would be difficult to put the figure much below £80 million in the light of the carefully prepared estimate by Ó Gráda of gross value added in Irish agriculture about 1845 of £43.4 million:[15] indeed, elsewhere Ó Gráda himself hazards the 'tentative guess' of £80–100 million for the total national income.[16] On the other hand, it is also difficult to reconcile a figure much in excess of £80 million with Irish experience relative to Britain over the previous 40 years.[17]

Such a figure implies an average income *per capita* for Ireland in 1841 of £9·8, or 40 per cent of the figure of £24·4 for Great Britain given in Deane and Cole.[18] How did this compare with other European countries? Bairoch gives estimates of real GNP *per capita* for many European countries at about this time and these are shown in Table 1.1 relative to the UK figure for the same year.[19] These estimates must be regarded as very fragile. Most of the figures relate to the year 1830, others relate to the year 1860, while the Irish figure relates to 1841. The comparison therefore is clearly not very precise. Nevertheless, it suggests that Ireland was one of the poorest countries of Europe in the years prior to the Great Famine. Among the countries for which 1830 data are available, the next lowest, Russia, still had a relative income *per capita* that was one-fifth higher than the Irish level. Among the countries for which 1860 data are the earliest available, a few — Romania, Greece, Yugoslavia and Bulgaria — had a slightly lower relative income *per capita* than the Irish figure for 1841.

While the figures in Table 1.1 confirm the relatively low living standards in Ireland just before the Famine, they do not perhaps fully account for the emphasis placed by contemporary foreign commentators on the degree of poverty in Ireland. It is possible, of course, that foreign visitors may have exaggerated the degree of poverty in pre-Famine Ireland because of differences in consumption patterns.[20] The Irish were indeed poorly clad and housed, but the Irish diet, in its energy content, was as rich as the best in Europe and there was also plenty of fuel in the form of peat. Foreigners might also be insensitive to the possibility that social tastes were quite different, as evidenced by the great preference in Ireland for large families. All of these points might suggest that Ireland was distinctive but not necessarily less well off. The extent of poverty is scarcely in doubt, however, given that the low overall average income *per capita* was probably combined with a very unequal distribution of income by West European standards. The distribution of income almost certainly deteriorated markedly in the 50 years or so before the Famine as rents rose considerably. At the same time there was also a significant transfer of income out of the country in rents to absentee landlords and investment income.[21] Finally, Mokyr mentions another factor which in his view greatly enhanced the *risk* of poverty, and even starvation — namely, the vulnerability of the society to exogenous shocks. According to this view, the standard of living was not only low but exceptionally precarious due to the extreme dependence of so many on one crop (the potato), the instability of tenure and the lack of alternative employment opportunities as a result of industrial backwardness.

The foregoing picture, taken in conjunction with that already given for the years immediately preceding the First World War, implies the surprising conclusion that average income in Ireland must have grown more rapidly than in the rest of Europe — and certainly than in Britain — in the second half of the nine-

Table 1.2: Average annual growth rates of total and *per capita* real product in Europe and other countries, 1830–1913, 1913–85

	1830–1913		1913–85	
	Total product	Product *per capita*	Total product	Product *per capita*
European countries (ranked in descending order of GNP *per capita* in 1913)	%	%	%	%
1. United Kingdom	2·3	1·3	1·8	1·4
2. Switzerland	2·3	1·6	2·6	1·8
3. Denmark	2·7	1·7	2·8	2·0
4. Belgium	2·4	1·5	2·1	1·8
5. West Germany	2·3	1·4	2·8	2·1
6. Netherlands	2·3	1·2	3·0	1·8
7. Sweden	2·2	1·3	3·0	2·4
8. Austria	1·9[a]	1·1[a]	2·2	2·1
9. France	1·4	1·1	2·5	2·0
10. Ireland	0·7[b]	1·6[b]	1·8	1·6
11. Norway	2·2	1·2	3·5	2·7
12. Finland	2·3	1·2	3·3	2·6
13. Czechoslovakia	n.a.	n.a.	2·8	1·9
14. Italy	1·4	0·8	2·9	2·2
15. Spain	0·9[a]	0·4[a]	2·8	1·9
16. Poland	n.a.	n.a.	n.a.	1·9[c]
17. Hungary	n.a.	n.a.	2·3	1·8
18. Romania	2·1[a]	1·0[a]	2·9	1·9
19. Soviet Union	1·9	0·8	3·3	2·4
20. Greece	2·6[a]	0·7[a]	3·1	2·4
21. Portugal	1·1	0·4	3·1	2·4
22. Yugoslavia	n.a.	0·5[a]	3·4	2·4
23. Bulgaria	1·4[a]	0·5[a]	3·5	2·5
Mean	1·9	1·1	2·8	2·1
Other countries				
United States	4·6	2·1	3·0	1·7
Canada	4·2	1·7	3·7	2·0
Australia	4·0[a]	1·2[a]	3·1	1·4
New Zealand	n.a.	1·2[a]	3·3	1·8
Japan	1·3	0·7	4·5	3·3

Notes: [a] 1860–1913; [b] 1841–1911; [c] 1929–85.
Sources: 1830–1913: The Irish figures for total real income, which relate to the whole country, are derived as explained in the text and notes, and the population data are from Census sources. Figures for other countries from Bairoch 'Europe's gross national product 1800–1975', *Journal of European Economic History*, vol. 5, no. 2 (Fall 1976), and 'National

economic disparities' in Bairoch and Levy-Leboyer (eds), *Disparities in economic development*. The population growth rates used to derive the total product growth rates for the US, Canada, Australia and Japan were taken from Maddison, *Phases of capitalist development*.

1913–1985: For all countries the sources are as in Table 1.1, cols (3) and (4). The sources for the Irish data (i.e. the Republic) covering the period 1926–85 are given later in Table 6.1, at which point the implications of the figures are also discussed. For the period 1913–26, we simply assumed that real product *per capita* was unchanged relative to the UK. In the main the concept of total product is GDP for all countries, except where Bairoch's figures are used, which relate to GNP.

teenth and early years of the twentieth century. This conclusion conflicts with the data in Feinstein[22] and in Matthews, Feinstein and Odling-Smee,[23] which suggest a lower growth in income *per capita* in southern Ireland, at least, than in the rest of the UK over the period 1855–1920. Indeed, Cullen has noted that most commentators 'have assumed that *per capita* Irish national income rose slowly in the nineteenth century', though he himself takes the view that 'from the Famine onwards, on the basis of practical evidence, Irish *per capita* incomes rose more rapidly than English'.[24] Cullen did not attempt to put a figure on the rate of growth in Ireland: this we try to do in Table 1.2, which shows rates of growth of total and *per capita* real product in European and some other countries spanning the periods 1830–1913 or 1860–1913, depending on data availability.

The Irish figure covering the period 1841–1911 relates to all Ireland and was derived as follows. To compare the 1841 figure of £80 million, which is best understood as a measure of net domestic income, with the 1911 estimate of £150 million for GNP at market prices, it is necessary first to reduce the latter figure in respect of depreciation, indirect taxes less subsidies and net factor income.[25] Secondly, it is necessary to consider changes in the price level. There is no separate overall price deflator for Ireland, but, in view of the close links between the two areas, the trend of British prices provides a reasonable indicator for purposes of assessing changes in Irish real *income* — though not necessarily in real *output* for reasons discussed below. On the basis of trends in British prices, we take the price level to be the same in 1911 as in the first half of the 1840s,[26] so that the change in nominal value gives a rough guide to the change in Irish real income between these two periods.

The mean growth of real GNP in European countries over the period 1830–1913 was 1·9 per cent per annum. Several of the Western European countries had annual growth rates of 2¼ to 2½ per cent, with Denmark at the top with 2¾ per cent. Ireland was at the bottom among European countries and, along with Spain, was the only country with a growth rate of less than 1 per cent per annum. Indeed, the Irish growth rate of total *output* must have been significantly less than the figure given in Table 1.2 of 0·7 per cent per annum, which is best taken as a measure of the growth of total real *income*.[27] The reason is that Irish agricultural prices almost doubled from 1850 to 1911, chiefly due to the favourable trend in store cattle prices.[28] This encouraged specialisation in the production and export of cattle, and the import of wheat, the price of which declined substantially. Taken in conjunction with the price trend of industrial goods, of which Ireland was a net importer, there was a substantial gain in the terms of trade. The increase in the volume of Irish output, therefore, must have been less than the increase in its real income, though it would be difficult to say by how much.[29]

Yet remarkably, Ireland had one of the highest *per capita* growth rates because of its different population experience. Whereas in Europe as a whole, and in many of the individual countries, population was rising at close to 1 per cent per annum, in Ireland population was falling at a similar rate. Thus, despite little progress in economic development — as indicated by the low rate of growth of total real income and the even lower growth of total real output — Ireland still experienced a greater rise in average income *per capita* — albeit starting from very low levels at the time of the Great Famine.

There are several reasons, of course, why changes in total real income *per capita* may not give a full picture of changes in living standards. In particular, the rise in average real income in Ireland after the Famine overstates the rise for the resident population, because it was associated with the disappearance of the poorest section of the population — through death or emigration. By 1911, the Irish population, at 4,381,000 was little more than half the level of 8,175,000 in 1841. Given the wide disparities in income levels in 1841, and the fact that the bulk of the population decline was concentrated in the poorer half of the population, a significant increase in overall average income *per capita* would emerge even if the better-off half of the population had experienced no improvement in income *per capita*. It would be wrong, of course, to imply that this statistical quirk accounted for most of the measured rise in average income *per capita*. Aggregate real income *did* increase somewhat, and was now shared more evenly among those who were not forced to emigrate. Moreover, if we are concerned with the total Irish-born population, rather than just those continuing to reside in Ireland, then the emigrants also in the main experienced an improvement in living standards compared with their former position.

This is not to say, however, that the improvement in living standards achieved in this manner represented a satisfactory form of economic development. Indeed, the improvement in Irish living standards in the second half of the nineteenth century is somewhat analogous to what happened in medieval Europe after the Black Death and the subsequent outbreak of bubonic plague.[30] The plagues occurred after a period of population growth and diminishing marginal productivity to labour on the land. The result was to raise the land/labour ratio so that there was a substantial improvement in the standard of living of the survivors, but with no real development or technical advances. Likewise in Ireland, while its average income *per capita* on the eve of the First World War, though well below the British level, compared favourably with that of much of the rest of Europe, this position had not been achieved through vigorous economic growth. Though there was some rise in total product over the period 1841–1913, the rate was less than in almost any other European country at that time. Rather, the improvement in living standards came about mainly through population decline and specialisation in favourably priced livestock production which intensified the population decline.

1.2.2 Incomes north and south

So far we have concentrated on average income levels in Ireland as a whole, but the area, Northern Ireland, that was to remain in the United Kingdom after independence was achieved in the remainder of the island, had experienced a considerable measure of industrialisation in the nineteenth century. Did this then mean that average income levels were substantially higher in that region than in the rest of the country? Though the evidence is scanty, it points to the surprising conclusion that average incomes may not, in fact, have been significantly higher in Northern Ireland at about the time of the First World War.

From Feinstein's two estimates for the United Kingdom in 1920,[31] before and after the exclusion of southern Ireland, it emerges that average GNP *per capita* in the south was just under 60 per cent of the level in the United Kingdom (including all Ireland). This is not much below the figure of just under 62 per cent mentioned earlier as the ratio of income *per capita* in Ireland as a whole to the UK level in 1911. It would suggest that, while average incomes were lower in the south than in the north, the deficiency was little more than about 10 per cent.[32] It would be unwise, however, to lean too heavily on this residual method of calculation from a source in which the prime focus is on the much larger entity, Great Britain.[33]

Johnson, who is directly concerned with comparative income levels in Ireland, puts the Northern Ireland level of income *per capita* in 1924 at 61 per cent of the level in Great Britain, implying a very small difference between average incomes in the two parts of Ireland.[34] Indeed, elsewhere he states that 'living standards in Ireland were on average much the same on both sides of the border around 1930'.[35] Cullen notes that whereas net output per worker in agriculture in the south (£96) was only slightly lower than in the north (£104), industrial output per worker in the south (£215) was substantially above the level in the north (£151).[36] Cullen takes the view that if in fact average income *per capita* was higher in Northern Ireland, it was largely due to the fact that only about a quarter of the work-force was engaged in the low-income agricultural sector there, as against just over half in the south. The sector for which information is almost wholly lacking is that of services, which in both areas accounted for about one-third of the work-force at this time. However, if the average income in services was broadly similar in both areas, and if the data on net output per worker for agriculture and industry can be taken as a measure of the relative scale of income *per capita* in these sectors, then it would imply that overall, average income *per capita* in the south was, at most, only about 10 per cent below the Northern Ireland level.

This is quite surprising given that, even before it experienced substantial industrialisation, the north was traditionally considered more prosperous. Must we now revise this viewpoint?

Or is it a case that, despite the considerable degree of industrialisation in the north in the century prior to the First World War, the growth of income *per capita* was no greater, or perhaps even less, than in the south? As to the first question, some modern economic historians have produced figures which cast doubt on the greater prosperity of Ulster in the first half of the nineteenth century. Mokyr puts *per capita* income in the province of Ulster around 1840 at slightly below the national average.[37] While Ulster includes, as well as Northern Ireland, the three counties of Cavan, Monaghan and Donegal, which were poorer than the rest of Ulster, nevertheless even the exclusion of these would not raise the Northern Ireland figure to greatly in excess of the national average. Kennedy notes that in the mid-nineteenth century, Ulster had a higher proportion of small holdings than the rest of the country, and a lower proportion of large holdings — with the corollary of relatively low incomes among the bulk of Ulster farmers.[38] Kennedy also notes that in the decades after 1815 poverty intensified in Ulster and inequality increased.

As to the relative growth rates, there can be little doubt but that the volume of total output grew faster in the north than in the south in the century or so up to the First World War. Certainly, even if *per capita* output rose no faster in the north, its overall growth rate must have been greater, given the smaller decline in population — 0·4 per cent per annum in the north from 1841 to 1911 as compared with 1 per cent per annum in the south. However, some features of the industrialisation of the north, in which were heavily concentrated highly competitive export-orientated activities, may have limited the growth of *per capita* incomes. The mechanisation of spinning and weaving in the first half of the nineteenth century demolished the domestic textile industry, concentrated the locus of production in the east of the province, and brought great pressure on wages of skilled workers — a pressure that was maintained by the highly competitive nature of the textile industry internationally. Net output per head in the linen industry, which accounted for half of the industrial work-force in the early twentieth century, was only a little higher than in agriculture. Since industrial, relative to agricultural, exports were much more significant in the north, it is likely that it did not enjoy as favourable a movement in the terms of trade as did the south.

Furthermore, industrial development in the north did not

result in a great enlargement of the local market. The low labour earnings in agriculture and textiles, combined with shrinking population, did not provide adequate demand for the development of spin-off consumer industries. Shipbuilding performed better in that regard, but the impact was highly concentrated in Belfast and was not diffused to the rest of the province. While the north was a copy-book example of export-led growth, its experience suggests that strong export orientation, without corresponding home-market development, may not only be highly vulnerable to foreign competition and the vagaries of world markets (as later experience was to demonstrate), but may also limit the gains in living standards. Seen in a European context, however, the growth in *per capita* income in the north — even if no higher than in the south — was impressive. The south represents the more anomalous case, in that it reached a respectable standard of living without industrialisation and with little growth of total output.

1.3 PLAN OF STUDY

In discussing the period since 1922, it is necessary to specify our use of the term Ireland in the remainder of the study. Up to now, that term has been used to designate the whole of Ireland since this formed a common political entity up to 1922. The rest of our study, however, covering the period since 1922, is primarily concerned with the 26 counties of Ireland which became independent in that year. This area, by far the larger part of the whole island, was first officially known as Saorstát Éireann (The Irish Free State), but on leaving the British Commonwealth in 1949 the official title became the Republic of Ireland. For simplicity, however, in the remainder of this study, the term 'Ireland' will refer to this area unless the contrary is explicitly indicated. The other Six Counties will be designated throughout by the official name, Northern Ireland. When speaking simultaneously of Northern Ireland and the rest of the country, we shall refer to the latter for brevity as 'the Republic'; and wherever the two areas are grouped together from now on we shall use the term 'all Ireland'.

The study is divided into two further parts. Part Two describes chronologically the course of the economy over time since 1922 and outlines the policies pursued in different phases.

The period is divided into three sub-periods which form the subjects of Chapters 2, 3 and 4, respectively. Chapter 2 discusses the quarter century from independence to the end of the Second World War, the period during which the economy moved from free trade to protectionism. Chapter 3 deals with the post-war period up to 1973, during which there was a gradual return to an outward orientation and free trade, culminating in accession to the European Community on 1 January 1973. Chapter 4 covers the troubled years since 1973, dominated by the oil crises and two world depressions. The economic experience of Northern Ireland since 1922 was different in many respects from that of the Republic, and while it is not our intention to examine the former in full detail, we provide a short account in Chapter 5. In Chapter 6 the overall growth record is compared with that of other European countries.

Part Three is devoted to a more detailed examination of key aspects of the economic development of the Republic since 1922. The chapters in this part deal successively with population and labour force, capital investment, foreign trade, agriculture and industry, culminating in a final chapter which attempts to give an overall assessment of Ireland's economic performance since independence.

NOTES

1. J. Lee, *The modernisation of Irish society 1848–1918* (Gill and Macmillan, Dublin, 1973), p. 3.

2. Ibid., p. 2.

3. For an extended discussion of this argument, see E. O'Malley, *Unequal competition: the problem of late development in Irish industry* (forthcoming, 1988). For a formal theoretical analysis, see W.B. Arthur, 'Industry location patterns and the importance of history', seminar paper delivered at The Economic and Social Research Institute, Dublin, August 1986.

4. E.R.R. Green, 'Early industrial Belfast' in J.C. Beckett and R.E. Glassock (eds), *Belfast: the origin and growth of an industrial city* (British Broadcasting Company, London, 1967), p. 86.

5. Lee, *The modernisation of Irish society*, p. 16.

6. Quoted in New Ireland Forum, *The economic consequences of the division of Ireland since 1920* (Stationery Office, Dublin, 1983), p. 4.

7. C.H. Feinstein, *National income, expenditure and output of the United Kingdom, 1855–1965* (Cambridge University Press, Cambridge, 1972).

8. Ibid., p. 212.
9. P. Bairoch, 'The main trends in national economic disparities since the industrial revolution', in P. Bairoch and M. Levy-Leboyer (eds), *Disparities in economic development since the Industrial Revolution* (St. Martin's Press, New York, 1981), pp. 3–17.
10. J. Lee, 'A third division team?', *Seirbhís Phoiblí*, vol. 6, no. 1 (January 1985), pp. 3–8.
11. It may also be noted that in comparing Ireland and Britain, a sizeable part of the gap in *per capita* income can be accounted for simply by the differing proportions engaged in agriculture — 53.5 per cent in the Irish Free State and 8.3 per cent in the UK (Great Britain and Northern Ireland) in 1926 — where income *per capita* in both countries was under 60 per cent of the total. On Duncan's figures, the exclusion of agriculture would raise the Irish/UK ratio from 57 per cent to 80 per cent — G.A. Duncan, 'The social income of the Irish Free State, 1926–38', *Journal of the Statistical and Social Inquiry Society of Ireland*, vol. 16 (1939–40). An earlier estimate by Kiernan for the same year put total *per capita* income in the Irish Free State at 67 per cent of the British level — T.J. Kiernan, 'The national income of the Irish Free State in 1926', *Economic Journal*, vol. 43 (1933), pp. 74–87, and 'The national expenditure of the Irish Free State in 1926', *Journal of the Statistical and Social Inquiry Society of Ireland*, vol. 15, no. 91 (1932–3). Excluding agriculture in this case would push the Irish/UK ratio up to 94 per cent. For this and other reasons, however, Kiernan's estimate seems too high.
12. J. Mokyr, *Why Ireland starved: a quantitative and analytical history of the Irish economy, 1800–1850*, 2nd edn (Allen and Unwin, London, 1985), p. 6.
13. See C. Clark, *The conditions of economic progress* (Macmillan, London, 1960), in which various estimates are mentioned. See also Feinstein, *National income, expenditure and output*; E. Larkin, 'Economic growth, capital investment and the Roman Catholic Church in nineteenth century Ireland', *American History Review*, vol. 72, April (1967), pp. 852–83; and Mokyr, *Why Ireland starved*.
14. Mokyr, *Why Ireland starved*, p. 11.
15. C. Ó Gráda, 'Irish agricultural output before and after the Famine', *Journal of European Economic History*, vol. 13, no. 1 (1984), pp. 149–65.
16. C. Ó Gráda, 'Poverty, population and agriculture' in *New history of Ireland* (Royal Irish Academy, Dublin, forthcoming).
17. Although there are no estimates for the period, it is doubtful if average real income *per capita* in Ireland was higher in 1841 than in 1801, whereas there was a significant increase in Britain. If we assume an unchanged *per capita* real income in Ireland, then taking the £80 million figure for 1841 and the figures on British net national income *per capita* in P. Deane and W.A. Cole, *British economic growth 1888–1959*, 2nd edn (Cambridge University Press, 1967), it would follow that Ireland's average real income *per capita* in 1801 (at 1841 prices) was 66 per cent of the level in Great Britain. This is a high, but not impossible, level. However, if we were to put the Irish national

income in 1841 at a significantly higher level than £80 million, while retaining the other assumptions, then we would quickly approach an implausibly high relative level of income *per capita* in 1801. A figure of £90 million in 1841, for instance, would imply a relative income *per capita* in Ireland in 1801 equal to 74 per cent of the British level, while a figure of £100 million would imply a ratio of 83 per cent. It is possible, of course, that real income *per capita* rose in Ireland over the period 1801–41, but given the large rise in population, this would imply a growth in total real product which would be hard to reconcile with the general historical picture, especially after 1815. It may be noted, however, that in a recent paper, Mokyr and Ó Gráda reached the tentative conclusion for the period 1815–45 that 'While economic conditions facing the Irish poor probably stagnated or even deteriorated, the population as a whole seems to have been able to hold its own and possibly even improve its lot' — J. Mokyr and C. Ó Gráda, 'From poor to poorer? Living standards in Ireland before the Famine', *Discussion Paper, Department of Economics, University of British Columbia*, no. 86–14 (April 1986).

18. Deane and Cole, *British economic growth*, p. 282.

19. This comparison slightly underestimates the Irish position relative to other countries in that the Irish ratio has been calculated by reference to Great Britain, whereas the figures for other countries are all at 1970 boundaries, which for the UK embraces Great Britain and Northern Ireland. The difference is unimportant, however, on any reasonable assumptions, given that the population in Northern Ireland amounted to less than one-tenth that of Great Britain in 1841.

20. On this, see Mokyr, *Why Ireland starved*, Chapter 2.

21. In contrast, during the second half of the nineteenth century, rent outflows were declining and, for this and other reasons, Ireland by the end of the 1870s was well on the way to becoming a creditor country, with a net inflow of invisible income. See L.M. Cullen, 'Germination and growth' in Bernard Share (ed.), *Root and branch: history of Allied Irish Banks* (Dublin, 1979), p. 43.

22. Feinstein is careful to note, however, that his implicit figures for southern Ireland are not a direct estimate for that region; and that while the margin of error is not significant in relation to the UK or Great Britain, it 'could easily be intolerably large relative to estimates for Southern Ireland' — *National income, expenditure and output*, p. 3.

23. R.C.O. Matthews, C.H. Feinstein and J.C. Odling-Smee, *British economic growth 1856–1973* (Clarendon Press, Oxford, 1982).

24. L.M. Cullen, 'Trends and problems in recent Irish historiography' (forthcoming).

25. The figure of £150 million was scaled down to £130 million using the information for 1920 in Feinstein, *National income, expenditure and output*, Tables 1 and 2.

26. From 1846 to 1911, the Rousseaux and the Sauerbach-Statist overall wholesale price indices declined by 10–15 per cent — B.R. Mitchell and P. Deane, *Abstract of British historical statistics* (Cambridge University Press, 1962), vol. 17, pp. 471–5. Data covering

the period 1855–1911 in Feinstein, *National income, expenditure and output*, Tables 1, 6, 61 and 65, indicate that the decline in retail prices was less than in wholesale prices, while the price deflator of GDP rose slightly.

27. On the other hand, the increase in real disposable income may have been higher. Emigrants' remittances and government net transfers probably rose relative to domestic income while net factor income changed from an outflow to an inflow.

28. M. Turner, 'Towards an agricultural prices index for Ireland 1850–1914', *Economic and Social Review*, vol. 18, no. 2 (1987), Appendix 2, and T. Barrington, 'Review of Irish agricultural prices', *Journal of the Statistical and Social Inquiry Society of Ireland*, vol. xiv (1925–6), Table I.

29. Lee, *The modernisation of Irish society*, p. 35, puts the Irish growth rate of national income from 1848 to 1914 at about 0.5 per cent per annum, but gives no indication of how his figure is computed. No attempts have been made in the literature to estimate changes in the volume of industrial or services output, while the figures offered for agriculture differ widely. H. Staehle suggests that the total volume of agricultural output changed little from 1847 to 1861, but rose by 27 per cent from 1861 to 1909 — 'Statistical notes on the economic history of Irish agriculture 1847–1913', *Journal of the Statistical and Social Inquiry Society of Ireland*, vol. xviii, no. 4 (1950–1). R. Crotty says there was no overall growth in agricultural production — *Irish agricultural production: its volume and structure* (Cork University Press, Cork, 1966), p. 68. The price and volume figures in Turner, 'Towards an agricultural price index', point to a volume fall of about 10 per cent.

30. I am grateful to D. Johnson for suggesting this analogy.

31. Feinstein, *National income expenditure and output*, Table 1.4, p. 10.

32. If, however, incomes rose more in Ireland than in Britain during the period 1911–20, as is possible, then the ratio of average income in all Ireland to the UK level would be higher than 62 per cent in 1920 and on this reckoning the gap between north and south could be somewhat wider.

33. Nevertheless, Feinstein's 1920 figure accords well with the more fully articulated estimate of national income in the south for 1926 in Duncan 'The social income of the Irish Free State, 1926–38'. Both suggest a very similar ratio of Irish to UK income *per capita*.

34. D. Johnson, 'The Northern Ireland economy 1914–39' in L. Kennedy and P. Ollerenshaw (eds), *An economic history of Ulster 1820–1939* (Manchester University Press, 1985), p. 202. Johnson's figure for Northern Ireland of 61 per cent of the British level is based on a comparison of his estimate of net national income *per capita* with Prest's figure in Deane and Cole, *British economic growth*, 2nd edn, p. 330. Johnson's actual figure for income *per capita* in Northern Ireland was £53. To compare this with Duncan's figure of £51.9 for the south in 1926, which relates to GNP, we have to deduct capital consumption from the latter. R.C. Geary suggests that the total of

depreciation was about £6 million — *Journal of the Statistical and Social Inquiry Society of Ireland*, vol. 16 (1939–40) p. 15. Allowing for this, the estimate of net national income *per capita* in the south in 1926 becomes £49.8 or 6 per cent below Johnson's 1924 figure for Northern Ireland.

35. D. Johnson, *The inter-war economy in Ireland* (The Economic and Social History Society of Ireland, Dublin, 1985), p. 43.

36. Cullen, 'Germination and growth' in Share (ed.), *Root and branch*, p. 58.

37. Mokyr, *Why Ireland starved*, p. 27.

38. L. Kennedy, 'The rural economy' in Kennedy and Ollerenshaw (eds), *An economic history of Ulster*, pp. 20–1.

Part Two

The Course of the Irish Economy
Since Independence

2

From Free Trade to Protection, 1922–46

The first 25 years of independence divide readily into three sub-periods. In the first decade the primary emphasis was on establishing and consolidating the new state, free trade with the United Kingdom continued, and economic policy concentrated chiefly on raising efficiency in agriculture. From 1932 to 1938, Ireland and Britain were engaged in an economic conflict which came to be known as the 'Economic War'. Its immediate effect was to reduce trade between the two countries at a time when trade was already hit by the world-wide economic depression, but it also contributed to the switch from a long established position of free trade to a radical experiment in protectionism and economic nationalism. No sooner was the Economic War brought to an end than the Second World War supervened. Although Ireland remained neutral, the shortage of import supplies dispelled all notions of economic development and the paramount need was to secure basic necessities.

It is no accident that the drastic shift from free trade to protectionism coincided with a change of government. The treaty under which the new state was established was accepted only by a narrow majority in the Dáil (Parliament). A split in the nationalist movement followed, leading to a civil war which lasted until August 1923. The more moderate nationalists forming the new government triumphed and continued in government until 1932, the major political party involved being known as Cumann na nGael (later reorganised and renamed Fine Gael). Most of the disaffected republicans re-entered democratic politics in 1927 under the leadership of Eamon de Valera, who founded the Fianna Fáil Party in that year. Though there were considerable economic differences in the policies, and in the bases of support, of the two main parties that have dominated the political scene in Ireland to this day, the initial division between them was primarily on nationalist issues. As these issues became blurred with the passage of time, both parties have competed more and more for the centre, following pragmatic economic policies that are often indistinguishable from each other. Irish politics has not provided a hospitable reception for strong economic ideologies, whether of the left or of the right. Even the very moderate socialism of the Labour Party in Ireland has never commanded the votes of more than one-sixth of the electorate.

2.1 THE FIRST DECADE

The policy of many European governments in the 1920s was to restore the 'normalcy' that had existed in the tranquil and stable half-century before the First World War. From that perspective, therefore, it does not seem at all strange that the new Irish government did not introduce any radical departures in economic policy. Besides, the First World War had a beneficial effect on the Irish economy, north and south, so much so that 'in economic terms, the last years of the Union were the best ones'.[1] Nevertheless, from the perspective of Irish history, the failure to implement the strongly held nationalist approach to economic development calls for explanation. The need for industrialisation, and the infant industry argument for tariffs as a means of achieving that aim, were prominent in the economic philosophy of nationalist leaders such as Arthur Griffith in the generation leading up to independence. Moreover, the nationalist rhetoric had never accepted emigration as a satisfactory way of solving the problem of surplus labour, and industry was seen as the key to providing more jobs at home. On these premisses, the case for industrialisation was all the greater after partition, because the only part of all Ireland with significant industry was located in the excluded Six Counties of Northern Ireland.

Yet the new Irish government took the view that the overall prosperity of the economy depended on agriculture, and that the prosperity of agriculture depended on the export market. This view was supported by the fact that the land provided the only major known natural resource, that agriculture at the time accounted directly for more than half of the labour force, and that exports of food and drink amounted to 85 per cent of total merchandise exports. Moreover, Britain provided a huge market for livestock products, though one that was highly competitive, given the world over-supply of agricultural produce. The overriding aim of policy was to raise agricultural productivity and reduce farm costs so that Irish export sales would be competitive and farm incomes would rise. It would be inconsistent with this approach to burden agriculture with higher prices for its purchases of inputs or consumer goods — a likely consequence of industrial protection.

In addition to its economic rationale, there were other important factors which influenced the adoption of this strategy. The civil war put a premium on re-establishing stability, and a drastic reorganisation of economic life would not be conducive to this. In restoring stability, the government was anxious to retain the goodwill and support of the British government. This might be eroded by an extensive network of tariffs mainly affecting British goods. Though Ireland accounted for only 6 per cent of British exports, it was still one of Britain's largest single markets — on a par with France as an importer of British goods. There were fears that a departure from free trade might cause a flight of capital which would be hard to stop, given the long-standing financial links with Britain. A conservative approach was also fostered by the bureaucracy and by academic opinion. Many of the civil servants had served under the British administration, and the new government was advised by 'civil servants and economists whose background and training had closed their minds to most ideas outside the British liberal and *laissez-faire* tradition.'[2] Paradoxically, it was left to a British economist, none other than Keynes himself, to articulate the case for industrial protection in Ireland. Delivering the first Finlay Lecture at University College, Dublin, in April 1933, Keynes, to the acute embarrassment of his academic hosts, expressed his sympathy with the new government's approach to greater self-sufficiency: 'Let goods be homespun wherever it is reasonably and conveniently possible, and, above all, let finance be primarily national.'[3]

The fact that in the 1920s the government was prepared to accept the expert advice tendered by academics and the civil service owed much to the political balance that existed after the civil war. Some of the leading nationalist proponents of industrialisation, such as James Connolly and Arthur Griffith, were dead. The abstention of the more extreme nationalist elements from the Dáil until 1927 greatly reduced effective political opposition to the government's economic policies. There was little demand for protection from existing industrial enterprises which had managed to develop under free trade. Furthermore, the most conservative section of the population, the better-off farmers and the professions, were heavily represented in the Cumann na nGael Party, and these believed they would be worse off as a result of tariff policies. The economic philosophy articulated so forcefully by the first Minister for Agriculture, Patrick Hogan — namely, that economic policy should aim at maximising farmers' incomes, that this would maximise national income, and that such a policy must take precedence over self-sufficiency and the reduction of unemployment[4] — was therefore not only an expression of his own convictions, but also responded to the interests of his party's core electoral support.

These, then, were the major reasons why in the first decade of independence the government made only limited use of protection to promote greater self-sufficiency or to stimulate industrial growth. The tariff protection that was granted was moderate and selective; it was as a rule preceded in each case by a full public inquiry; the onus of proof lay with the applicant to show why the benefits of free trade should be foregone; and efforts were made to offset the adverse effects of tariffs on production and living costs by reducing duties on other goods as a compensatory measure.[5] Government policy stressed the need to increase competitiveness and to provide better access to capital. Efforts were also made to develop the industrial infrastructure, the most notable achievement being the building of the Shannon electrification scheme, which was begun in 1925 and completed in 1929. In general, however, the government did not favour a large public sector and was anxious to reduce taxation. In the first few years of independence, the civil war required maintenance of a sizeable army, but once demobilisation was effected the government took the opportunity to cut the standard income tax rate from 25 per cent in 1924 to 15 per cent in 1927. Farm incomes were already exempt from income taxation and there were relatively few income tax payers — about 60,000 in the mid-1920s. Income and supertax receipts amounted to only 3 per cent of GNP, and nearly three-quarters of total tax revenue came from indirect taxes, chiefly customs and excise duties and local authority rates on property.

2.1.1 Economic impact

What was achieved in the first decade of independence? Given that the central focus of economic policy was on agriculture, it is here that one would look first for progress. In the early years of the state, however, agriculture faced difficult supply and trading conditions. The turmoil of the civil war affected production, and was followed by very poor harvests in 1923 and 1924 due to exceptionally poor weather conditions. Most important of all, however, was the collapse of agricultural prices following the wartime boom. The agricultural output price index to base 1911–13 = 100, fell from 288 in 1920 to 160 in 1922 and by 1931 had reached 110.

In the event there was little or no progress in agriculture. Notwithstanding the slogan of the time — 'one more cow, one more sow, one more acre under the plough' — no increase took place in the number of cows, other cattle or pigs, while the area under crops fell by nearly one-fifth between 1922 and 1932. The volume of gross agricultural output in 1924/5 was 13 per cent below the level of 1912/13, and although it had recovered by over 10 per cent in 1929/30, it was still 4 per cent below the pre-war level.[6] Livestock and livestock produce had increased their dominance still further, while crops and turf accounted for only 16 per cent of the value of gross output in 1929/30 as against 22½ per cent in 1912/13. The value of net output — the closest proxy for farm incomes at this time — was 5 per cent less in 1929/30 than in 1924/5.

These results seem disappointing in the light of the primacy attached by the government to agriculture, but in practice the government was stronger in its determination to avoid placing burdens on agriculture than in undertaking active measures. No direct support for agricultural prices was provided. An active government policy directed to raising farming efficiency might have been expected to lay great stress on agricultural education. However, the numbers of students involved remained trivially small — less than 300 throughout the 1920s. The amount of state expenditure on agriculture in 1922/3 was only £400,000, or less than 2 per cent of government expenditure. The figure showed little change from this level in the next decade except in one respect. In 1925/6 grants of £0·6 million per annum were introduced to relieve local authority rates on agricultural land — a form of assistance that was of dubious benefit in raising agricultural output and efficiency.[7] State expenditure on forestry doubled during the decade, but the amounts involved were very small. The same held true for fisheries. The Land Act of 1923 completed the transfer of land from landlords to small peasant owners, a process that did nothing to dynamise production or marketing. A semi-state body, the Agricultural Credit Corporation, was set up in 1927 to provide loans to farmers, but little use was made of its facilities until very much later. Perhaps the greatest achievement of agricultural policy in this period was that of restoring the reputation for quality of Irish agricultural exports on the British market — a reputation that had been damaged through supplying inferior quality products in the aftermath of the First World War. This achievement was brought about by establishing standards for the testing, grading and packing of eggs and butter, and by the licensing of bulls used for breeding.

The first figures available for industrial output relate to 1926. In the three years 1926–9, the total volume of industrial output rose by 8½ per cent, but in the following two years there was a considerable slowing down, the rise from 1929 to 1931 being less than 2 per cent. There are no comprehensive figures, except for 1926, on total employment, but the available indicators suggest that it fell. A small gain in industrial employment was far more than offset by the decline in numbers engaged in agriculture. There is little solid information on trends in services employment, but it is unlikely that it rose much if at all. A very tight control was maintained on numbers in the civil service, and the sizeable army establishment of the civil war period was reduced by two-thirds by 1931. As might be expected from the lack of progress in employment creation, there was also no success in reducing emigration. In fact emigration in the decade 1921–31 averaged 33,000 per annum, higher than the figures for either of the two previous decades, 1911–21 (19,000 per annum) or 1901–11 (26,000 per annum). True, there was exceptionally high emigration of 88,000 in 1921–2 related to British withdrawal, but even excluding this the average for the 1920s would still be higher than in the two preceding decades. The estimated decline in population from

1922 to 1931 was 89,000, or nearly 10,000 per annum — again greater than in either of the decades 1911–21 or 1901–11.

Pressure for a change of policy was mounting even before the de Valera government took office in 1932. The impact of the Great Depression on Ireland was delayed, partly because of the absence of heavy industries but more particularly because of the livestock basis of Irish agricultural production and exports. The prices of cereals and feeding-stuffs which Ireland imported declined more than those of livestock products which Ireland exported. Although both export and import prices fell sharply from 1929–31, the latter fell far more and the improvement in the terms of trade since 1924 was sustained. The volume of exports held up in 1930, but fell sharply by 10 per cent in 1931. Ireland, unlike many other countries, was not constrained by the balance of payments, since it held substantial external assets accumulated through the large export surpluses during the First World War.

Rising unemployment, however, created pressure for trade restrictions. Emigration dropped due to the tightening of US immigration laws and the decline in job oppportunities abroad as a result of the depression. In 1931 emigration was less than 9,000, and for the first time since the Famine the movement to the US became insignificant, falling to 801 in 1931 and just 256 in 1932. The total population, which had fallen every year since independence, rose by 11,000 in 1931 and continued to rise until the middle of the decade. The need to create jobs became even more urgent. Given the conservative fiscal attitudes of the time, expansionary fiscal measures were not canvassed widely: on the contrary, the fiscal response, as in Britain, was one of retrenchment. Pressure for protective duties mounted, however, and the Cumann na nGael government was forced to yield to this to the extent that it took power in 1931 to impose anti-dumping duties to prevent a threatened dumping of goods in Ireland.

In evaluating Irish economic policy in the first decade, Meenan took the view that

> the aims of economic policy have never since been so clearly defined, nor its methods so exactly adapted to those aims, as in the first ten years of the State when priority was given to the encouragement of agriculture and agricultural policy was directed by Patrick Hogan.[8]

The aims were certainly clearly defined but one might question whether the methods were adequate to the chosen aims, and, even more fundamentally, whether the aims themselves were not too narrow. The achievements of government in the first decade of independence lay in the political rather than in the economic sphere — in establishing the framework of democratic government and in peacefully handing over the reins to another government with a quite different outlook on economic policy.

2.2 THE PROTECTIONIST PATH

Fianna Fáil took office on 9 March 1932 with an avowedly protectionist policy. The motivation underlying this policy was partly nationalist — to reduce economic dependence on Britain, even at the price of a lower living standard:

> If the servant was displeased with the kicks of the master and wanted to have his freedom, he had to make up his mind whether or not he was going to have that freedom, and give up the luxuries of a certain kind which were available to him by being in that mansion.[9]

More pragmatically, however, the policy was also aimed at providing employment and reducing emigration. This was also the motive force behind the policy of increasing tillage: 'We should get for our own people the necessities of life and try to maintain our population.'[10] This advocacy of protectionism, unlike that of Griffith, was not directed towards the establishment of infant industries which would ultimately be expected to be competitive internationally. Indeed, de Valera frankly admitted that he saw little hope of establishing export industries, apart from food. Nor did he conceal his view that the maintenance of a large community in Ireland would involve material sacrifice: he simply counselled the people to 'forget as far as we can, what are the standards prevalent in countries outside this'.[11]

The Finance Act of May 1932 began to give effect to this policy by imposing *ad valorem* duties ranging from 15 to 75 per cent on 38 classes of goods, with specific duties on five other classes. While the nationalistic and employment-creating objectives of the policy had considerable emotional appeal, the corollary of material frugality, however, enjoyed much less support. It is doubtful, therefore, if de Valera could have persisted with this approach were it not for the so-called Economic War with Britain which began in July 1932: as Hancock put it, 'The revival of the old quarrel with England had created the atmosphere of emotional fervour which he needed for launching a drastic experiment in economic nationalism.'[12]

2.2.1 The Economic War

The Economic War stemmed from a dispute about which government, the British or the Irish, should receive the land annuities collected from Irish tenant purchasers. These annuity payments arose out of various Land Acts under which the British government arranged funds to enable Irish tenants to purchase their holdings from the landlords, with the tenant purchaser undertaking to repay the principal and interest over a long period. Prior to the establishment of the new Irish state, those annuity payments which later became the subject of dispute were collected from the tenant purchasers and passed through the National Debt Commissioners to the holders of Irish land stock. In February 1923 the Irish government specifically agreed to pay over to the appropriate fund the full amount of the annuities, making itself responsible for their collection from the tenant purchasers. Subsequently, when Ireland was released in 1925 from liability for any part of the public debt of the United Kingdom, the two governments were in no doubt that this did not absolve the Irish government from continuing to hand over these land annuities. Indeed, the Irish government's continued obligation in that regard was explicitly recognised in an agreement made in March 1926 between Mr Blythe, the Irish Minister for Finance, and Mr Churchill, the British Chancellor of the Exchequer.

Mr de Valera took a different view, however, and advanced legal, technical and moral arguments to support the claim that the annuities belonged to the Irish Exchequer. Whether valid or not, these arguments were ingenious and nationalistically appealing, but our concern here is with their economic impact rather than their merits. The retention of the annuities formed

41

one of the main planks in de Valera's election platform in 1932, and on 1 July 1932 the new Fianna Fáil government withheld the half-yearly instalment due on that date. The payments withheld amounted to about £5 million per annum, equivalent to one-seventh of Irish merchandise exports in 1931, or about one-fifth of tax revenue. The sum was obviously of far less consequence to Britain, though its loss could scarcely be welcomed at a time of depression and balance of payments difficulties.

Nevertheless, the British reaction was exceptionally sudden and severe. Rejecting arbitration as an approach to resolving the matter, the British government replied on 12 July 1932 by imposing an *ad valorem* duty of 20 per cent on imports of Ireland's main agricultural exports, with a view thereby to collecting a sum equal to the annuity payments. The duties were raised by a further 10 per cent in November 1932. In addition, the exemption of Irish exports from the general 10 per cent duty imposed under the Import Duties Act 1932 was revoked. In 1933 specific duties were imposed on cattle so that by 1934, the worst year of the Economic War, the duties amounted to up to two-thirds of the value of the animal, depending on age. Irish exports to Britain were also subject to quota restrictions which came into force on 1 January 1934. These quotas involved a complete prohibition of Irish beef and veal, a 50 per cent restriction compared to 1933 on fat cattle, and a complete restriction on store cattle. The British government, however, held that these restrictions derived entirely from British agricultural policy and not at all from the dispute.

The Irish government did not remain inactive, but rather entered the fray with alacrity. On 13 July 1932, the day after the British imposed the special duties, the Emergency Imposition of Duties Bill was introduced and became law on 23 July, enabling the government to impose discriminatory duties by statutory order. The Minister for Finance claimed that the measure was one of 'self-defence' rather than of 'retaliation and aggression'. The first order made under this Act imposed duties on British coal, cement, iron and steel goods and certain other items. The total of these items covered about one-third of the import trade from Britain and was widely regarded as a relatively moderate reply. As we shall see below, however, it was only the beginning.

The Economic War lasted until 1938, when it was finally

settled by the Defence, Financial and Trade Agreements signed on 25 April 1938. However, some of the most damaging features of the conflict had earlier been modified by the coal–cattle pacts starting in January 1935. Some historians suggest that de Valera fomented the conflict as a means of implementing his protectionist policies.[13] That is probably going too far. It would be nearer the mark to conclude that the Fianna Fáil government made use of the Economic War once it had begun to hasten that government's policy. What is undeniable is that the severity of the British government reaction rallied Irish public opinion behind the actions of the Irish government to a degree that would otherwise have been difficult to achieve.

2.2.2 The extension of protection

Following Ireland's reply to the British levies in July 1932, further impositions followed in October 1932 involving *ad valorem* duties ranging from 15 per cent to 75 per cent on a further 29 classes of goods and specific duties on seven commodities. In subsequent years the annual Finance Act was used for the introduction of new duties. Most of these impositions were not retaliatory but rather in pursuance of the government's protectionist policy. An indication of the range of goods involved may be seen from the fact that in January 1936 the official import list containing nearly 2,000 categories showed over half of them subject to tariffs, many in the range 50 to 75 per cent. The average tariff level rose from 9 per cent in 1931 to 45 per cent in 1936, while an index of the tariff level in Ireland relative to other countries for 1937, indicates that the Irish level was 1½ times that in the UK, about twice as high as in the US, Japan, Belgium and France but about one-third less than in Germany.[14]

Considerable use was made of quotas, import licences, compulsory milling regulations and other non-tariff barriers to shelter the domestic market further from external competition. A number of quotas was introduced where there was already a substantial import duty which had proved insufficiently protective. A further step in the pursuit of the nationalist economic policy was the attempt through the Control of Manufactures Acts 1932 and 1934 to keep Irish production in Irish hands. This legislation provided that in the case of all new manufacturing companies, Irish nationals must hold 51 per cent of the nominal share capital and two-thirds of shares with voting rights — unless specifically exempted by the Minister for Industry and Commerce.[15]

The Fianna Fáil government did not confine its protectionist policy to industry alone, but also attempted to make Ireland more self-sufficient in agricultural produce. Duties were levied on various agricultural imports, and bounties were paid to encourage the production of wheat, flax and other products. Moreover, it became necessary to pay substantial subsidies on Irish exports to Britain during the course of the Economic War, since otherwise the British penal duties would have effectively destroyed the Irish export trade.

There was also a considerable extension of state-sponsored bodies in industry and commerce in the 1930s. The Cumann na nGael government had begun this approach in 1927 with the Electricity Supply Board, the Dairy Disposal Company and the Agricultural Credit Corporation. The 1930s saw the establishment of Comhlucht Siúicre Éireann in 1933 to manufacture sugar from home-grown beet;[16] the Turf Development Board in 1934 (later to become a statutory body, Bord na Móna, in 1946) to develop native peat resources; the Industrial Credit Company in 1933; Ceimici Teoranta, a chemicals manufacturer, in 1934; Aer Lingus, the Irish airline, in 1936; and the Irish Life Assurance Company and the Irish Tourist Board in 1939.

2.2.3 Impact of the Economic War and protection

The course of the Irish economy in the 1930s was dominated by three factors — the Economic War, the protectionist policy and the impact of the Great Depression. It would be difficult to distinguish the separate effects of these factors, nor would it be altogether appropriate to do so given that they were to some degree interdependent. All three factors militated against trade. The volume of merchandise exports, which had already fallen by 10 per cent in 1931, declined by a further 29 per cent between 1931 and 1933. Remarkably, the 1930 volume of merchandise exports was not reached again until 1960. Even more remarkably, the ratio of exports to GNP was only superseded in 1968. Export prices also fell drastically, by 33 per cent between 1931 and the low point in 1934. By 1938, export prices had not recovered to the 1931 level, which in turn was 15 per cent below the 1929 level. The average annual value of exports in the years between 1932 and 1938, £21.3 million, was less than half the average in the preceding seven years (1925–31), £43.1 million.

Exports of live animals were hardest hit, declining in value terms from £19.7 million in 1929 to a trough of £6.1 million in 1934. Exports of foodstuffs of animal origin fell in the same period from £14.5 million to £5.2 million, and even the reduced level depended to a considerable extent on export subsidies. Since these agricultural exports were the products affected by the Economic War, it is tempting to ascribe a large part of the decline to that factor. It should be noted, however, that, as shown later in Chapter 10, British food imports fell considerably in the 1930s, so that Ireland would have suffered a decline in exports even apart from the Economic War. Nevertheless, the substantial fall in the Irish *share* of UK imports owed much to the Economic War. Moreover, had Ireland at that time 'exploited to the full its resources of diplomacy and finesse and the advantages of its geographic situation'[17] rather than antagonised the British government at a sensitive time, it is possible that it could have concluded a preferential agreement with Britain. This is by no means certain, of course, since British agricultural policy was in transition, and as Keynes put it, 'The exclusion of Irish agricultural produce suits extremely the present trend of British agricultural policy.'[18]

While import prices also declined, they fell much less after 1931 than export prices, so that the terms of trade deteriorated by more than a quarter between 1931 and 1934, and even by 1938 had recovered only to within 20 per cent of the 1931 level. Large movements in the terms of trade have always strongly affected the prosperity of Ireland, as might be expected in a country with such a high trade ratio. The volume of imports did not decline nearly as much as the export volume. This was partly due to the need for imports of machinery for the new industries. A further factor was that many of the new protected industries consisted in the assembly of goods formerly imported in finished form. Thus, while imports of manufactured goods fell from £32.2 million in 1931 to £24.1 million in 1938, imports of raw materials or simply prepared goods had risen from £13 million to £15.4 million. In some respects this made the country even more dependent on the international market since now employment, as well as consumption, depended on being able to import — an ironic result given the emphasis on self-sufficiency underlying the move to protection. As might be expected, imports from the UK declined more than total imports. Despite the increase in the visible trade gap, Ireland did not experience a serious balance of payments constraint. Apart from the fact that external reserves were substantial, the invisible items (notably, investment income, British pensions, emigrants' remittances and sweepstake receipts) held up well, aided by the retention of the annuities of about £5 million a year.

Turning to production, the total volume of gross agricultural output fluctuated in the 1930s around a static level. The share of output exported in 1938-9, at 36½ per cent in value terms, was well below the 1929-30 level of 51 per cent, a level that was not reached again until the early 1970s. Wheat and sugar beet were the only important agricultural products in which a substantial increase in output was attained, and this expansion proved useful in anticipating wartime shortages of these products. The slowing down in the outflow of persons from agriculture in the 1930s, however, owed more to the curtailment in emigration than to the small net increase in tillage, since the expansion in wheat and beet was largely offset by a decline in the acreage of oats. Farm incomes were squeezed on a number of fronts. The price of agricultural output in 1935 was 40 per cent below the 1929 level, as compared with a fall of 28 per cent in the same period in the price of the inputs of feeds, seeds and fertilisers. The overall cost-of-living price index fell by much less than this and since the decline in the food component was considerable, the non-food consumer items purchased by farmers scarcely declined at all. The squeeze on farm incomes affected investment which delayed recovery in output even when output prices improved.

The volume of industrial production grew rapidly — by nearly 50 per cent between 1931 and 1938. Given that the purchasing power of agriculture was depressed, and that the world economy was in turmoil, it is highly improbable that an expansion on this scale, albeit from a low base, would have been achieved at that time without the protectionist measures. Not all of the increase is attributable to protection, however, since there was also a substantial expansion in building activity due largely to the government's housing policy: over 70 per cent of all new house construction from 1923 to 1938 was undertaken after 1932.[19]

The increased industrial production was almost entirely directed to the home market, and there was no progress in expanding industrial exports. Indeed, Ireland's chief industrial export, Guinness beer, was permanently impaired by the turmoil associated with the Economic War and the protectionist policy. The Guinness Company, the dominant Irish brewer, was 'in the peculiar difficulty of being a Protestant firm and Ireland's biggest manufacturing industry, with a big English trade'.[20] The industry in fact accounted for 30 per cent of total manufacturing value added in Ireland in 1926, and exported nearly three-quarters of its output. Considerable uncertainty had been posed for the company during the War of Independence, and by the establishment of the new Irish state with its separate tax system. Nothing was done in the first decade, however, to disturb the company's freedom of access to its main market. With the Economic War and the new protectionist policies, however, the company's fears revived. Moreover, although the penal duties did not apply to beer, Irish exports became subject to the general 10 per cent import duty imposed in Britain in 1932. The Guinness Company decided to safeguard its market in Britain by building the Park Royal brewery near London, which came into operation in 1936. The decline in Irish exports from 1·3 million barrels in 1935 to 0·8 in 1938 closely matched the increase in output at the Park Royal brewery. Irish beer exports, although they revived in the post-war period, have never again reached the 1935 level, which was itself about 10 per cent below the levels of the 1920s.

Total industrial employment, as measured in the Census of Industrial Production,[21] rose from 110,600 in 1931 to 166,100 in 1938, an annual average growth rate of over 6 per cent. Labour productivity improved little, however, and indeed declined slightly in manufacturing — a remarkable fact, given the rapid growth in output which would normally be expected to increase productivity. The total population rose in the first half of the 1930s from 2,927,000 in 1930 to 2,971,000 in 1935, but had fallen back again to 2,936,000 by 1939. The rise in the first half of the decade, an unusual experience for Ireland, was due entirely to the fall off in emigration. From June 1930 to June 1940 emigration averaged only 14,000 per annum, compared with 35,000 in the previous ten years, and indeed there was a small net inflow in 1932. This reduction in emigration, however, must be ascribed more to the Great Depression and US immigration policy than to domestic activity or policy. While the increase in total employment was probably the first since the Famine, it was nevertheless slight. No definitive statement can be made about the trend of unemployment in view of the major changes that took place in the administration of the unemployment compensation schemes. However, it is clear that despite the gains in industrial employment, unemployment remained very high and at the peak in January 1936 there were some 145,000 on the unemployment register. Once conditions began to improve abroad, emigration picked up again in 1937 and 1938 to the levels of the 1920s, though the main destination had shifted from the US to Britain.

Gross national product at constant prices was about 10 per cent higher in 1938 than in 1931.[22] This increase was much less than in the UK where, despite a sharp decline from 1929 to 1931, the volume of GNP in 1938 was 18 per cent above the 1929 level. The Irish population changed little during the 1930s, but with a sharp decline in the terms of trade, the gain in average real income *per capita* was slight.

We shall have more to say in Part Three about the effects of the policy changes made in the 1930s. While these changes were substantial, however, it would be wrong to overstate their radical nature. Certainly, there was often a pragmatic, rather than an ideological, basis underlying the changes. The new industrial and commercial state bodies, for instance, were established only where it was abundantly clear that private enterprise would not or could not operate. Land policy essentially reflected the same pragmatic approach, social in outlook but definitely not socialist. Division and reallocation of holdings continued on the basis of providing small peasant proprietorships for rural landless men in their own locality. While this did not necessarily lead to innovative farming or the most economically efficient use of land, the country's chief natural resource, it undoubtedly reflected political realities arising from the values of the vast majority of the population.

2.2.4 The Anglo-Irish Agreements of 1938

The Economic War was brought to a conclusion as part of the

1938 Defence, Financial and Trade Agreements. What caused the parties to agree then to a settlement? From the Irish viewpoint, the policy of self-sufficiency had been implemented about as far as it could sensibly go, if not further, and once this had been accomplished there was no good reason to prolong a conflict that was now needlessly damaging. Moreover, the failure to achieve any substantial redirection of trade had underlined the essential dependence on the British market. From the British viewpoint, there had been economic losses in the reduction in Irish imports of coal and machinery, but political considerations — in particular its desire to retain Ireland within its sphere of influence — were probably of even greater consequence to Britain. It seemed foolish to Chamberlain, the British Prime Minister, to persist in an economic dispute with its nearest neighbour at a time of crisis in Europe which was likely to culminate in war.[23]

The objects of the financial and trade agreements were to achieve 'a final settlement of all outstanding financial claims' and 'to facilitate trade and commerce'. The arrangement substantially accorded victory to Ireland on the annuities question, with the Irish government agreeing to pay £10 million before 30 March 1938 in final settlement of all British claims, the capitalised value of which was estimated at £80–100 million. Ireland undertook to abolish the emergency duties on certain imports, while the UK agreed to abolish the penal duties imposed under the Special Duties Act 1932. Under the trade agreement, the Irish government agreed to discontinue the export bounties and subsidies that were introduced to counter the British penal duties. Commonwealth preferential duties were re-established between the two countries. In general, Irish agricultural produce was allowed access to the British market, though a preferential subsidy was retained by Britain in favour of domestic cattle. The agreement recognised the desire of each country to protect certain of its products. Broadly the overall outcome was that Ireland regained access for agricultural produce, the bulk of its exports, while retaining most of its protective, as distinct from its penal, duties on imports.

2.3 THE WARTIME EXPERIENCE

Trade relations with the UK had hardly been normalised in

1938 before the outbreak of the Second World War produced the next serious disruption to the Irish economy. Although Ireland remained neutral during the war, its imported supplies of fuel, raw materials, machinery and many foodstuffs were severely curtailed, and economic survival took over from economic development as the main thrust of policy. Protective duties were suspended for all practical purposes in 1942 and many quotas were in abeyance. Nevertheless, Ireland now had imposed upon it external pressure to produce as much as possible at home — the goal pursued voluntarily during the 1930s. However, even the most extreme nationalist would not have wished to go so far in the direction of autarky, which was bound to impose a drastic cut in living standards in a small island economy, with very limited natural resources.

Although still producing a large agricultural surplus, Ireland nevertheless experienced an acute shortage of many foodstuffs which could no longer be imported in sufficient quantities or adequately substituted for domestically. Because of food shortages in Britain, there was now a ready market for whatever Ireland could or would supply in the way of agricultural produce. However, the possibility of expanding agricultural output was severely constrained for two main reasons. Firstly, because of supply shortages abroad, fuel, fertiliser and feeding-stuffs were very scarce, and it was extremely difficult to get machinery, or even parts for old machinery. Secondly, in order to widen the range of foodstuffs for the home market, it was necessary to extend and diversify the amount of tillage, with adverse implications for productivity. In the event, the total volume of gross agricultural output was maintained during the war at about the immediate pre-war level. This in itself was a remarkable achievement, given the large drop in inputs of materials: in 1942–3, the volume of such inputs was less than one-fifth of the pre-war level.

Industry was also severely hit, not only by the shortages of fuel and machinery, but also by the scarcity of materials — given that much of the new industry of the 1930s involved the final processing and assembly of semi-finished goods imported from abroad. The volume of manufacturing output fell to a low point in 1942, nearly 25 per cent below the 1939 level, and only in 1946 was the 1939 overall level surpassed again — and indeed, only later still in some branches of industry. Activity in building and construction was hit even harder, and the number of new houses completed in 1945–6 was only 1,300 compared with 12,300 in 1939–40. Industrial employment was better maintained than output, so that labour productivity fell, partly because of the difficulty in replacing or expanding capital equipment. With no shipping fleet of its own, Ireland was more dependent than ever on Britain for import supplies. These were provided, though in greatly diminished volume, in British ships up to the end of 1941 in return for much-needed supplies of Irish meat and meat products. When British ships were withdrawn from transporting goods to Ireland, it became necessary for the Irish government to establish Irish Shipping, a state-sponsored body, to try to maintain essential supplies. At the low point, 1942, the volume of imports was less than one-third of the 1939 level. Export volume never fell anything like as much as imports, so that Ireland had a substantial current balance of payments surplus, and built up sizeable external reserves. Exports were now almost totally concentrated on the UK, with less than 1 per cent going to other countries.

Total employment was maintained at about the pre-war level. Even though Ireland remained neutral, there was a threat of invasion and the numbers in the defence forces were increased substantially: the regular armed forces rose from 7,500 in 1939 to a peak of 38,000 in 1942. The outflow from agriculture was held back, partly because many had nowhere else to go, and partly because of the switch to greater tillage at a time when mechanisation was constrained by supply scarcities. The total area under tillage rose to over 2½ million acres at the peak in 1944, a level not previously seen since the 1870s. Emigration during the war, at an average of about 26,000 per annum, was twice as high as in the 1930s. Some of these were volunteers to the British armed forces, and by the end of the war there were an estimated 50,000 persons from the Republic serving in the British forces. However, the bulk of the rise in emigration was in response to the demand for labour in war-production factories in the UK. The increase in the rate of emigration, however, was not such as to cause a reduction in population, which in 1946 was fractionally higher than in 1939.

The volume of GNP was about the same at the end of the war as at the beginning, as was also real GNP *per capita*. This stability, of course, masks a decline in the standard of living due to the much more limited choice of goods available. Tea, sugar, bread, butter and clothing were rationed, private motoring was eliminated in 1943, cigarettes and tobacco were in very short supply, and many tropical and sub-tropical fruits were no longer available. These privations, however, were much less severe than in many other European countries. Ireland's ability to cope reasonably satisfactorily with the difficult conditions enforced by the war was helped by the agricultural policies of the 1930s, which gave a head-start in diversifying the range of production needed during the war. The longer-term effects of the policies are more questionable, however. Perhaps the most important lesson of the war years was that the strenuous protection of industry and agriculture in the 1930s had succeeded in changing only the *nature*, but not the *fact*, of Ireland's dependence on the outside world.

NOTES

1. D. Johnson, *The inter-war economy in Ireland*, (Economic and Social History Society of Ireland, Dublin, 1985), p. 5.
2. P. Lynch, 'Ireland since the Treaty 1921–66' in T.W. Moody and F.X. Martin (eds), *The course of Irish history* (The Mercier Press, Cork, 1967), p. 334.
3. J.M. Keynes, 'National self-sufficiency', *Studies*, vol. xxii, June (1933). It should be added, however, that Keynes also warned — though the warning largely went unheeded — of the dangers to be avoided in the pursuit of economic nationalism, which he classified as *silliness, haste*, and *intolerance*.
4. G. O'Brien, 'Patrick Hogan, Minister for Agriculture, 1922–32', *Studies*, vol. xxv, September (1936).
5. See W.J.L. Ryan, 'The nature and effects of protective policy in Ireland, 1922–39' (unpublished doctoral thesis, Trinity College, Dublin, 1949), p. 68, and Commission of Inquiry into Banking, Currency and Credit, *Reports* (Stationery Office, Dublin, 1938), p. 55.
6. These and the remaining figures in this paragraph are taken from R. O'Connor and C. Guiomard, 'Agricultural output in the Irish Free State area before and after independence', *Irish Economic and Social History*, vol. xii (1985), pp. 89–97.
7. R. Crotty, *Irish agricultural production: its volume and structure* (Cork University Press, Cork, 1966), pp. 126–9.
8. J. Meenan, *The Irish economy since 1922* (Liverpool University Press, Liverpool, 1970), p. xxix.
9. E. de Valera, *Fianna Fáil and its economic policy* (National Executive of Fianna Fáil, Dublin, 1928), p. 3.
10. Ibid., p. 7.
11. Ibid., p. 8.
12. W.K. Hancock, *Survey of British Commonwealth affairs:*

problems of nationality (Oxford University Press, London, 1937) vol. 1, p. 350.

13. See, for example, N. Mansergh, *The Irish Free State: its government and politics* (Allen and Unwin, London, 1934), and Hancock, *Survey of British Commonwealth affairs.*

14. Ryan, 'The nature and effects of protective policy', p. 225.

15. In support of this legislation, it was argued by the Minister that subsidiaries of foreign companies 'would never attempt to do more than supply this market' — Dáil Debates, 14 June 1932, vol. 42, cols 1236–7. In this respect they would be no different from native firms, given de Valera's earlier contention that he saw little hope of Irish industries being able to develop exports, other than food. Still, the restriction on foreign firms could be given an economic rationale: recent theoretical work suggests that international capital mobility nearly always adds to the cost of protection — see J.P. Neary and F.P. Ruane, 'International capital mobility, shadow prices and the cost of protection', *Working Paper, Centre for Economic Research, University College, Dublin*, no. 32 (1984).

16. This was an extension of a development initiated by the previous government which encouraged the establishment of a privately operated factory in Carlow in 1925.

17. O'Brien, 'Patrick Hogan', p. 363.

18. Keynes, 'National self-sufficiency', p. 190.

19. J.P. Neary and C. Ó Gráda, 'Protection, economic war and structural change: the 1930s in Ireland', *Working Paper, Centre for Economic Research, University College, Dublin*, no. 40 (1986), p. 8.

20. J. Vaizey, *The brewing industry 1886–1951: an economic study* (Pitman, London, 1960), p. 31.

21. The Census of Industrial Production (CIP) did not cover all industrial employees as recorded in the Census of Population. For various reasons the proportion covered by the former expanded over time, so that the growth in industrial employment derived from this source exceeds the growth of numbers as defined in the Census of Population — see K.A. Kennedy, *Productivity and industrial growth: the Irish experience* (Clarendon Press, Oxford, 1974), pp. 37–8. Thus, for example, the rise in industrial employment between 1926 and 1936 was 51,600 on a CIP basis and 44,200 on a Census of Population basis. A number of scholars have gone further in suggesting that a sizeable part of the rise in CIP employment was illusory on the grounds that it represented no more than an improvement of the coverage of the CIP — see Johnson, *The inter-war economy*; G. FitzGerald, 'Mr Whitaker and industry', *Studies*, vol. xlviii (1959); and N.J.J. Farley, 'Determinants of establishment size in Irish manufacturing industries: some notes on the Irish case 1931–1972', *Economic and Social Review*, vol. 6, no. 2 (January 1975). There are a number of grounds, however, for doubting whether this factor accounted for much of the rise in CIP employment in the 1930s. Certainly, one would expect that the more obvious omissions were picked up by 1931, by which time three censuses had been carried out.

22. The only national income figures covering the period are the

unofficial estimates of G.A. Duncan, 'the social income of the Irish Free State, 1926–38', *Journal of the Statistical and Social Inquiry Society of Ireland*, vol. 16 (1939–40) and 'The social income of Éire, 1938–40', *Journal of the Statistical and Social Inquiry Society of Ireland*, vol. 16 (1940–1). Duncan's figures put the growth of real GNP over the period 1926–38 at 13–17 per cent, but suggest that nearly all of this was concentrated in the years 1926–31. The figures for the 1930s have been questioned by Neary and Ó Gráda, 'Protection, economic war and structural change', who do not, however, provide alternative estimates. Our own examination of the position leads us to the view that, while Duncan's growth rate for the full period 1926–38 is plausible enough, the distribution of the growth within the period is not plausible. In particular the time pattern of real output growth is distorted by the price index used by Duncan for industry. Correction for this gives an increase of about 10 per cent in real GNP from 1931–8, with the increase from 1926 to 1931 correspondingly reduced. Such a pattern also accords much better with other available indicators of output growth in the sectors.

23. N. Mansergh, *Survey of British Commonwealth affairs: problems of external policy 1931–39* (Oxford University Press, Oxford, 1952), p. 310.

3

Outward Re-orientation, 1947–72

As normality returned after the war, the development challenge had to be taken up afresh. There was considerable innovation in economic policy in the next decade or so, but not all of these developments came to fruition until later. Serious structural weaknesses had to be overcome, and policies to deal with these took time to devise and implement, and even longer to bear fruit. Progress was retarded by the fact that the initial phase of fiscal expansion in the years 1947–51 was followed by a deflationary fiscal stance for most of the remainder of the 1950s. Ireland's overall growth performance in the 1950s was one of the worst in Europe, emigration reached record levels for this century, and confidence about the viability of the economy reached an all-time low.

Nevertheless, the 1950s marked an important transition in Ireland's economic development. The strategy that was slowly and painfully evolved then was to hold sway over the next three decades — though of course it was refined and extended over time. It led to continuous economic expansion from the late 1950s to the early 1970s at a pace not witnessed previously in Ireland for such an extended period. Total GNP nearly doubled, the decline in population was arrested, living standards increased markedly, the structure of the economy was transformed, and entry to the EEC in 1973 signalled the final stage of the reopening of the economy. Yet major structural problems remained unresolved which left the economy still vulnerable in the face of the troubled world conditions that were to follow.

3.1 POST-WAR ADJUSTMENT PROBLEMS

The decade or so after the war was to pose the greatest challenge to Ireland's ability to survive and prosper as an independent economic entity. That this should be so may seem surprising in a European context. The Western world entered a phase of rapid recovery which was sustained by expansionary domestic policies underpinned by international economic co-operation on monetary, trade, and development issues. Ireland had not suffered war damage, it had not accumulated war debts but rather had built up considerable monetary reserves, and it had a plentiful supply of labour.

Why was Ireland also not lifted by the rising tide of international prosperity? One reason was that Ireland remained very much an agricultural country. The post-war climate of international co-operation extended primarily to industrial trade rather than agricultural, and most countries strongly protected their own agriculture. Ireland's only important export market, the United Kingdom, was by no means an ideal one on which to be so heavily dependent. The UK was one of the most slowly growing Western countries — the 'sick man' of Europe — and the manner in which it protected its own farmers, by income supports, was designed to keep prices low. Moreover, since it was one of the few major markets to which there was wide freedom of access, competition was intense. Irish agriculture, following the upheavals of the 1930s and 1940s, was ill-fitted to compete in many products, while the memory of the Economic War in the 1930s and of Ireland's neutral stand during the Second World War was not calculated to predispose the British favourably to accord special status to Irish supply.

The overriding constraint in manufacturing lay on the supply side. Though the home market was small, there were virtually unlimited markets in Europe and beyond, if Ireland was capable of supplying them. However, much of Irish manufacturing was small-scale, technologically unsophisticated, and with little or no experience of export marketing. It was clear enough that these problems needed to be overcome, but not so clear how it was to be done. Serious deficiencies also existed in social and infrastructural facilities. Having remained neutral during the war despite considerable pressure from Britain and the United States, Ireland could not expect to be the beneficiary of substantial recovery aid. In the event, Ireland received only

£46 million in Marshall Aid and all but £6 million of this was in the form of loans, though at a very favourable interest rate of 2½ per cent. The outflow of labour from agriculture, restrained in the 1930s and during the war, was bound to increase substantially as a result of the inevitable reduction in the abnormally high tillage levels, the availability of new machinery and a backlog of labour-saving techniques.

To these pressures on the social fabric can be added another, impossible to quantify but no less real on that account — namely, the demonstration effect from abroad. A poor economic record could be excused and accepted more readily when performance abroad was not strikingly good. However, with the welfare state, full employment and rapid growth in living standards becoming a reality in the industrialised nations with which Ireland, by reason of its location, inevitably compared itself, major deficiencies in Irish economic progress were more likely to provoke dissatisfaction — especially now that league tables of comparative economic growth rates were regularly published. Given Ireland's history and ease of access to labour markets abroad, such dissatisfaction was likely to be reflected in higher emigration rather than in creative pressures to adopt more radical development measures.

3.1.1 The policy response

The policy response to these challenges was initially quite enterprising in some areas. The most far-reaching development was the launching of a large programme of public capital expenditure. Much of this was devoted to building badly needed infrastructural facilities — some social, such as houses, schools and hospitals, but also a significant volume in power, transport and communications. This made good sense not only in providing basic development facilities, but also in absorbing the prevailing high unemployment in the construction industry and the outflow of unskilled labour from agriculture. The approach further ensured a high growth of demand for domestic manufacturing supplies.

The early post-war years witnessed a considerable degree of economic recovery and progress. The total volume of GNP had surpassed the highest pre-war level by 1947, and in the following four years rose at an average of 3 per cent per annum.

Industrial production was the most buoyant element. Having surpassed the pre-war level in 1946, it grew in the five years from 1946 to 1951 at an average annual rate of 10.7 per cent. Construction activity rose particularly rapidly in response to the expanding Public Capital Programme, but manufacturing activity was not far behind with an average annual rate of 9.4 per cent. Little of the increased manufacturing output was exported, however. Protection was restored, with some new tariffs added, and the expansion of output was fuelled by the buoyancy of domestic demand, led by revival in consumer demand repressed during the war. The performance of agriculture was erratic. As might be expected tillage declined once the war was over and production of cattle and beef expanded, but there was no progress in expanding the overall volume of output.

The outflow from agriculture rose substantially to a total of 70,000 from 1946 to 1951, nearly as much as in the whole of the preceding 20 year. Despite this, however, the overall level of employment declined by less than 10,000, due to the large rise in industrial employment. Though the emigration rate was somewhat higher than in the previous 20 years, so also was the rate of natural increase, and the population rose slightly between 1946 and 1951. The unemployment rate fell from 9.3 per cent in 1947 to 7.3 per cent in 1951, while the rate in building and construction fell from 15.4 to 11.4 per cent. This performance, while perhaps modest in comparison with contemporary European experience, was much better than what had gone before in Ireland, or what was to follow during most of the next decade.

There were two major and interrelated lacunae in the immediate post-war strategy. The first was that buoyant home demand was bound to encounter balance of payments difficulties unless measures were taken to secure a complementary development of exports to match the inevitable large increase in imports. The second, and partly related, lacuna was the absence of a sense of direction on future industrialisation, given that there was no scope for extending significantly the type of protection used in the 1930s.

Serious balance of payments problems did not emerge for a few years, however, and were then due as much to international as to domestic factors. True, the volume of imports nearly trebled between 1945 and 1947, bringing them well above the immediate pre-war level, while at the same time, the volume of exports was unchanged — leading to a very large trade deficit of £92 million in 1947. Ireland had a substantial surplus in invisibles, however, and was at this time experiencing a tourist boom, consisting largely of British tourists seeking a good meal: rationing continued in Britain up to 1949 while foreign exchange restrictions limited travel to non-sterling areas. In addition, the big increase in imports was largely due to post-war restocking, and once this was completed the growth of imports tapered off. On the other hand, after 1947 the volume of exports recovered strongly up to 1953, when they were almost twice the 1947 level. The current balance of payments deficits experienced up to the end of 1950 were largely offset by sizeable private capital inflows, and taking account of the Marshall Aid funds, the external reserves were somewhat higher in 1950 than in 1946.

The position deteriorated sharply in 1951 when a large current payments deficit of £62 million, equal to nearly 15 per cent of GNP, coincided with reduced capital inflows due to exhaustion of the Marshall Aid funds. This led to a decline of nearly one-sixth in external reserves. Underlying the deficit was a large increase in imports from mid-1949 to mid-1950, due to sharply rising import prices following the 1949 devaluation of sterling, to which the Irish pound remained linked, and US involvement in the Korean War in June 1950, which caused a large increase in world raw materials prices. A further important factor was that tourist receipts declined after 1948 as conditions in Britain improved.

While these developments could be said to be largely externally determined, the onus was nevertheless on Ireland to anticipate such problems by measures to develop its own exports. The 1948 Trade Agreement with Britain achieved further relaxation in the restrictions in the UK on Irish agricultural exports. However, given the UK determination to achieve a greater measure of agricultural self-sufficiency, and the intense competition on the British market from the traditional suppliers, agricultural exports were unlikely to grow fast enough to preclude balance of payments difficulties. What was most required was the development of manufactured exports. The Trade Agreement of 1948 provided substantial free entry to the large British market for most Irish manufactured goods, while permitting Ireland to maintain most of its own protective tariffs. However, access to a large market was of little value if Irish manufacturers were not geared to compete in that market. There was little evidence that this would happen spontaneously; and it was only gradually as the 1950s progressed that policy measures were taken to assist Irish manufacturing towards export competition.

It should also be noted that, even with more expeditious measures, manufacturing exports could only become significant from a balance of payments viewpoint with some lapse of time, due to the negligible starting base. However, the balance of payments constraint depended not only on the growth of exports but also on the willingness to use external reserves and/ or to borrow abroad to finance worthwhile development at home. By the standards of most countries Ireland had considerable latitude in this regard. External reserves in 1949 were equivalent to 20 months' purchase of imports of goods and services, far higher than the generality of European countries. With little foreign debt, it would not have been imprudent for Ireland to sustain its expansionary path longer by resort to foreign borrowing or repatriation of foreign reserves. In the event, however, fiscal and monetary conservatism prevailed. The response to the large balance of payments deficit of 1951 was one of fiscal retrenchment which further retarded development in the 1950s.

3.2 THE TRANSITION IN THE 1950s

The 1950s have been viewed as a period of great trauma in Irish economic and social life, which at the time inspired titles like *The vanishing Irish* and to which phrases have been applied subsequently like 'national malaise' and 'symptoms . . . resembling the "death wish" of a society'.[1] It is certainly true that economic performance was poor, being characterised by two serious depressions and a decline in population over the seven years between 1951 and 1958 nearly twice as great as in the whole of the preceding period since independence. It is also true, however, that during this period the basis of the development strategy was laid which propelled the economy towards unprecedented growth in the 15-year period 1958–73.

Despite the buoyancy in world trade, there were a number of unfavourable external developments from the Irish viewpoint.

The terms of trade had deteriorated sharply in 1951 with soaring import prices due to the Korean War. Although the rise in import prices slackened, export prices drifted downwards due to poor agricultural prices, so that most of the 1950s was characterised by falling terms of trade, which in 1957 were 14 per cent below the 1949 level. The volume of exports was also sluggish, rising by less than 6 per cent between 1953 and 1958. Many categories of processed agricultural exports were subject to the vagaries of the British market and were liable to considerable fluctuation. Manufactured exports were rising at a rapid proportionate rate, but the initial base was so low that this had only a small, though increasing, impact. Tourist receipts stagnated as rationing and restrictions on travel to non-sterling areas eased in Britain.

The domestic fiscal policy response compounded the external difficulties. Even though the adverse 1951 balance of payments position was already improving by the time the 1952 budget was introduced, whereas industrial output was falling and unemployment rising, the budget adopted was highly deflationary, adding further to the recessionary conditions that already existed. This check to growth would not in itself have proved serious had expansionary measures been resumed once the balance of payments deficit was under control by the end of 1952. Such was not the case, however: instead, the Public Capital Programme was maintained in the next four years at about the same nominal level as in 1952, implying a fall in real terms.

Worse was to follow. In 1955 there was a temporary consumer boom, leading to a large rise in imports. This coincided with a cyclical fall in cattle and beef exports, which, together with a decline in the net capital inflow, led to a drop of one-fifth in external reserves. To deal with this situation, special import levies were introduced in March 1956 and raised in July to 60 per cent full rate (with a 40 per cent preferential rate for UK and Commonwealth goods). These measures quickly brought the trade balance under control, but inevitably also depressed activity, since so much of domestic industrial production depended on imports. Moreover, manufactured exports which had been growing rapidly suffered a decline in 1956 due to the disruptive effects of the Suez crisis. The economy was already in the throes of recession when the 1957 budget was introduced. Instead of seeking to provide an offsetting stimulus, however, the budget was highly deflationary, with a cut of nearly one-

61

third in the Public Capital Programme and an especially large reduction in housing expenditure. The restrictive fiscal stance continued in 1958.

Predictably, economic progress was severely retarded. The volume of GNP in 1958, further depressed by a large decline in agricultural output due to bad weather conditions, was 2½ per cent below the 1955 level, and only 6½ per cent above the level of seven years earlier. The decline in numbers engaged in agriculture continued at a rapid rate, but was now augmented by a substantial fall in non-agricultural employment. Total employment declined continuously from 1951 to 1958, the cumulative decline amounting to over 12 per cent. The overall non-agriculture unemployment rate rose to 9 per cent, and was over 19 per cent in building and construction. Indeed, the unemployment rate would have been far higher were it not for the fact that emigration increased to rates not previously seen since the 1890s.

3.2.1 The evolving development strategy

Given the performance described above, it is small wonder that gloom bordering on despair, prevailed at this time, and that the period has remained in the consciousness of those who experienced it as the nadir of Irish economic performance since independence. Yet there was another side to the picture. Throughout the decade a number of important steps were taken to establish the basis of an export-orientated strategy. In 1951 a state-sponsored body, Córas Tráchtála (Irish Export Board) was set up to assist exporters in marketing their products abroad. However, the problem lay not only in marketing but also in the range and quality of products and in the efficiency of production. It was accepted that indigenous firms were unlikely to undertake the necessary investment without financial help from the state and without enhanced incentives, and further-more that domestic enterprise would need to be supplemented by foreign enterprise. In 1952 the Industrial Development Authority (IDA), a state-sponsored body initially established in 1949 to review the operation of tariffs and quotas in specific industries, was given the role of attracting foreign industry as well as encouraging the establishment of new indigenous industry. In the same year, still another state-sponsored body,

An Foras Tionscail (the Underdeveloped Areas Board) was set up with powers to give grants towards the capital and training cost of new industries in the west and south-west of the country. The grants could cover the full cost of factory site and buildings, up to 50 per cent of the cost of plant and the full cost of training workers. In 1956 the Board was given power to offer grants in the rest of the country in respect of site and buildings up to two-thirds of the cost.

Although such grants were not formally limited to export-orientated industries, this was certainly the intention and that is how it worked out for many years. Indeed, it would have been politically difficult to operate a grant scheme in any other way at that time because of the objections which would have arisen from competing domestic industries, whereas new production for exports could not reasonably be opposed as threatening the market of existing firms. This is not to say that there were not complaints from the established tariff-protected industries about the new direction of policy. Indeed, the slowness in developing an export-orientated strategy was not due solely to the time taken to devise new instruments but also to the political need to build support for the new approach in the face of this lobby.[2]

Probably the most important incentive of all in attracting foreign enterprise — it also applied to indigenous industry but with less response — was the export profits tax relief scheme initiated in 1956, and enlarged and extended in the Finance Acts of 1957 and 1958. The effect was to give complete tax exemption for a period of ten years, later extended, on profits derived from new or increased manufacturing exports. A variety of other incentives to industry was introduced during the period. More favourable depreciation allowances for industrial buildings (including hotels) were introduced in 1956, and for plant and machinery in 1958. The Industrial Credit (Amendment) Act 1958 extended the powers and the resources available to the Industrial Credit Company in providing capital for industry. A customs free area was established at Shannon Airport in 1947 but the venture did not begin to reap its full potential until the formation of the Shannon Free Airport Development Company in 1959 which went on to develop a large industrial estate. Of considerable symbolic importance was the first step taken in 1958 to dismantle the Control of Manufactures Acts of 1932 and 1934 which sought to keep control of Irish industry in Irish hands. Although this legislation had been circumvented readily enough, it had nevertheless given formal expression to a mentality that was prejudicial to attracting foreign enterprise.

It was not only in manufacturing that new initiatives were undertaken. A large programme of land reclamation was launched in 1949 designed to improve neglected land, and involving a planned state capital expenditure of £40 million over ten years (partly financed by the Marshall Aid funds). Although from a strictly economic viewpoint it would have made more sense to devote the moneys to raising output and efficiency on the better land, the scheme did nevertheless represent a substantial effort to develop resources, and had important psychological and distributional benefits for depressed areas.[3] The Bovine Tuberculosis Eradication Scheme was started in 1954. Important developments took place in the agricultural advisory services, and in 1958 An Foras Talúntais (the Agricultural Institute) was established which was to play a large role in applied agricultural research and in disseminating this research, both directly and through the advisory services. In tourism, two state-sponsored bodies were set up in 1952, one with responsibility for developing facilities and the other for promotional activities. The two were amalgamated into one body, Bord Fáilte Éireann (Irish Tourist Board) in 1955. The establishment of the sea fisheries board, Bord Iascaigh Mhara, dates from 1952.

Social and infrastructural facilities to underpin economic development had also been greatly enhanced. The provision of new hospitals and the improvement in the health services had helped, *inter alia*, radically to reduce the death-rate due to tuberculosis. State investment had also resulted in a vast improvement in the housing stock, and had brought electric power to 75 per cent of rural areas, as well as greatly expanding the generating capacity. While these investments did not yield an economic pay-off in the short term, it is difficult to see how subsequent economic progress could have been possible without them.

These developments took place in a piecemeal fashion. Moreover, at first implementation was not always effective. This was due partly to the need for experimentation and partly to inadequate funding, but it also arose from the fact that no coherent strategy linked the disparate measures. That coherence was supplied from a source, the Department of Finance, which was not previously noted for favouring development initiatives involving greater public expenditure or foreign indebtedness. On the contrary the Department, which held the same status in the Irish civil service as the Treasury in the British, had acted impeccably from the foundation of the state along conservative Treasury lines. In 1958, however, the Department published a remarkable study entitled *Economic development*, organised and written with government approval by its new Secretary, T.K. Whitaker.

This study aimed to 'work out an integrated programme of national development for the next five or ten years',[4] taking the view that the most urgent need was to identify in concrete terms the productive purposes to which resources should be devoted, and where these resources were to come from. A specific set of investment proposals was made covering in particular the activities with export potential — agriculture, fisheries, industry and tourism. In this respect more than any other, perhaps, the study differed from much previous economic advice which was cast in generalities or else looked for economic salvation to a single measure or activity. As regards financing, the study favoured reducing social expenditure so as to release resources for productive investment.[5] However, it also broke with the traditional financial conservatism of the Department of Finance in arguing that 'If sufficient capital is not available from home sources, every effort should be made to obtain it abroad on reasonable terms.'[6] As regards the overall thrust of economic policy, the study gave a new impetus to the often tentative steps taken in the previous ten years towards an export-orientated direction.

3.3 THE REOPENING OF THE ECONOMY

The favourable experience of the economy from 1958 to 1973 was not due solely to domestic policies. The period was one of faster and steadier growth in the world economy generally, with nothing quite so disruptive as the Korean War and the Suez crisis in the preceding period. Ireland's terms of trade improved considerably and in 1973 were 39 per cent above the 1957 level. There was a great increase world-wide in direct investment abroad by multinational companies, which made it easier to attract some to Ireland.

Nevertheless, domestic influences also played a major role in sustaining expansion. A consistently expansionary fiscal policy was pursued, led by an increasing Public Capital Programme. The decline in so-called social public investment, emphasised so much in the 1950s and envisaged as essential in *Economic development* to release resources for productive investment, did not in fact take place. Rather, both components rose substantially faster than anticipated, and this was important both in increasing the capacity to supply goods and services and in securing adequate home demand. It is true, of course, that this approach could not have been sustained had adequate attention not been paid to expanding exports, and had conditions abroad not been so favourable. Nevertheless, the authorities generally showed greater willingness than in the 1950s to persist with an expansionary approach in years when export growth slowed.[7]

In sharp contrast with the earlier phases since independence, there was a broad political and social consensus in favour of according primacy to economic development, and of the general thrust of the strategy needed to achieve it. The economic planning exercises played a role in mobilising this consensus. The *First Programme of Economic Expansion* adopted by government was based largely on *Economic development* and covered the period 1959–63. This was followed by a more ambitious attempt at planning in the *Second Programme*, covering the years 1964–70, which set detailed quantitative targets for all major branches of the economy. The targets were based on the assumption that Ireland would be a member of the EEC by 1970, but the document had hardly been published when it transpired, following the breakdown of negotiations between Britain and the EEC, that this assumption would not be fulfilled. The programme was abandoned two years later when the programme goals looked as if they would not be achieved. In 1969 a *Third Programme* was launched for the years 1969–72, covering social as well as economic development. The targets of this programme were not reached either — the short-fall in employment was particularly great — and no further plan was attempted for most of the remainder of the 1970s.

While many valid criticisms can be made of the national planning efforts of the 1960s,[8] the planning process itself was important in disseminating knowledge of the requirements of economic growth and the disciplines of free trade, and in developing communications between industry, trade unions and the public service. In this context a significant part was played by the National Industrial and Economic Council (NIEC), established in 1963 and comprising representatives of government, trade unions and employers. The NIEC reports helped to reinforce the broad consensus in favour of the new directions of policy, and particularly the progression towards free trade.

3.3.1 The move to free trade

At the time *Economic development* was being written, free trade was a very live issue in Europe, culminating in the Treaty of Rome in 1958 which established the Common Market between the original six countries. *Economic development* was emphatic that 'sooner or later, protection will have to go and the challenge of free trade be accepted,' since 'There is really no other choice for a country wishing to keep pace materially with the rest of Europe.'[9] The immediacy of the challenge receded, however, following the breakdown of the negotiations for a wider European community including Britain. Britain's accession to the European Free Trade Association (EFTA) in 1959, which Ireland did not join, had no significant effect on Ireland's access to the British market, though it did threaten greater competition in that market. The EFTA applied largely to industrial goods only, and left countries free to maintain their own arrangements with third countries. When negotiations were resumed with the EEC in 1961, Ireland applied for membership, but this move collapsed once negotiations between Britain and the EEC broke down in 1963.

To maintain momentum towards free trade, however, Ireland undertook two unilateral reductions in tariffs in January 1963 and January 1964, amounting to 10 per cent each. These moves were largely symbolic because of the height of most tariffs. A much more significant step on the way to dismantling protection took place in 1965 with the negotiation of the Anglo-Irish Free Trade Area Agreement (AIFTAA) to take effect from mid-1966. Ireland obtained substantially improved access to the British market for agricultural exports and the removal of the small remaining restrictions on industrial exports. In return

Ireland undertook to phase out tariffs on British industrial goods over a ten-year period, with some exceptions for particularly vulnerable activities, like assembly of motor vehicles. Finally, in the early 1970s, when Britain again resumed negotiations with the EEC, Ireland also gained entry with effect from 1 January 1973. Under the terms of entry, Ireland agreed to establish free trade with member countries over a period of five years by means of cuts in existing tariffs of 20 per cent per annum.

By the time Ireland joined the EEC, a number of domestic policy measures had been implemented during the previous decade to prepare and adapt Irish industry for free trade. In June 1961 a Committee on Industrial Organisation (CIO) was set up, with membership drawn from industry, the trade unions and the public service, to study in detail the extent to which Irish industry was equipped to cope with free trade. Similar reviews of the agricultural processing industries were carried out by the Department of Agriculture. Surveys of 26 industries were speedily completed by the CIO, which found native industry ill-prepared for free trade. Specific recommendations were made on the steps that needed to be taken to prepare to meet foreign competition. An adaptation grants scheme was announced in 1962 providing up to 25 per cent of the cost of investment needed to modernise buildings and plant. To achieve quick results, the scheme was to apply only up to March 1965, though it was subsequently extended to end-1967, and it was followed in February 1968 by a re-equipment grants scheme on similar lines. A Committee on Industrial Progress was then set up to concentrate in particular on deficiencies in product policy and marketing. Earlier the national dairy marketing board, An Bord Bainne, was established in 1961, while the functions and resources of Córas Tráchtála were expanded.

Ireland's growth of manufactured exports from 1958 to 1973 — averaging 23 per cent per annum in value and 18 per cent in volume — was well in excess of the growth of manufactured imports in the UK. This high growth rate was achieved not only by increasing the share in the UK market but also by penetrating other markets. As a result, the proportion of Irish manufactured exports going to the UK had fallen in 1972, the year immediately before Ireland joined the EEC, to 58 per cent, compared with almost 80 per cent in 1958, while the share going to the six countries then comprising the EEC had risen from 6 per cent in 1958 to 16 per cent in 1972. At the latter date manufactured exports amounted to 30 per cent of total manufacturing output as compared with about 5 per cent 20 years earlier. Much of the export growth came from new foreign enterprises, as discussed more fully in Chapter 11. However, the indigenous firms also benefited from the strong growth in home demand, and total industrial output was over 2½ times higher in 1973 than in 1958.

Though manufactured exports grew by far the fastest, exports of livestock and livestock produce also expanded considerably. Moreover, they continued to be of major importance to the balance of payments because of their low import content — 10 per cent for livestock, and 26 per cent for food, as against 53 per cent for manufactured exports in 1968.[10] Within agricultural exports there was a substantial shift from live cattle to meat and meat preparations. Exports of dairy produce also increased strongly from negligible proportions in the late 1950s. These exports were of doubtful value then since they were a by-product of the policy of expanding livestock numbers and the resulting milk surplus had to be disposed of in subsidised export sales — until Ireland entered the EEC.

The volume of gross agricultural output, which had been stagnant since the First World War, was 50 per cent higher in 1972 than in the late 1950s. Livestock and livestock produce grew fastest, at 3.4 per cent per annum, as against an annual growth rate of 1.2 per cent for crops. There were three main factors underlying this expansion. Firstly, important domestic policy measures, involving substantial state expenditure, were adopted, in the course of the *First* and *Second Programmes* to stimulate farmers to expand output — notably, the calved heifer subsidy, the subsidies to export milk supplies, and the lime and fertiliser subsidies. The last-mentioned subsidies helped to stimulate a large increase in the volume of farm inputs, which grew by 6½ per cent per annum between 1960 and 1973, so that the volume of net output rose much less than gross output. Secondly, there were the more favourable arrangements concluded with Britain, especially through the AIFTAA, for the sale of Irish livestock and butter in the British market. Thirdly, the price of agricultural output world-wide rose strongly in the late 1960s and early 1970s, augmenting farmers' incomes and giving farmers both the stimulus to, and the resources for, effecting improvements in farming. Between

1967 and 1973, the agricultural price index doubled, while livestock prices went up 2¼ times. The value of net output in agriculture trebled between 1960 and 1973, and with consumer prices only doubling in the same period, and the numbers engaged in agriculture continuing to decline at about 3 per cent per annum, the real incomes of farmers improved substantially.

Invisible exports also rose rapidly up to 1968 — until tourism was badly hit by the outbreak of the Northern Ireland conflict in 1969. Somewhat surprisingly, in view of the large capital inflows throughout the post-war period, and especially from the early 1960s, receipts from foreign investment income almost kept pace with payments. The reason is that there was as yet little or no outflow of earnings then in respect of the substantial amount of foreign direct investment. Emigrants' remittances also continued to hold their own as a proportion of total invisible earnings despite falling emigration — presumably because the stock of recent emigrants remained large even though the flow was declining.

Given Ireland's history of secular population decline in the previous 100 years or so, the reversal of this trend represented an even sharper break with the past than the improvement in GNP growth. Though emigration began to fall after 1958, the population continued to decline up to 1961, when an all-time low of 2·8 million was reached. The fall in emigration was maintained thereafter and by the early 1970s there was small net immigration. As a result, the population rose at an increasing rate during the 1960s, averaging ½ per cent per annum over the decade. Other peculiarities of Irish demography also changed. The marriage rate, which had never before in this century been above 5·5 per thousand, rose to 7.2 per thousand — almost 'normal' in comparison with the generality of European countries at that time. This was associated with a fall in the age at marriage and a higher proportion marrying in each age-group, and both of these factors are attributable, in part at least, to improved living standards.

3.4 REMAINING STRUCTURAL WEAKNESSES

By 1972, the eve of entry into the EEC, Ireland had moved in many respects during the previous 15 years from being an agricultural to an industrial country. Manufactured exports were now almost equal to agricultural exports whereas in 1958 they were only about one-quarter the size of the latter. Industrial employment now accounted for 30 per cent of the total work-force and exceeded agricultural employment by about one-fifth. The GDP arising in industry was nearly double that in agriculture. Yet despite all these accomplishments, the economy had by no means overcome all of its structural weaknesses, which still left it highly vulnerable to an unfavourable turn of events.

Perhaps the greatest disappointment was the fact that total employment did not rise by very much. While employment in industry and services rose, this increase was largely offset by the continuing rapid decline in numbers engaged in agriculture. The failure to achieve a significant increase in total employment did not become a cause of undue concern until the late 1960s, since unemployment was falling up to the mid-1960s. Indeed, the non-agricultural unemployment rate in 1964 dipped below 5 per cent for the first time ever in the history of the state; and in 1966 the NIEC, with some credibility, produced a report charting possible paths towards full employment.

In retrospect the slow growth of employment was a cause for greater concern than was realised then, since the impact of rising population on the future labour force was masked for a time. A scheme of free secondary education was introduced in 1966 which in the next few years led to a great rise in educational participation. When this once-for-all change came to an end, however, as it inevitably had to, then the growth of the labour force would certainly resume. In addition, enhanced education at secondary level, when it did not lead to a particular skill or professional qualification, was itself likely to lower the willingness to emigrate, at least in the traditional manner to the more readily available unskilled jobs abroad. This factor was compounded by the improvements in unemployment benefits which were possible in consequence of rising living standards. The participation of married women in the labour force had always been very low and even in 1971 amounted to only 8 per cent. With rising living standards, falling marriage fertility, and changing attitudes, however, it was inevitable that participation would soon begin to increase sharply. By the early 1970s, as unemployment began to rise — due to slackness in the demand for labour in Britain — it was beginning to emerge that popula-

71

tion growth without a corresponding growth in employment was not an unmixed blessing.

Another unresolved problem was the comparative failure of indigenous private enterprise to respond to the incentives which had proved successful in attracting foreign enterprise. This failure threatened large job losses once protection of the home market was progressively dismantled. Indeed, the figures on industrial job losses were already beginning to mount in the early 1970s, offsetting much of the gains in employment in new enterprises. Moreover, given the sensitivity of foreign investment to world economic conditions, the heavy reliance on foreign enterprise meant that any major shock to the international system would affect not only the demand for Irish products, but also the supply of new enterprise. A further adverse development towards the end of the period was the outbreak of hostilities in Northern Ireland in 1969, which was to prove damaging to the economy of the Republic in a number of ways — taking up a great deal of the time and energy of government, and raising the cost of security. The immediate impact, however, was most visible with regard to tourism. Earnings from foreign visitors rose by over 5 per cent per annum in real terms between 1959 and 1968, but had fallen to two-thirds of the 1968 level by 1972. The decline was concentrated chiefly in tourism from Northern Ireland and Britain, and would have been much greater were it not for the continued rapid growth in tourist receipts from continental Europe.

A further problem was the lack of any sign that there would be a tapering off, even in the future, in the demands on the state to finance economic and social development. Nearly half of total investment was financed by the state — either through capital formation by the public sector itself or loans and grants to the private sector. Little of this produced a direct return to the Exchequer so that the loans had to be serviced through taxation. While revenue buoyancy increased with economic activity, it was not enough to keep tax rates from rising, given the many other demands on the Exchequer. At this time the state was able to escape a sizeable part of the burden of its borrowing through inflation, but it was unlikely that lenders would continue indefinitely to provide loans at low or negative real interest rates. A development strategy involving an ever-increasing Exchequer burden clearly could not be sustained for ever; yet there was no tendency in business towards greater self-reliance.

From the late 1960s, Ireland, like many other countries, experienced an acceleration in inflation. The consumer price index rose at an annual average rate of 8.3 per cent between 1968 and 1972, about double the average rate previously experienced since the Second World War. The major impetus came from external factors, beginning with the sterling devaluation of November 1967 and sustained by world-wide inflation. Domestic wage demands also soared, however, and settlements were high, even in real terms, in comparison with previous experience. There was also considerable industrial unrest, and the number of man-days lost due to industrial disputes in 1969 and 1970 was close to one million each year compared with an annual average of about 400,000 during the 1960s. A further domestic influence on inflation was the large increase in indirect taxation to finance the now rapid growth of public expenditure. These factors suggest that expectations were rising even faster than the resources available to satisfy them. This tension was to increase in the succeeding period when expectations remained high but economic growth was sharply curtailed.

NOTES

1. J.A. O'Brien (ed.), *The vanishing Irish* (McGraw-Hill, New York, 1953; W.H. Allen, London, 1954); F.B. Chubb and P. Lynch (eds), *Economic development and planning* (Institute of Public Administration, Dublin, 1969), pp. 1–2.

2. For an account of the evolution of policy from this perspective, see P. Bew and H. Patterson, *Seán Lemass and the making of modern Ireland 1945–1966* (Gill and Macmillan, Dublin, 1982).

3. P. Lynch, 'The Irish economy in the postwar era' in K.B. Nowlan and T.D. Williams (eds), *Ireland in the war years and after, 1939–51* (Gill and Macmillan, Dublin, 1969), p. 198.

4. Department of Finance, *Economic development* (Stationery Office, Dublin, 1958), p. 227.

5. Whether the cut in social expenditure was necessary or desirable is open to debate — see K.A. Kennedy and B.R. Dowling, *Economic growth in Ireland: the experience since 1947* (Gill and Macmillan, Dublin, and Barnes and Noble, New York, 1975), pp. 225–30.

6. Department of Finance, *Economic development*, p. 44.

7. Thus, even when deflationary measures were taken to deal with the large fall in reserves in 1965, the authorities engaged in significant foreign borrowing to avoid a more serious reduction in public capital spending — Kennedy and Dowling, *Economic growth*, pp. 233–6.

8. See K.A. Kennedy, 'The Irish economy: the challenges and

options', *Management* (Journal of the Irish Management Institute), vol. xxi, no. 5 (May 1974), and *Reprint Series,* no. 37 (Economic and Social Research Institute, Dublin); D. Norton, *Problems in economic planning and policy formation in Ireland, 1958–1974,* Broadsheet Series no. 12 (The Economic and Social Research Institute, Dublin, 1975); O. Katsiaouni, 'Planning in a small economy: the Republic of Ireland', *Journal of the Statistical and Social Inquiry Society of Ireland,* vol. xxiii, part v (1977–8).

9. Department of Finance, *Economic development,* p. 2.

10. E.W. Henry, *Irish input–output structures, 1964 and 1968,* General Research Series no. 66 (Economic and Social Research Institute, Dublin, 1972), p. 16.

4

Oil and Troubled Waters, 1973–87

The danger signs mentioned at the end of the last chapter were only dimly seen at the time. Certainly no one at all foresaw the shattering consequences that would follow from the two oil crises, and associated world depressions. On the contrary, Ireland entered the EEC on 1 January 1973 in a confident, even exuberant, mood. It had behind it 15 years of economic progress unparalleled in its own history, which had brought about a considerable rise in living standards and an end to the secular decline in population. Great benefits for agriculture were anticipated under the Common Agricultural Policy (CAP). In manufacturing, while it was recognised that the older industries would be threatened by increasing competition, there was every confidence that this would be more than counter-balanced by free access to the EEC market and Ireland's enhancement as a location for new foreign enterprise. That expectations were so high made it all the harder to cope with the reality which emerged during the next decade and a half. In 1987, as we conclude our study, unemployment and the national debt are at all-time high levels, living standards are depressed, substantial emigration has resumed, and the future outlook is problematic.

4.1 THE OIL CRISES AND THE DOMESTIC POLICY RESPONSE

The two major oil price increases — the first towards the end of 1973 and the second beginning late in 1979 — raised the price of oil about ten-fold, and the prices of other imported energy rose in tandem, though not by the same amount. For a country like Ireland, which imported over 70 per cent of its primary energy requirements, such an increase in price was bound to have a large effect on the balance of payments. Energy is price inelastic in the short to medium term, and there were no known domestic substitutes to supplant the bulk of import needs. Thus, despite the attempts, partly successful, to economise on energy, to switch from oil to cheaper coal, and to develop domestic energy sources, the ratio of the value of energy imports to GDP rose from 2·6 per cent in 1973 to 7·2 per cent in 1974, and after being reduced to 5·5 per cent in 1978, rose again to 8·8 per cent in 1980 and 1981. The balance of payments impact was only one of the problems presented by the oil price increases. In addition, the enormous rise in price of a major necessity — oil — was inflationary in its impact on the general price level at the same time as being deflationary in its impact on demand — both by cutting real income at home and by depressing demand abroad due to the inability of the oil producers to spend their gains sufficiently quickly.

4.1.1 The response to the first oil price increase

The primary demand-deflationary impact would have been exacerbated had the governments of oil-importing countries attempted to dampen the price-inflationary spiral by further restricting home demand. Instead, the Irish government, like many other governments, responded by accepting the price-inflationary consequences and trying to offset the demand-deflationary implications through increased Exchequer borrowing. In 1972 the budgetary convention of balancing current expenditure with current revenue, which had been strictly adhered to since independence, had been formally abandoned, but the current budget deficit as a percentage of GNP was still only 0·4 per cent in 1973. It rose sharply to 6·9 per cent in 1975, while the Exchequer borrowing requirement rose in the same period from 8·6 per cent to a massive 16 per cent. In order to finance the larger borrowing, it was necessary to increase the proportion borrowed abroad to nearly half the total for the years 1974–6. Not all of this came about solely as a counter-cyclical measure, however. A Fine Gael/Labour coalition government had come to power in March 1973 with the belief that resources would not be constrained following entry to the

EEC. In the event, the government fulfilled election commit-
ments to cut local authority rates and abolish death duties and
also greatly increased public services and social welfare
benefits.

In the 1976 and 1977 budgets, the government cut back the
growth of public expenditure and reduced the borrowing
requirement. The current budget deficit as a proportion of GNP
was reduced from 6·9 per cent in 1975 to 4·4 per cent in 1976
and 3·8 per cent in 1977; while the Exchequer borrowing
requirement fell from 16 per cent in 1975 to 11·1 per cent in
1976 and 10 per cent in 1977. Although it would have been
better had rather less of the retrenchment taken place in 1976
and rather more in 1977, nevertheless the move was generally in
the right direction, given that the world economy had begun to
revive in 1976. Had the policy been continued in 1978–9, then
the public finances would have been largely restored to order
before the world economy turned down again in 1980.

In fact, however, a new Fianna Fáil government came to
office in June 1977 with a programme of increasing public
spending and reducing taxes in order to bring down the then
prevailing high level of unemployment. It was accepted that this
would initially increase the Exchequer borrowing rate, but it
was argued that once full employment approached it would be
possible to bring borrowing down again. The best that can be
said for such a strategy at this time is that it was well inten-
tioned. It ignored so many harsh realities that it was bound to
run into problems. The borrowing requirement and the balance
of payments deficit were already at a high level when the
strategy was initiated, while the world economy was expanding
quite rapidly. From a counter-cyclical viewpoint this was not
the best time, given the public finance and balance of payments
position, to boost demand still further. Moreover, the economy
was now much more open than in the past, so that the impact of
fiscal expansionism was likely to spill over into imports more
quickly and to a greater degree than heretofore. Finally, while
the strategy recognised the need for pay restraint by setting a
very low target for pay increases, no instruments were devised
to achieve this target. Without such instruments, the stimulation of demand was likely to intensify wage pressures, and in
the event the target for pay restraint was substantially
breached.

It is possible that the strategy might have been justified by events, had the world economy entered on a sustained expansion as in the 1960s. Even then, however, some check on the rate of domestic demand expansion would have been necessary. By 1979, even before the world economic downturn, the balance of payments deficit amounted to 13½ per cent of GNP,[1] the current budget deficit was nearly 7 per cent of GNP, the Exchequer borrowing requirement was over 13 per cent of GNP, and the state-sponsored bodies were engaged in further substantial borrowing for capital purposes. The servicing of government debt appropriated an increasing share of total tax revenue, rising to 25 per cent in 1979.

4.1.2 The second oil price increase and the subsequent depression

The response by the Western world to the second oil price increase at the end of 1979 was rather different from the first. Fears about price inflation, the balance of payments and the public sector deficit dominated over concern for unemployment. Governments of the major economies were determined to resist the price-inflationary impact of the oil price increase through restrictive fiscal and monetary policies — even at the cost of further reducing output growth and increasing unemployment. In the event the winding down of inflation proved to be a more protracted process than had been anticipated, and was accompanied in Europe in particular by a prolonged depression and a substantial rise in unemployment.

Ireland was ill-prepared to cope with this situation. Even before the depression began to take effect, the parlous state of the public finances pointed to the need for retrenchment, and this was acknowledged by the new Fianna Fáil Taoiseach, Mr Haughey, in a televised address to the nation in January 1980. Such a course, however, would exacerbate still further the rise in unemployment that would in any event be inevitable as a result of the spill-over of the world depression. In practice, Mr Haughey's government chose to maintain an expansionary fiscal stance in 1980 and 1981, and in particular to sustain infrastructural investment. Despite a restrictive supplementary budget introduced by a new Fine Gael/Labour coalition government in July 1981, the current budget deficit for that year amounted to 7½ per cent of GNP, the Exchequer borrowing requirement had risen to nearly 16 per cent of GNP, while the balance of payments deficit reached almost 15 per cent of GNP. The demand management approach adopted by Mr Haughey's government in 1980 and 1981 has been widely condemned by economic commentators. Yet two extenuating points can be made. Firstly, the policy was not in essence different from that followed in the previous recession in 1974–5. That it put the public finances in greater jeopardy was due partly to the earlier mismanagement of the public finances in the years 1977–9, which was a much more suitable time for corrective measures. Secondly, no one foresaw that the second world recession would be so severe or would last so long.[2] Its severity may be seen from the fact that the volume of private investment fell by 25 per cent from 1979 to 1982, and only because of the increased public investment was the volume of total investment maintained.

The attempt to maintain activity and employment in the face of a collapse in private investment undoubtedly helped to mitigate the impact of the depression at a time when the Irish population and labour force were expanding at record rates. Given that the scope for prudent counter-cyclical action had already been pre-empted, however, it did so at a cost of seriously jeopardising the public finances and postponing the adjustment in prices, wages and the balance of payments. Moreover, there were other features of economic policy which exacerbated the position. The rapid expansion of the Public Capital Programme included projects which, while alleviating unemployment in the short term, were of doubtful long-run value to the economy. Even more objectionable, perhaps, were the large increases in pay awarded at this time to several major categories of public sector employees — especially when unemployment was rising rapidly and the public finances were in dire straits. Average pay in the public service almost doubled in the three-year period 1978–81; and since the propensity to spend these income gains on imported goods and foreign holidays was quite high, they could scarcely be justified as the most suitable means of maintaining demand for domestic output — quite apart from their adverse impact on costs and competitiveness.

By 1982 all the major political parties subscribed to the need for 'fiscal rectitude'. Mr Haughey, in government again in 1982, produced a medium-term economic plan, *The way forward*, proposing to eliminate the current budget deficit by 1986. Before any of the proposals could be implemented, however, a general election in November 1982 brought to power another coalition government, which deferred the date for elimination of the deficit by one year to 1987. Subsequently, in 1984, this government produced a new medium-term plan, *Building on reality*, which adopted a more relaxed target of reducing the deficit to 5 per cent of GNP by 1987. Furthermore, the deficit was to be allowed to rise in 1985 and all of the correction was to be accomplished in 1986 and 1987 — a highly improbable scenario given that a general election would then be imminent. In practice, no lasting progress was made in reducing the current budget deficit, which in 1986 was 8½ per cent of GNP. Some progress was made, however, in lowering the Exchequer borrowing requirement from 16 per cent of GNP in 1982 to 13 per cent in 1986, mainly through a substantial real reduction in the Public Capital Programme. The wisdom of cutting borrowing for investment purposes while continuing to borrow heavily for day-to-day expenditure is open to question, assuming that worthwhile investment projects existed.

That there was so little progress in reducing the current budget deficit was partly due to the depression, which added to the demands on the Exchequer while dampening revenue buoyancy. Furthermore, the annual borrowing rate was so high in the early 1980s that the cuts which were made did not go far enough to stop the accumulated national debt from rising further relative to GNP — so that the debt service burden went on rising. This situation was seriously aggravated by higher real interest rates, which were negative in the 1970s and early 1980s, but became strongly positive from 1983. As a result of rising national debt and rising interest rates, the service of public debt had by 1985 risen to 35 per cent of total tax revenue. In effect, a progressively greater part of government borrowing was going to service past debt, so that fiscal policy was highly deflationary in its impact on the demand for goods and services, despite a continued high level of borrowing. The reduction in fiscal demand (excluding interest payments) from 1981 to 1985 was close to 9 per cent of GNP, which inevitably depressed the economy.

While little progress was made in correcting the public finances, the current balance of payments deficit was reduced substantially from the peak of 15 per cent of GNP in 1981 to just

2 per cent of GNP in 1986. This was mainly due to the massive decline in home demand aided by some improvement in the terms of trade, as import prices rose more slowly and began to fall in the second half of 1985 with the collapse in oil prices. Energy imports relative to GDP fell from 8·8 per cent in 1981 to 3·8 per cent in 1986, and price inflation also declined considerably. In common with all Western countries, Ireland had experienced a sharp acceleration in inflation following each of the two oil price rises. The average annual rate of increase in consumer prices between 1973 and 1982 was 16·2 per cent — greater than in any other EEC country except Greece and Italy. By the end of 1986, however, the annual rate of increase in Ireland was down to 3 per cent, close to the EEC average.

Looking at demand management since 1973, the irony may be noted that a Keynesian approach was used so extensively even though it had much less prospect of success than in the 1950s when it was not used at all. In the later period not only was the economy itself more open, so that a greater part of any demand stimulus would spill over into imports, but other European countries were not expanding their demand at anything like the same rate, which further diminished the chances of success.

4.2 THE DECLINE IN ECONOMIC GROWTH

All OECD countries have suffered a major decline in economic growth since 1973 compared with preceding post-war experience.[3] Ireland is no exception, though the scale, nature and timing of the decline has differed in important respects. The first oil price shock was followed by a marked slowing down in Irish economic growth in the years 1974–6. Recovery was very strong, however, in the years 1977–9, led by favourable demand conditions abroad and expansionary fiscal policies at home, so that the average annual growth rate of the volume of GDP from 1973 to 1979 was, at 4·1 per cent, not much below that of the 1960s and early 1970s. In the prolonged depression that followed the second oil price increase, however, the volume of GDP rose by only 1½ per cent per annum between 1979 and 1986, or about the same as the average for OECD Europe. Thus, as far as GDP is concerned, the decline in the Irish growth rate between 1973 and 1986 was less than in most

OECD countries, and was concentrated much more in the 1980s.

For several reasons the decline in the growth of GDP does not adequately indicate the degree to which Ireland's total real income was affected by developments after 1973. First, there was a huge increase in net factor income outflows due to interest payments on public foreign borrowing and repatriation of profits earned by foreign enterprise in Ireland, which is examined more fully in Chapter 9. Secondly, in contrast with the period 1960–73, when the terms of trade improved, the oil price increase led to a substantial deterioration. Thirdly, working in the opposite direction, Ireland benefited from sizeable EEC transfer payments. When these influences are quantified, as in Table 4.1, it emerges that the growth rate of real gross national disposable income, which was nearly 5 per cent per annum between 1960 and 1973, was almost halved from 1973 to 1979, and fell to 0·3 per cent per annum between 1979 and 1986. Moreover, as will be discussed in the next section, the impact on real income *per capita* was further aggravated by demographic developments.

Table 4.1: Average annual growth rates of real product, various periods, 1960–86

	1960–73 %	1973–9 %	1979–86 %
Gross Domestic Product (GDP)	4·4	4·1	1·5
Gross National Product (GNP)	4·3	3·4	−0·3
GNP adjusted for terms of trade	4·8	2·2	0·2
Gross National Disposable Income (GNDI)	4·9	2·8	0·3
Population	0·6	1·5	0·7
GNDI *per capita*	4·2	1·2	−0·4

Sources: A. Punch, 'Real gross national disposable income adjusted for terms of trade 1970–1984', *Quarterly Economic Commentary (ESRI)*, April (1986). The figures have been extended to other years using *National income and expenditure*, various issues. The difference between GDP and GNP arises from the inclusion in the latter of the outflow of net factor payments, while GNDI further includes transfer payments received from abroad as well as the terms of trade adjustment.

Clearly, this was a disappointing performance, given the buoyant expectations that prevailed on Ireland's entry into the EEC. Nowhere were these expectations more optimistic than in agriculture, which anticipated huge gains from access to more remunerative market outlets under the CAP. Paradoxically, Ireland was not long in the EEC before a cattle crisis developed in 1974 because of the glut in the world market due to the build-up of stocks in the preceding years and the fall in demand during the general economic depression. Young cattle which were worth £70–80 a head in October 1973 were selling a year later at just £20–30 a head. Due to the EEC intervention system, however, the prices of finished cattle did not fall nearly as much, and the crisis was short-lived. Moreover, dairy farmers were enjoying greatly enhanced prices for milk, and the CAP yielded substantial benefits to Irish agriculture in the period up to 1978. Real agricultural income per person engaged was over 40 per cent higher in 1978 than in 1972, the year preceding EEC entry. The higher prices, improved income prospects, and increased investment resources available to farmers led to a considerable increase in production, especially milk. The volume of gross output was one-sixth higher in 1978 than in 1973, though with inputs of farm materials increasing even faster, the rise in the volume of net output was slightly lower.

It began to seem as if prosperity had finally dawned for Irish agriculture. Farming confidence knew no bounds, large debts were incurred by farmers to develop their land, to increase their herds and purchase more land as well as machinery. The price of land was pushed up to totally unrealistic levels which could not be justified by productive returns, and made sense only if capital gains accrued through a continuation of rapidly rising land prices. Yet when expectations were most buoyant, farmers suffered one of the sharpest income declines in the years after 1978 that they had ever experienced. Between 1978 and 1980, real income per person engaged dropped by nearly one-third. There was subsequently some improvement and the volume of output increased considerably between 1981 and 1984. Never-theless, in 1986, following two years of exceptionally bad weather conditions, farmers' real income *per capita* was only slightly above the pre-EEC level, even though the numbers engaged had fallen by one-third.

What went wrong? Three major factors changed after 1978. Firstly, the transition phase was now ended during which Ireland had benefited more than the generality of EEC farmers as Irish prices were adjusted to EEC levels. Secondly, entry into the European Monetary System (EMS) in 1979 largely deprived Ireland of the so-called 'green pound' devaluations, which were granted when the Irish pound depreciated along with sterling, and which had effectively adjusted Irish farm prices to match the relatively high domestic inflation rate. Irish farmers were now limited to much the same price increases for agricultural produce as their EMS partners, whereas they continued to face a much higher rate of domestic price inflation. Thirdly, and most serious of all for Ireland from a long-term viewpoint, the squeeze on the Community budget arising from growing food surpluses brought increasing pressure to limit production both by cutting real prices to producers and by imposing levies on surplus production.

The growth of manufacturing output also slowed down considerably. Between 1973 and 1979 it averaged just over 5 per cent per annum, compared with 6½ per cent from 1960 to 1973, and fell further to 4·1 per cent between 1979 and 1986. Though reduced, Ireland's manufacturing growth rate was considerably better than the generality of OECD countries. The performance of manufactured exports remained good, averaging a growth rate in volume terms of over 11 per cent per annum between 1973 and 1985. The main explanation lies in two related factors: access to EEC markets and the attraction of new foreign enterprise to take advantage of that market. The share of Irish manufactured exports going to the EEC Six rose from 16·7 per cent in 1972 to 36 per cent in 1985, and the latter figure exceeded the share going to the UK, 30·3 per cent. Although other exports also performed well, the share of manufactures in total Irish merchandise exports rose from 41 per cent in 1972 to 64½ per cent in 1985. Manufactured imports also rose rapidly, with the result that, as we shall discuss in more detail in Chapter 11, the older protected industries were subject to severe competition and fared badly.

The increasing openness of the economy is perhaps best illustrated by the fact that the ratio of total exports plus imports of goods and services to GNP almost doubled from 73 per cent in 1972 to 138 per cent in 1985. For the first time ever, apart from wartime conditions when import supplies were not available, Ireland had a surplus on merchandise trade in 1985. However, it no longer had a surplus on invisibles, despite the sizeable transfers received from the EEC. Although tourist receipts grew in real terms after 1972, they never surpassed the level prevailing in 1968 prior to the outbreak of the Northern Ireland conflict. On the other hand, there was a marked increase in the propensity of Irish people to holiday abroad, so much so that by 1980 tourist expenditures abroad exceeded receipts — though afterwards with the prolonged depression the volume of Irish tourist spending abroad again declined. The more substantial change affecting invisibles, however, was the vast increase in factor payments abroad in respect of the service of government external borrowing and repatriation of profits by foreign enterprises.

4.3 THE DEMOGRAPHIC TRANSFORMATION

Given its past history, perhaps the most striking feature of all about the Irish economy in the 1970s was the rate of growth of population and labour force. As stated in the previous chapter, a sustained rise in population had begun in 1961 due to the fall in net emigration. There was still enough emigration to keep population growth at a modest average annual level of 0·5 per cent over the period 1961–71. From the late 1960s, however, net emigration declined sharply and, with greater numbers of former emigrants returning, turned into sizeable net immigration averaging over 10,000 per annum between 1971 and 1981 so that population grew in the 1970s at an annual rate of 1½ per cent. This was a very high rate by any standards, whether compared with Ireland's past experience, or with contemporary Europe where the population in many countries was stable or even declining slightly.

The most obvious consequence was that any given growth in total real income now had a greatly reduced impact in terms of raising *per capita* incomes. This was compounded by the fact that the growth of total real income fell sharply after 1973. Thus, faster population growth, slower GNP growth, unfavourable terms of trade and greatly increased factor payments abroad all conspired radically to attenuate the increase in living standards. As may be seen from Table 4.1, the growth rate of real gross national disposable income *per capita* fell from over 4 per cent per annum between 1960 and 1973 to only a little over 1 per cent per annum between 1973 and 1979, and there was a decline of close to ½ per cent per annum between 1979 and 1986. The faster population growth also exerted a strong upward pressure on public expenditure: more schools, hospitals, houses and other social facilities were needed, and needed quickly, to cope with the sudden population explosion. In addition, it provoked a greater need for social welfare transfers, and particularly unemployment compensation.

The transformation in labour force experience was even greater than in population. For reasons discussed at the end of the last chapter, the moderate increase in population in the 1960s was muted in its impact on the labour force, which rose by only 34,000, or 0·3 per cent per annum between 1961 and 1971. In the following decade, however, the rise in the labour force outstripped the rise in population. From 1971 to 1981 population growth was concentrated heavily in the younger active age-groups, with the population aged 15–24 increasing at an average annual rate of 2⅓ per cent, and the population aged 25–44 by as much as 3 per cent per annum. Furthermore, the number of married women in the labour force almost trebled from 37,000 in 1971 to 105,000 in 1981. In this decade the overall labour force rose by 162,000, nearly five times the rise in the previous decade. Clearly, it would not be an easy matter to cope with such an increase at any time, let alone in very troubled world economic conditions.

In fact, the decade 1971–81 witnessed an unprecedented rise in employment of 97,000, or on average nearly 1 per cent per annum. Given that agricultural employment continued to decline at an annual rate of over 3 per cent, the increase in non-agricultural employment was spectacular — 173,000 or over 2 per cent per annum. Yet despite these very considerable gains in employment, the pressure of labour force growth was such that unemployment in 1981, at 126,000, was more than double the 1971 level. While the unemployment rate in Ireland in the early 1980s was near the top of the range for EEC countries, the increase between 1973 and 1981 was nevertheless less than for the EEC as a whole, and very much less than in countries such as Belgium, the United Kingdom, Denmark and the Netherlands. This was a remarkable achievement, given that the labour force was growing so much more rapidly in Ireland. Whereas total employment in the entire EEC was slightly less in 1981 than in 1973, in Ireland it was 8 per cent higher — again, quite a remarkable achievement, given that Ireland had a relatively large share in the declining agricultural sector.

Unfortunately, however, it did not prove possible to maintain expansion in employment in the depression following the second oil price increase. Too much of the expansion had depended on the public sector to be sustainable. About half the total rise in non-agricultural employment over the period 1971–81 was concentrated in the public sector, involving an average annual increase of 4½ per cent. Subsequently, the numbers in the public sector were reduced in the interests of restoring order to the public finances. In addition, the substantial reduction in the volume of the Public Capital Programme severely depressed employment in building and construction. These developments limited domestic demand for manufactures supplying the home market, while the flow of new foreign enterprise declined and was more heavily concentrated in activities with high labour productivity. From 1980 manufacturing employment declined steadily and by the end of 1986 was 20 per cent below the 1979 peak.

By April 1987, total employment had fallen by almost 100,000 since 1980 and was back to the level prevailing immediately before EEC entry. Unemployment had risen to almost 250,000, or nearly one-fifth of the labour force, and the deterioration was much greater in Ireland in the 1980s than in any of its EEC partners. Indeed, the rise in unemployment in Ireland would have been even greater had it not been for the fact that, as labour market conditions worsened, emigration resumed again at an increasing rate and by 1986 was almost equal to the natural increase in population.

4.4 THE GROWTH OF GOVERNMENT

Like most other Western economies, the evolution of the Irish economy has been accompanied by a vast increase in the degree of government involvement in the economy. The extent of the change can be seen most succinctly in the fact that the total expenditure of public authorities (including transfers) has risen relative to GNP from less than 25 per cent in the mid-1920s to nearly 70 per cent in the mid-1980s.[4] While there were sharp upward shifts in the ratio of public expenditure to GNP in the early 1930s and from 1947 to 1951, the really large increase in the ratio has taken place since 1960, when it was 32 per cent, and more particularly in the period 1973–85 when the ratio rose from 42 per cent to 67 per cent.

The rise in public expenditure since 1960 has been dominated by two main components, social expenditure and national debt interest. Together these items accounted for just over half of total public expenditure in 1960, but by 1985 they had risen to 70 per cent of the total. Social expenditure rose from 14 per cent of GNP in 1960 to 22 per cent in 1973 and 34 per cent in 1985; while national debt interest, which was less than 4 per cent of GNP in 1973, had risen to 12 per cent in 1985. The largest single component of social expenditure has always been income maintenance, consisting of social security and welfare payments. Since 1960 it has risen by 10 percentage points relative to GNP, with the greater part of the increase occurring since 1973.

It is not surprising, given that it accounted for so much of the rise in public expenditure, that analysts have directed particular attention to social expenditure. One study[5] attempted to decompose the rise in public social expenditure from 1960 to 1981 into a number of components. The frequently observed tendency for the price of public services to rise more than prices in general was found to be comparatively small: on average the price deflator for social expenditure was about 1 per cent per annum above the GDP deflator, though the effect was greater for both education and health. Increases in the relevant population to which the programmes applied accounted for a real annual increase of 1 per cent between 1960 and 1975 and nearly 2 per cent thereafter, due mainly to the large increase in unemployment. Extension of the proportion of the relevant population covered by benefits — either through wider eligibility or increased take-up — also accounted for a real annual increase of about 1 per cent, though the effect varied between programmes. By far the biggest component of the overall increase, however, consisted in the increase in the average real level of state expenditure per recipient. This was true for all the individual programmes, except for unemployment compensation over the period 1975–81 when the growth in numbers unemployed predominated. Since 1981 the large increase in unemployment has continued to be a significant factor in raising public expenditure as well as in eroding the tax base.

The rapid rise in the public expenditure to GNP ratio was accompanied by a large increase in the tax burden. In the post-war period up to 1960 tax revenue was fairly stable as a proportion of GNP at about 22 per cent. Thereafter, it rose to

Table 4.2: Irish national debt, various years, 1926–86

| | Total national debt £m | Ratio to GNP at current market prices | |
		Total national debt %	Foreign debt %
1926	19	11·2	–
1931	35	20·3	–
1938	58	31·7	–
1947	109	33·8	1·3
1951	204	49·9	12·1
1960	414	64·0	7·4
1973	1,480	54·5	6·8
1980	7,291	81·0	24·5
1983	14,773	109·4	52·0
1986	23,045	142·2	60·2

Sources: National debt figures from 1960 onwards are taken from the Department of Finance Databank. Figures for earlier years have been derived from the *Finance accounts*. Local authorities' indebtedness and liabilities under the Land Acts are excluded throughout. The only foreign debt prior to the Second World War consisted of foreign holdings of national loans. A figure for this is not available, but it was undoubtedly only a small proportion of the total. The GNP figures are taken from *National income and expenditure*, various years, and K.A. Kennedy, *Productivity and industrial growth: the Irish experience* (Clarendon Press, Oxford, 1971). The data in the latter, which relate to GNP at factor cost, have been adjusted to a market price basis, using the figures on indirect taxes less subsidies in the *Irish statistical survey 1957*, and M. O'Donoghue and A.A. Tait, 'The growth of public revenue and expenditure in Ireland' in J.A. Bristow and A.A. Tait (eds), *Economic policy in Ireland* (Institute of Public Administration, Dublin, 1968).

31 per cent in 1973 and 43 per cent in 1985. The largest increase was in taxes on income. Even as late as 1960, such taxes amounted to less than 6 per cent of GNP and accounted for little more than a quarter of total tax revenue, but by 1985 they had risen to 23 per cent of GNP and accounted for more than half of the much heavier tax burden. The higher income tax burden has fallen on persons rather than on companies. Largely because of the tax incentives for manufacturing investment and export profits, company taxes have never yielded much — usually less than 2 per cent of GNP. On the other hand, the increasing share of non-agricultural employees in the total

89

work-force, their rising real incomes, the inadequate adjustment of tax bands and allowances in the face of accelerating inflation, and substantial discretionary increases in both employers' and employees' contribution rates to social insurance, all contributed to a rapid increase in the other elements of direct taxes. Taxes on expenditure also increased considerably relative to GNP — though not as rapidly as taxes on income — due to the introduction of retail and wholesale taxes which were subsequently replaced by value added tax applying to most expenditures except food. Taxes on capital, wealth and property have declined substantially. This was due to the abolition of estate duties, local authority rates on dwellings and motor registration duties and the fact that the various partial replacements have yielded far less revenue.

The very substantial rise in tax revenue was quite insufficient, however, to match the pace of the increase in public expenditure since 1973, resulting in a vast amount of public borrowing, as already described in section 4.1 above. Not surprisingly, the scale of public borrowing since 1973 has had a dramatic impact in raising the national debt, but an increasing national debt to GNP ratio is not a new phenomenon. As may be seen from the figures in Table 4.2, it has characterised most of the history of the state, though the pace of the increase since 1973 has been such as to dwarf the earlier rise.

Ireland started off in a highly favourable position as regards national debt, having been released in 1925 from liability for any share of the public debt of the United Kingdom. In 1926 the national debt amounted to little more than one-tenth of GNP, but by 1938 had risen to nearly one-third. The large increase in public capital expenditure after the Second World War brought the debt/GNP ratio to 50 per cent in 1951, and despite the cutbacks in the 1950s the ratio had risen to 64 per cent by 1960. During the 1960s the ratio stabilised in the region of 62–6 per cent of GNP and declined in the early 1970s to 54 per cent by 1973. This decline, however, had much to do with the acceleration in inflation and the fact that interest rates were fixed at a time when inflationary expectations were much lower, so that there was a massive expropriation in favour of the Exchequer at the expense of holders of government bonds.[6] This relief to the state finances could hardly have continued indefinitely.

After 1973 new factors entered which caused a massive rise in the debt/GNP ratio, despite a very high rate of inflation up to 1983. Firstly, as outlined earlier, borrowing increased substantially to finance not only a rising Public Capital Programme but also a substantial current budget deficit: in the early 1980s as much as one-third of the greatly enlarged level of public expenditure was financed by borrowing. Secondly, borrowing on this scale required extensive recourse to foreign borrowing, and the real value of such debt could not so easily be eroded through inflation since it was denominated in foreign currencies: a relatively high domestic inflation rate was bound to be reflected, sooner or later, in a depreciation of the Irish currency. Thirdly, both domestic and foreign lenders became less willing to lend at fixed interest rates, so that increasing interest rates began to raise not only the cost of current borrowing, but also of past borrowing. Indeed, the general level of real interest rates world-wide rose to unprecedented levels from 1982. Ireland was now extremely vulnerable to such a rise because of the high debt/GNP ratio. To some degree it might be said that the government had been seduced into borrowing more than it might otherwise have done by reason of the low or negative real interest rates prevalent up to 1980. The rapid turnaround in the level of real interest rates was such that even with a much tighter fiscal policy — involving reduced capital spending and a significant surplus on current spending apart from interest payments — the debt/GNP ratio continued its explosive upward course.

The net result was that in the 13-year period between 1973 and 1986, the national debt/GNP ratio rose by nearly 90 percentage points, or much more than the increase in the whole of the previous history of the state. Furthermore, while Ireland had incurred very little foreign debt up to 1973, apart from the low interest Marshall Plan loans, in 1986 over two-fifths of the national debt represented foreign debt. This large burden of foreign debt had the additional disadvantage of involving an unrequited outflow which reduced national product — unlike the service of domestic debt which involved only an internal transfer. In the mid-1980s national debt interest payments abroad amounted to over 5 per cent of GNP. The enormous scale of Ireland's national debt — over 1½ times GNP at the end of 1987 — constitutes a major constraint on further development measures by the government.

4.5 AN ECONOMY IN CRISIS?

In early 1987 a sense of crisis prevailed. The most obvious indications of this crisis were the massive unemployment, the resumption of heavy emigration, falling living standards and the intransigent public finance imbalances. The mood of depression was heightened by developments in 1986 when an expected recovery failed to materialise. At the beginning of 1986, with oil prices falling and international interest rates coming down, it was expected that economic activity would benefit from a revival in consumer demand and that the public finance position would be alleviated by lower interest payments. In the event, these hopes were sadly disappointed and 1986 brought new woes. The rate of inflation did fall but not as much as expected and there was no consumer boom. Like the rest of Europe, Irish tourist receipts from US visitors were severely affected by the Chernobyl nuclear explosion and fears of terrorist reprisals following the US bombing of Libya. In addition, exceptionally bad weather for the second year in succession depressed agricultural output and peat production.

Moreover, while international interest rates were lower, domestic rates were forced up. This arose chiefly from pressure on the Irish exchange rate within the EMS as sterling floated downwards. The appreciation of the Irish pound against sterling threatened the competitiveness of manufactured exports to the UK and there was continuing speculation that the Irish pound would be devalued. From the fourth quarter of 1985, large unspecified capital outflows took place totalling over £2,000 million by the end of 1986. A devaluation of 8 per cent in July was not sufficient to stem these outflows: on the contrary, it probably confirmed speculators in their view that the Irish pound would still tend to follow sterling downwards. Confidence was also damaged by a substantial overrun on the current budget deficit. Domestic interest rates were pushed up to record levels in real terms. In the last quarter of 1986, the ordinary overdraft rate was 17 per cent, whereas the inflation rate was only 3 per cent. This clearly had a very depressing effect on investment and on borrowing for purchases of consumer durables.

What was perhaps most damaging to confidence in the unstable political and economic situation at the beginning of 1987 was the absence of any clear sense of purpose about the future direction of economic policy. The outcome of the general election in February 1987, which failed to provide a majority government, did not at first promise much in the way of decisive action. In the event, the minority Fianna Fáil government which took office under Mr Haughey proceeded to tackle the public finance crisis with great firmness. A restrictive budget was introduced designed to cut the current budget deficit from 8½ per cent of GNP in 1986 to 6·9 per cent in 1987, and to reduce Exchequer borrowing from 13·0 to 10·7 per cent of GNP. This was followed by a severe pruning of public expenditure with a view to a further substantial improvement in the public finances in 1988. These actions did much to restore financial confidence, and domestic interest rates fell somewhat, though remaining at extraordinary high levels in real terms. The balance of payments in 1987 was in surplus and a larger surplus is predicted for 1988. Furthermore, there was a recovery in economic activity from the depressed level of 1986, the estimated growth rate of GNP in 1987 being over 4 per cent compared with a fall of 1½ per cent in 1986.

Nevertheless, while fears of a financial crisis have been averted, the economic problems remain very formidable. Even with substantial fiscal retrenchment, it will probably take at least until 1990 to stop the national debt from rising as a proportion of GNP. Despite substantial emigration, unemployment remains stubbornly at about 250,000 or nearly one-fifth of the labour force, and there is little prospect of much increase in total employment over the next few years. The medium-term prospects for agriculture under the CAP are not bright. The indigenous manufacturing base is still weak, while there is greater competition in Europe for the available flow of mobile foreign enterprises.

Faced with this situation the government published a *Programme for National Recovery* in October 1987 covering the period to 1990. The fact that this programme, unlike many previous ones, is not just a statement of government intentions, but rather an agreement worked out between the government and the major interest groups, could help considerably in securing its implementation. The programme embodies a firm commitment to stabilise the national debt/GNP ratio no later than 1990, and includes a moderate pay agreement covering the next three years which should effect a significant improvement in competitiveness. On the assumption that the programme and

93

associated fiscal measures are fully implemented, and that there is no recession in the world economy over the next few years, the ESRI in its *Medium-term Review 1987–1992*, published in December 1987, predicted a considerable improvement in the economy by the early 1990s. The annual GNP growth rate would then be about 3½ per cent and the national debt/GNP ratio would be falling. No reduction in the level of unemployment would take place, however, despite assumed emigration averaging 27,000 per annum. As throughout its history over the last 150 years, the scarcity of employment opportunities remains Ireland's most intractable economic problem.

NOTES

1. At the time, the statistics showed the balance of payments deficit relative to GNP to be about 3 percentage points lower than this, but nevertheless at a very high level. The later adjustments related mainly to profit outflows which had not been correctly identified for several years.
2. Indeed, towards the end of 1980 some economic commentators were confidently predicting that the economy would be picking up by mid-1981, and criticised the expansionary fiscal approach on the grounds that it was pro-cyclical! (See C. McCarthy and B.M. Walsh, 'The coming crisis in the public finances', *Irish Times*, 29–30 September 1980.)
3. A. Maddison, 'Growth and slowdown in advanced capitalist economies', *Journal of Economic Literature*, vol. xxv, no. 2 (June 1987).
4. The figures for public expenditure relate to public authorities (i.e. central and local government, including extra-budgetary funds) on a national accounts basis, excluding redemption of securities and loan repayments. GNP figures are at market prices.
5. M. Maguire, 'Social expenditure in Ireland and other European OECD countries: past trends and prospective developments', *Public social expenditure — value for money?* — papers presented at ESRI Conference (Economic and Social Research Institute, Dublin, 1984).
6. R. Bruton, *Irish public debt*, General Research Series no. 94 (Economic and Social Research Institute, Dublin, 1978).

5

Northern Ireland, 1920–87

The partition of Ireland in the early 1920s meant that the area comprising the six north-eastern counties, Northern Ireland, remained part of the United Kingdom. The status of Northern Ireland was, therefore, essentially that of a region of the United Kingdom. Even though it had a separate Parliament up to 1972, which had rather greater power to influence the economy of the area than local authorities in other regions of the UK, these powers were nevertheless subject to the dominant economic policy formulated by the Westminster Parliament. Thus, unlike the Republic, Northern Ireland was unable to impose tariffs or quotas, to conclude trade agreements with other countries, or to establish its own monetary and exchange rate policies. Even in fiscal policy, although Northern Ireland benefited from the net transfers that tend to favour poorer areas in developed countries, it was constrained by what the UK authorities were willing to finance. For all of these reasons, as well as the fact that there was relatively little economic interdependence between the two parts of Ireland, Northern Ireland's experience was far more influenced by what happened in Britain than by what happened in the Republic.

Yet there are good reasons why a study primarily devoted to the Republic should still consider Northern Ireland's experience. The two areas formed a common unit for so long before the Republic achieved independence that it is of interest to examine how they fared afterwards under separate regimes. Northern Ireland is so small and so peripheral relative to the UK that it tends to be neglected in studies dealing with that country. Finally, a significant minority of the population of Northern Ireland, and the vast majority of those in the

Republic, aspire to a united Ireland. While political and economic considerations make it doubtful that this aspiration will be realised in the foreseeable future, nevertheless in the meantime the consequences of political instability and violence in Northern Ireland have significant spillover effects on the economy of the Republic. In this chapter, then, we outline the demographic and labour force experience of Northern Ireland, the degree of progress achieved in the main sectors of the economy, and the major events and policies that influenced these developments.

5.1 POPULATION AND LABOUR FORCE

The land area of Northern Ireland is about one-fifth that of the Republic and two-thirds that of Wales. With a population in 1981 of 1½ million, the population density is over twice that of the Republic, but less than half that of the UK. Although Northern Ireland shared in the general decline of the Irish population after the Famine, the fall there was much less than in the rest of the country. In the period 1841 to 1921, the population of Northern Ireland had fallen by a little less than a quarter, whereas the population of the rest of the country had more than halved. Thus, at the time of partition the Northern Irish population amounted to 29 per cent of the population of all Ireland, whereas 80 years previously it had amounted to only 20 per cent.

The decline in population in Northern Ireland had largely ceased in the 20 years before partition. Thereafter, the population increased in most years up to the early 1970s, and in 1971 was 22 per cent greater than in 1921. This was in marked contrast with the experience of the Republic, where population was declining for most of the period after independence, so that in 1971 Northern Ireland accounted for 34 per cent of the population of all Ireland. A reversal of the pattern has taken place since then, with the population of the Republic growing strongly while that of Northern Ireland has changed only marginally. Indeed, the long-term demographic experience of Northern Ireland has been very similar to that of the eastern province of the Republic, Leinster, which contains the capital, Dublin, and resembles Northern Ireland in size and density. In both areas the population is back to within 10 per cent of the pre-Famine levels, whereas in the rest of Ireland the population is little more than one-third of the pre-Famine level.

The different population experience in Northern Ireland compared with the Republic was almost entirely due to differences in the rate of emigration. Like the Republic, Northern Ireland has experienced net emigration for most of the period from the Famine, and since 1921 the total has amounted to over 300,000. Nevertheless, the rate was much lower than in the Republic up to the early 1970s, and was generally less than the rate of natural increase after the 1920s. The position was reversed in the 1970s, with the Republic now experiencing net inward migration, while in Northern Ireland the outward migration rose in the first half of the decade to a level that in some years exceeded the natural increase in population. As a result, Northern Ireland experienced little or no growth in population[1] at the very time when the Republic was experiencing unprecedented population growth.

The overall figures on net emigration for Northern Ireland conceal a very different pattern between the Roman Catholic and Protestant populations. A major consideration in determining the boundary of Northern Ireland was that of including the areas where there was a significant Protestant population, but without bringing in enough Roman Catholics to threaten the overall Protestant majority. Nevertheless, in 1926 Roman Catholics amounted to 33·5 per cent of the total population of Northern Ireland, and their birth-rate was higher. There were continual fears among the Protestant community that Roman Catholics would eventually constitute a majority. In fact, this did not happen, and the Roman Catholic population in 1961, at 34·9 per cent, was only slightly higher than in 1926. The reason was that the emigration rate among Roman Catholics was more than twice that of Protestants.[2] In turn, this was linked with much higher levels of unemployment among Roman Catholics in Northern Ireland, who are more heavily concentrated in the areas and occupations of high unemployment. In the last 20 years, however, the proportion of Roman Catholics in the total population has risen to 37 per cent in 1971 and about 39 per cent in 1981.[3] Their labour market prospects continued to be relatively unfavourable, however, and with their fertility rates declining rapidly, the prospect of an eventual Roman Catholic majority remains very remote.[4]

5.1.1 Employment and unemployment

The structure of employment in Northern Ireland in the 1920s was very different from that of the rest of the country. In 1926, one-third of employment there was in industry compared with only 13 per cent in the area of the Republic. Even compared to Leinster, the most highly urbanised part of the Republic, the contrast was considerable (Table 5.1). Agriculture was somewhat less important in Northern Ireland than in Leinster, while in non-agricultural activities, services dominated in Leinster and industry in Northern Ireland. Up to 1971 Northern Ireland fared better than the Republic with regard to total employment. This, however, was due chiefly to the smaller share in agriculture in Northern Ireland, so that the decline in agricultural employment there had considerably less impact on the growth of total employment. In fact, the rate of growth of non-agricultural employment in the two areas was not very different up to 1971, and was considerably higher in the Republic in the 1970s.

Northern Ireland's initially strong manufacturing base proved to be heavily concentrated in activities subject to structural decline. While the Second World War provided a stay of execution on shipbuilding and many new multinational industries were later established, there was nevertheless no rise in manufacturing employment in the 1950s and 1960s. Since 1974 there has been a continuous and rapid decline in manufacturing employment from 172,000 to 105,000 in 1986. The decline in manufacturing was offset by a massive rise in services employment, which increased by two-thirds from 1958 to 1980. Most of this was in the public sector and depended heavily on the extension to Northern Ireland of the British welfare state. The share of all employees in Northern Ireland now engaged in services is remarkably high for a non-metropolitan area: in 1985 it was greater than in any other region of the UK except the South-east, which includes London. Among all persons engaged in services in Northern Ireland, three in every five are employed in the public sector. With the more restrictive policies on public expenditure in the UK in recent years, however, services employment has not grown much further. Construction activity has also been badly affected and employment in the industry has fallen from 45,000 in 1980 to 32,000 in 1986.

Although the trends in the sectoral employment shares in

Table 5.1: Comparison of population and employment trends in Northern Ireland, Leinster and the rest of Ireland

	1841	1926	1961	1971	1981	1986
Population ('000)						
Northern Ireland	1,649	1,257	1,425	1,536	1,538	1,567
Leinster	1,974	1,149	1,332	1,498	1,791	1,853
Rest of Ireland	4,555	1,823	1,486	1,480	1,653	1,688
Employment ('000)						
Northern Ireland	n.a.	505	540	555	567	549
Leinster	n.a.	459	484	535	615	575
Rest of Ireland	n.a.	762	534	514	531	505
Sectoral employment Shares % Agriculture:						
Northern Ireland	n.a.	29	16	11	8	8
Leinster	n.a.	35	20	14	9	9
Rest of Ireland	n.a.	65	51	39	26	23
Industry:						
Northern Ireland	n.a.	34	42	42	30	27
Leinster	n.a.	19	32	36	33	29
Rest of Ireland	n.a.	10	18	25	31	28
Services:						
Northern Ireland	n.a.	37	42	47	62	65
Leinster	n.a.	47	48	50	58	63
Rest of Ireland	n.a.	25	32	36	44	49

Sources: Northern Ireland: *Digest of statistics*, DMS *Gazette*, *Census of Population*, *Regional trends*, *Annual abstract of statistics*, and Northern Ireland Economic Council, *Annual report 1985–86*, Belfast, Report No. 62, October 1986. Leinster and Rest of Ireland: *Statistical abstract of Ireland*, *Census of Population*, and *Labour Force Survey*.

Northern Ireland and the Republic have been very different, the result has been to produce a much closer convergence in the distribution of employment. Northern Ireland still has a rather lower proportion than the Republic engaged in agriculture, its industrial share is now slightly less, while its share in services is greater. The convergence with the province of Leinster, shown in Table 5.1, is particularly striking.

Unemployment rates in Northern Ireland have always been much higher than the UK average. In the 1920s unemployment

99

in the insured labour force averaged close to 20 per cent and rose in the 1930s to an average of 27 per cent. Even with the advent of low unemployment in the UK generally in the post-war period, the rate in Northern Ireland remained high, only rarely falling below 6 per cent when most other regions of the UK were at 2 per cent or less. In the 1970s, with unemployment rates rising generally in the UK, the absolute gap widened. By 1985 the unemployment rate of 21 per cent in Northern Ireland compared with a UK average of 13½ per cent.

Any precise comparison with unemployment rates in the Republic in the pre-Second World War period is impossible due to differences in economic structure and in the basis of recording unemployment. For the post-war period the broad picture is that unemployment was generally somewhat higher in the Republic until the mid-1970s. The much more severe increase in Northern Ireland's level of unemployment from the mid-1970s reversed the position for a number of years. Unemployment increased more rapidly in the Republic after 1981 and both areas had close to one-fifth of the total labour force unemployed at the end of 1986.

5.2 TRADE AND PRODUCTION

It has been said that 'One of the few safe generalisations in international economics is that the degree of a country's participation in the international economy varies inversely with the size of its domestic market.'[5] It would not be surprising, then, to find that when Ireland was partitioned, the much smaller area of Northern Ireland would emerge with *relatively* greater external trade than the south. What is perhaps surprising is that Northern Ireland's external trade was *absolutely* greater, even though its population and total income were less than half of that in the south. To some extent this reflects the inadequacies of the Northern Ireland trade statistics which are overstated due to the inclusion of transit trade. However, it also reflects the more highly industrialised structure of Northern Ireland and the character of that industrialisation.

The two areas have never been heavily involved in trade with each other, particularly if the movement of live animals is excluded. Prior to partition, however, Belfast was a major port for the export of goods from all over Ireland. Due to the political and sectarian tensions following partition, this trade was severely curtailed and many areas on both sides of the border were also cut off from their natural hinterland. However, the south never constituted a significant outlet for the north's highly specialised manufactures, which needed access to larger markets, particularly Great Britain. Free trade was also favoured by northern industry to facilitate the purchase of materials and equipment from the cheapest source, and to keep down the cost of living. Quite apart from the overriding political considerations, therefore, the north was opposed on economic grounds to being part of an independent Ireland, with its ambition to achieve economic development through protectionism and self-sufficiency.

Table 5.2: Total merchandise exports, Northern Ireland and the Republic, selected years, 1926–85

| Year | Value of merchandise exports | | | Ratio to GDP at current factor cost | |
	(1) Northern Ireland £m	(2) Republic £m	(3) Ratio (1) to (2)	(4) Northern Ireland %	(5) Republic %
1926	54·4	41·3	1·32	81·0	29·1
1938	47·1	24·2	1·95	67·1	16·3
1946	127·7	39·0	3·27	76·4	14·3[a]
1958	301·7	131·3	2·28	89·2	27·0
1974	1,367·9	1,134·3	1·21	90·5	42·9
1985	n.a.	9,743.0	n.a.	n.a.	63·0

Note: [a] 1947
Sources: The merchandise exports figures for Northern Ireland are taken from *Digest of statistics* and K.S. Isles and N. Cuthbert, *An economic survey of Northern Ireland*, (HMSO, Belfast, 1957), pp. 100 and 611. It should be noted that the Northern Ireland trade data make no distinction between ordinary trade and transit trade, which leads to some overstatement in the figures. Furthermore, since no customs documentation is required for trade with Great Britain, it became increasingly difficult with the growth of container traffic to compile accurate figures, and publication of the data was terminated after 1974. Merchandise exports figures for the Republic are taken from *Statistical abstract of Ireland*, and *Trade statistics of Ireland*. The sources of the GDP data are given later in Tables 6.1 and 6.2.

As already described in Chapter 2, partition did not greatly affect external trading conditions facing the two parts of Ireland for the first decade. However, the situation changed in the early 1930s with the adoption of protectionist policies in the south and in the UK. As may be seen from Table 5.2, Northern Ireland's exports did not fall nearly as much as in the Republic during the 1930s and they expanded more during the Second World War so that by 1946 they were over three times greater than in the Republic. This pattern was gradually reversed in the post-war period, however, as the Republic won more favourable marketing arrangements for its agricultural products and shifted to an export-orientated strategy of industrial development. The Republic's merchandise exports grew much more rapidly than those of Northern Ireland, particularly after 1958. By 1974, the north's exports exceeded those of the Republic only by one-fifth, about the same disparity as had existed 50 years earlier. Although there are no comprehensive figures available since then for Northern Ireland, it is certain that the value of merchandise exports of the Republic, which rose ninefold between 1974 and 1985, are now considerably greater than those of Northern Ireland. However, the ratio of exports to GDP still remains higher in Northern Ireland.

Manufactures have always accounted for upwards of two-thirds of Northern Ireland's merchandise exports, and this position changed little. In contrast, agricultural exports dominated in the Republic at the time of independence. With the move to free trade in the Republic since the Second World War, however, and the remarkable rise in its manufactured exports, the structure of merchandise exports is now very similar to that of Northern Ireland. Thus, as regards both the export/GDP ratio and the composition of exports there has been a substantial convergence in the position of the two areas. The north, however, has been much less successful than the Republic in diversifying the destination of its exports, which remain heavily concentrated on the British market.

As regards invisibles, tourist revenues grew rapidly in Northern Ireland in the 1960s, but it was never as important as in the Republic. It suffered a drastic decline in the four-year period 1969–72, due to the conflict situation, and has only partially recovered since then. There are no official figures on Northern Ireland's balance of payments, but it has been estimated[6] that the current account was probably in surplus for much of the post-war period, with small deficits in trade and services being more than matched by transfer payments from the UK Exchequer. The British subvention to Northern Ireland has grown enormously from £87 million in 1970 to £1,280 million in 1983.[7] The balance of payments position, of course, has less explicit significance for a region like Northern Ireland than for an independent country. Assuming, however, that the current account was in surplus, it would follow that there must have been a net outflow on the capital account. In the absence of data, it is not possible to identify the nature of the net outflow, other than to say that it must have occurred on the private capital account, since the net flow was inwards on the government account.

5.2.1 Agriculture

Agriculture has long been much less significant to the Northern Ireland economy than to the Republic's. The agricultural share of GDP has declined in both areas, but in 1984 still accounted for 12½ per cent of the total in the Republic, compared with only 5 per cent in Northern Ireland. The disparity is even greater in absolute terms if the farm supply and food processing industries are included. Nevertheless, the structure of agriculture is rather similar in both areas, with grasslands enterprises dominating, and a high proportion of agricultural output exported. In 1912 the major difference in structure was that Northern Ireland had a greater proportion of the land under cereals and other crops (26 per cent) than in the Republic (14 per cent). The difference was mainly due to the more extensive growing of oats and potatoes in the north, and to the production of flax for the linen industry. The size of holdings in the north tended to be considerably smaller.

Partition did not initially alter trade conditions or bring about much change in the structure of production in the two areas. In the 1930s, however, as trade barriers developed, Northern Ireland's agriculture enjoyed more favourable access to the British market and this situation continued after the Second World War when the north had the advantage of the UK deficiency payments system. In the 1960s, however, this relative advantage was eroded as the Republic gained more favourable access to the British market. Entry to the EEC in 1973 further

Table 5.3: Index numbers of volume and price of agricultural output in Northern Ireland and the Republic, 1912–85

Year	Volume of gross output		Price		
	Northern Ireland	Republic	Northern Ireland	Republic	Price ratio NI/Rep
1912	100	100	100	100	100
1926	85·8	94·4	136[a]	136[a]	100[a]
1934	91·4[b]	94·1	97	84	116
1939	111·9[c]	94·9	122	121	101
1946	113·3[d]	87·4	275	225	122
1962	274·6	120·6	388	370	105
1972	280·9	156·9	556	662	84
1985	329·0	207·3	1,906[e]	2,839[e]	67[e]

Notes: [a] average, 1927–9; [b] average, 1930/1–1934/5; [c] average, 1935/6–1939/40; [d] average, 1945/6–1949/50; [e] 1984. It should be noted that since the price indices are in national currencies, the relative price deterioration in Northern Ireland from 1972 to 1984 shown in the table was largely offset by the depreciation of the Irish pound relative to sterling since the Republic joined the EMS in 1979.

Sources: Northern Ireland: The data are taken from various issues of *Report on the agricultural statistics of Northern Ireland, Statistical review of Northern Ireland agriculture* and *Annual abstract of statistics*. The output change from 1912 to 1926 was taken from S.J. Sheehy, J.T. O'Brien and S.D. McClelland, *Agriculture in Northern Ireland and the Republic of Ireland* (Co-operation North, Dublin and Belfast, Paper III, 1981), Table 2.5a, which gives an estimate of the change in volume of net output. It was assumed that the price change in Northern Ireland from 1912 to the late 1920s was the same as in the south.

Republic: Various issues of *Statistical abstract of Ireland* and *Irish statistical bulletin*, and R. O'Connor and C. Guiomard, 'Agricultural output in the Irish Free State area before and after independence', *Irish Economic and Social History*, vol. xii (1985).

improved the relative market position of southern farmers due to the different approaches of the national governments. The UK as an importer sought to keep food prices down, which redounded to the disadvantage of Northern Ireland farmers, whereas the Republic, as a net exporter, took advantage of green pound devaluations to secure better prices for its farmers. In the late 1970s, however, the balance swung back somewhat in favour of the north as a result of the entry of the Republic into the EMS, the strength of sterling, and the lower general inflation rate in the UK.

Table 5.3 illustrates the trends in the volume and price of agricultural output in Northern Ireland compared with the Republic since 1912. The volume of gross output has more than trebled since then in the north, whereas it just doubled in the south.[8] The volume of output rose in Northern Ireland in the 1930s when it was stagnant in the south. While this was no doubt helped by the more favourable marketing conditions for northern suppliers to the British market, it should be noted that Northern Ireland agriculture also outperformed British agriculture at this time. The period of most rapid expansion in northern agriculture, however, was in the post-Second World War period up to the early 1960s when the volume rose by 2½ times, whereas in the Republic it was only recovering to the First World War level. The *trend* of relative prices in this period favoured the Republic, but the north still enjoyed a higher price *level*[9] and unrestricted market access to Britain. Subsequently, with improved price and market access for the Republic, agricultural output has risen faster than in the north.

The structure of Northern Ireland's agricultural production has changed somewhat since the First World War. Tillage declined due to the demise of flax and the import of cereals. Farmyard enterprises in pigs, poultry and eggs developed under the UK policy of free grain imports and support prices for output. In the 1970s such enterprises accounted for about a quarter of agricultural production in the north as against one-tenth in the south. These enterprises were adversely affected from the mid-1960s, however, by the UK policy of protecting home-based cereal production, and since 1973 by similar protection within the EEC. The overall trend of developments in the north and south has operated to bring about an even closer convergence in the structure of agriculture in the two areas — in terms of both the composition of output and the size of holdings.[10] The same is true with regard to agricultural incomes and productivity. While incomes grew faster in the north up to the mid-1960s, since then growth has been much more rapid in the south, and the productivity gap between the two areas has narrowed.[11] With the difficulties facing the EEC's CAP, the future outlook for agriculture is not promising in either area.

5.2.2 Manufacturing

As outlined in Chapter 1, Northern Ireland had a large industrial sector at the time of partition, revolving around two basic industries, shipbuilding and linen. These were augmented by engineering, especially marine engineering and textile machinery. Linen and shipbuilding depended almost entirely on sales outside Northern Ireland, while a significant proportion of textile machinery was also exported. Clothing had also become important from the beginning of the century, at first mainly for the home market, but with major exports after the First World War.

Northern Ireland's industry was highly exposed and vulnerable to fluctuations. The province had no natural resources or raw materials, except agricultural products, and relied heavily on imports for fuel and raw materials. Even in linen, by the 1920s only about 30 per cent of the flax used came from domestic production, and in the years prior to the Second World War, the proportion had fallen to 10–12 per cent. The north's peripheral location meant that transport and handling costs were relatively high. The structure of industry, with its heavy weighting of capital goods, was such that it was particularly liable to fluctuations, while the north's main consumer goods products in textiles and clothing were more prone to fluctuations than the generality of consumer goods because they were of a semi-luxury type. The foregoing considerations need not, however, have precluded continued strong industrial advance. The more fundamental problem was that, as in Great Britain, a high proportion of manufacturing was concentrated in declining industries — though this only became clear with the passage of time. Indeed, the position of Northern Ireland was worse in that regard than Great Britain: it has been estimated that in 1924, almost 60 per cent of Northern Ireland's industrial work-force was located in declining industries, as against just over 40 per cent in Great Britain.[12]

Northern Ireland's industries benefited from the boom in activity during and immediately after the First World War, but suffered in the subsequent depression. The effect was mild, however, compared with the impact of the Great Depression beginning in 1929 which had disastrous consequences for Northern Ireland's export industries. Shipbuilding employment, which had reached an all-time peak of almost 30,000 in the post-First World War boom, had fallen to one-third of this level by the mid-1920s. The problem arose from world-wide over-capacity in shipping, resulting in intense competition and poor demand for new ships. The moderate recovery that followed was short-lived. From July 1930 to July 1933, ship-building employment in Northern Ireland plummeted by 85 per cent, and the firm of Workman Clark ceased operations permanently in 1935. Recovery was protracted: the 1930 level of employment in shipbuilding was not reached again until 1939 and then only as part of the preparation for the Second World War, which brought booming demand for ships and ship repair work.

Shipbuilding activity was reasonably well maintained in the early post-war years due to replacement of war losses, and lack of competition because of the devastation of competitors' yards and restrictions on shipbuilding in the defeated nations. In 1948, the UK produced nearly half of world gross tonnage and Northern Ireland accounted for 8½ per cent of UK output.[13] Subsequently competition intensified, and by 1976 UK output, although about 25 per cent greater than in 1948, accounted for less than 5 per cent of world production. Northern Ireland's share of the world market also declined considerably, though not by as much as total UK output, and in 1976 it accounted for nearly one-third of UK production. In an industry where productivity was increasing rapidly, this performance was still not nearly enough to maintain employment. In the second half of the 1970s, the bottom fell out of the world market, and cut-throat competition developed, with all countries selling below cost. Northern Ireland suffered an even greater decline than the UK as a whole, and by 1980 employment in Harland and Wolff was down to 7,400, or less than one-third of the level that prevailed in 1950. The secular decline in shipbuilding in Northern Ireland is part and parcel of the decline in the industry in the UK. This decline has been attributed not only to competition from lower-cost countries and unstable demand, but also to poor management of the industry generally in the UK, which manifested itself in the inability to adapt to changing market conditions and changing techniques of production.[14]

As regards Northern Ireland's major traditional textile industry, linen, the basic problem here was a secular decline in world demand for the product due to changes in consumer tastes and social habits. In the 1920s there was still strong

107

demand for dress linens in the US although it was hit by the return of the UK to the gold standard in 1925. Production in Northern Ireland in the second half of the 1920s was about one-third down on the pre-First World War peak.[15] The US market was severely affected by the Great Depression and the industry never really recovered fully again in Northern Ireland. In 1938, half the work-force was unemployed. During the war, the industry was hit by disruption of its markets and by difficulties in obtaining supplies of imported flax. The factories were used for producing wartime supplies of clothing and textiles. Afterwards there was some recovery in linen production up to the early 1950s from the depressed wartime levels, but subsequently the trend was downward. Over the period 1960–79, linen production fell by over 60 per cent and the depression since then has further exacerbated the position.

Even granting that Northern Ireland was unfavourably placed in 1920 in the structure of its manufacturing, nevertheless a strong industrial performance might have been obtained by diversifying into other activities with better growth potential. In the 1920s and 1930s, however, such a course faced difficulties which were common to many other regions of the UK. With high unemployment everywhere, there was no particular attraction for firms to relocate in areas of specially high unemployment. On the contrary, the activities that were then expanding — consumer products and services — had a decided preference for proximity to the larger and wealthier centres of population in the south of England. The Northern Ireland government began attempts at diversification in the 1930s. The New Industries Development Acts of 1932 and 1937 provided the government with powers to encourage industrial development through interest-free loans and grants to new undertakings. The powers were limited, however, and failed to have much impact. The only notable achievement in diversification at this time was the establishment by Short Brothers and Harland of an aircraft factory in 1937, which some years later was to employ over 30,000 at the wartime peak.

An Act of 1945 gave increasing powers to the government to develop industry and further legislation in 1951 and 1956 enabled the government to grant-aid existing firms in respect of up to one-third of the cost of re-equipment and modernisation. Much of the emphasis of policy, however, was on the attraction of external investment. This was greatly helped by the strengthening of UK regional policy in the 1960s, involving a wage subsidy, the regional employment premium and the industrial development certificates which had the effect of restricting planning permission for industries wishing to locate in the more prosperous regions.[16] A large new man-made fibre industry developed from 1958, and in the period 1958–68 the volume of manufacturing output rose by 5 per cent per annum. In the same period, annual private manufacturing investment rose by 9 per cent in real terms.[17] Much of this investment was concentrated in highly capital- and energy-intensive activities, notably man-made fibres and shipbuilding. Furthermore, this pattern of development was a high-risk one in that 'it depended on a sustained demand for products which, historically, had exhibited a cyclical pattern'[18] — though it must be conceded that alternative projects were not readily available.

The outbreak of conflict in 1969 seriously hampered efforts to maintain the flow of inward investment. The problem was aggravated by the 1973 oil price shock and by the weakening of UK regional policy. While industry in the Western world generally was badly affected by the oil crisis, there were a number of factors which compounded the problem in Northern Ireland. Firstly, the province was much more heavily dependent on oil than the rest of the UK, with over three-quarters of its energy deriving from oil in 1973 as against less than half in the UK. Secondly, its major manufacturing industries were energy-intensive. Thirdly, the inflow of manufacturing investment, around which the industrial strategy was built, dried up in the face of the disturbed conditions in the world economy, the unstable political situation and the emerging strength of sterling arising from the exploitation of North Sea oil.

The volume of manufacturing investment fell by 9 per cent per annum between 1973 and 1978, while output dropped by 11 per cent in the two years 1973–5 and was stagnant thereafter up to 1979. In the wake of the second oil shock in 1979, the volume of output fell by a further 16 per cent to the trough in the fourth quarter of 1982. The high energy prices had rendered man-made fibre production totally uneconomic and the industry all but vanished. Recovery in manufacturing since 1982 has been uneven and slower than in Great Britain, and the volume of output in 1986 was still about 15 per cent below the 1973 level. Over the post-war period as a whole, Northern Ireland's manufacturing output increased much less than in the Republic, where it rose nearly 5½ times from 1950 to 1985, as against a doubling of output in Northern Ireland. Furthermore, due partly to the high capital-intensity of its new projects, labour productivity growth was high in Northern Ireland up to 1973, so that its relative employment performance in manufacturing was also much inferior to the Republic. With the decline in inward investment, greater attention has been given in Northern Ireland to the Local Enterprise Development Unit established in 1972 to develop small, largely indigenous, manufacturing enterprises. While some success has been attained, the impact on total manufacturing employment has been swamped by the collapse in the larger enterprises.

5.3 CONCLUSIONS

Since 1920 the structures of the two economies in Ireland have converged in many important respects. Indeed, it is ironic that the convergence was greater in some ways than if the two areas had operated in a common political regime. It is doubtful, for instance, whether the sectoral employment shares would now be quite so similar, had the country not been partitioned. If both areas had remained part of the United Kingdom, the dominance of Leinster over Northern Ireland in services employment would have continued. Equally, an independent united Ireland simply could not have afforded the vast expansion in public services which took place in Northern Ireland, while its industrial development strategy would have had to be shaped differently to build on the larger initial industrial base in that part of the country.

Northern Ireland, like the south, failed to cope satisfactorily with its labour surplus, and unemployment remains the most fundamental economic problem in both areas. The problem in the north is greatly exacerbated by its highly uneven incidence, unemployment rates being twice as high among Catholics as among Protestants and much higher in the western than in the eastern part of the province — and these differences have persisted even though industrial location policy has been absolved of any unfairness on the basis of religion.[19] Moreover, the nature and extent of structural change has been such that it has pushed up unemployment even when the overall level of employment was maintained. Thus, for example, though there was little change in the total number of employees (excluding self-employed) from 1971 to 1986, the number of female employees rose by about 40,000, while the number of males fell by a similar amount. In 1986, females accounted for 47 per cent of all employees, and male unemployment was twice that of females. This owed much to the fact that the public sector jobs, which replaced the lost manufacturing employment, offered far fewer opportunities to male manual workers.

Northern Ireland is a classic case of an area that was highly specialised in a narrow range of industries, which were vulnerable due to secular decline in world demand (linen) or to increasing competition from newly industrialising countries with cheaper costs (shipbuilding). Industrial survival for such an area depends on adaptation to higher value products, generally based on new technologies. Northern Ireland essentially failed to adapt, so that it has experienced massive de-industrialisation. The contrast with the Republic is quite striking in that regard. As recently as 1950, despite the considerable increase by that year in protected manufacturing industry in the Republic, manufacturing employment in Northern Ireland was still absolutely greater than in the Republic, but by the mid-1980s it had fallen to half the level in the Republic.

Northern Ireland's inability to adapt its industry more successfully must be ascribed largely to the fact that its fate was so much bound up with that of the UK, which was itself one of the slowest-growing economies in Europe. Even within the UK, Northern Ireland was very much a peripheral region. In the inter-war period, it was circumscribed in the range of policy instruments available to it for adapting its industrial base. However, even the more vigorous measures adopted since the Second World War have not succeeded in establishing a self-generating process of expansion. A considerable number of new jobs were indeed created: 48,000 were employed in 1980 in manufacturing projects begun since 1951, amounting to 37 per cent of total manufacturing employment.[20] A detailed study of the individual projects launched over that period, however, showed that employment typically reached a peak in these projects after about six years and then began to fall.[21] Because of this, and the fact that the old-established industries were in decline, more new projects were continually needed just to maintain existing levels of manufacturing employment.

In the 1970s the situation deteriorated in two further

respects. The flow of new projects diminished while in those already established the decline in employment came earlier and more sharply. The only consoling feature is that the north's adverse industrial structure, arising from the predominance of declining traditional industries, has been largely eliminated: the numbers engaged in shipbuilding and textiles had fallen to less than 19,000 in 1984 as compared with 83,000 in 1960. Accordingly, there should be much less negative drag on future measures to expand manufacturing employment.

The divided nature of the Northern Ireland community has also been adverse to the economic development of the province. Even before the current campaign of violence began in 1969, the community tensions were inimical to the building of a strong social consensus for development, and since then the problem has been greatly exacerbated. Estimates have been made of the cost of violence since 1969, and while these are inevitably problematic, they do at least give a broad indication of the magnitudes involved. The New Ireland Forum[22] estimated that the total economic cost of violence in 1982 was over Ir£1,630 million, of which Ir£1,300m fell on the north and Britain, and Ir£330m on the Republic. Relating these figures to GDP at factor cost in Northern Ireland and the Republic, they work out at 23 per cent and 3 per cent, respectively. This, however, tends to underestimate the relative cost of violence to the south, since the north's economy has been partly cushioned by being part of the UK. If, at the other extreme, we relate the estimate of damage borne by the north and Britain to the GDP of the UK in 1982, it works out at under ½ per cent, much less in relative terms than in the Republic. Clearly, this in turn grossly understates the impact on the north, where the violence has been preponderantly concentrated; but it does underline the fact that the spill-over on the south has not been inconsequential.

Another study[23] has tried to isolate the impact of violence on employment in Northern Ireland from the other major factors affecting employment. The estimated impact of the violence on manufacturing employment was very severe, involving a loss of 40,000 jobs from 1971 to 1983, or nearly a quarter of total manufacturing employment in 1971. Offsetting this, however, the conflict led to the creation of about 24,000 jobs in security activities, public and private. In addition, an unknown part of the large increase in UK public expenditure in the province might not have taken place in the absence of the conflict, so that the overall net impact of the violence on employment may even be slightly positive.[24] If so, however, the outcome has still undermined Northern Ireland's capability for autonomous development, and has greatly increased its dependence on the UK Exchequer. This dependence is perhaps most forcefully illustrated by the fact that 40 per cent of all persons at work in Northern Ireland are now engaged in the public sector, and that the 20 per cent of the labour force who are unemployed must also be supported through taxation. Clearly, this situation would be impossible to sustain without large fiscal transfers to the region.

It is not surprising, of course, that Northern Ireland, as part of a much larger and richer country, should benefit from net fiscal transfers. Such interregional transfers take place all the time within the UK, as in every other country: the difference in Northern Ireland's case is that the transfers are more explicit. Historically, although the principle of equality with Britain in rates of taxation and social benefits was established early on in Northern Ireland, the mechanisms for financing this arrangement evolved slowly. Thus, in the 1920s and 1930s, when unemployment was very high in the north, its public finances were constantly in difficulties. It was only in 1938 that the British government agreed to make good any deficit in the budget of Northern Ireland arising from the maintenance of parity of services. After the Second World War the principle of parity was extended to a wider range of social services. While subsequently the expansion of the public sector in Northern Ireland was similar to the UK generally up to 1970, the level of public service provision still lagged behind, so that Northern Ireland was then treated less well than other areas of the UK.

Since 1970 public expenditure has grown much more rapidly in Northern Ireland. The rise can be regarded as a catching-up process to raise public service provision to British levels, but the cost was enlarged by the fact that the needs themselves were growing rapidly at this time. Because of these greater needs, total public expenditure *per capita* in Northern Ireland in the early 1980s was 1¼ times that in Great Britain,[25] even though its GDP *per capita* was about 30 per cent lower. Less than two-thirds of public expenditure in Northern Ireland could be financed out of its own tax revenue, and the British subvention had grown from under 10 per cent of GDP in 1970 to 27 per cent in the mid-1980s.

113

In the next chapter, where we examine the economic growth record of the Republic since independence, we shall compare its record with that of Northern Ireland, and consider how overall living standards in the two areas have been affected by the developments we have outlined in this, and the earlier chapters of Part Two.

NOTES

1. The precise figure for the Northern Ireland population in 1981 has been a matter of debate. The latest revised official figure used in Table 5.1 suggests that there was virtually no change in 1981 compared with 1971. See also Northern Ireland Economic Council, *Demographic trends in Northern Ireland*, Report no. 57 (Northern Ireland Economic Development Office, Belfast, 1986), Chapter 1.

2. J. Simpson, 'Economic development: cause or effect in the Northern Irish conflict' in J. Darby (ed.), *Northern Ireland — the background to the conflict* (Appletree Press, Belfast, 1983), p.102.

3. D. Eversley and V. Herr, *The Roman Catholic population of Northern Ireland in 1981: a revised estimate* (Fair Employment Agency, Belfast, 1985) and P.A. Compton and J.A. Power, 'Estimates of the religious composition of Northern Ireland local government districts in 1981 and change in the geographical pattern of religious composition between 1971 and 1981', *Economic and Social Review*, vol. 17, no. 2 (January 1986).

4. P.A. Compton, 'An evaluation of the changing religious composition of the population of Northern Ireland', *Economic and Social Review*, vol. 16, no. 3 (April 1985).

5. D. McAleese, 'The foreign sector' in N.J. Gibson and J.E. Spencer (eds), *Economic activity in Ireland: a study of two open economies* (Gill and Macmillan, Dublin, 1977), p. 115.

6. Ibid. p. 135.

7. New Ireland Forum, *The macroeconomic consequences of integrated economic policy, planning and co-ordination in Ireland*, a study by Davy, Kelleher McCarthy Limited, Economic Consultants (Stationery Office, Dublin, 1984), p. 51. By 1986 the subvention had risen to almost £1,600 million, not including £150 million for the 'extra cost of the Army's task in Northern Ireland' — written answers to Questions in the House of Lords, *Hansard*, 2 July 1987.

8. The increase in the volume of net output was probably somewhat less in both areas. Estimates made by S.J. Sheehy, J.T. O'Brien and S.D. McClelland, *Agriculture in Northern Ireland and the Republic of Ireland* (Co-operation North, Dublin and Belfast, Paper III, 1981), Table 2.5a imply that there was no increase at all in the volume of net output in Northern Ireland from 1912 to 1979, but this is difficult to believe — see G.W. Furness and T.F. Stainer, 'The performance of agriculture in Northern Ireland and the Republic of Ireland', paper

presented to a Co-operation North Conference, Queen's University, Belfast, 10 September 1981, pp. 2–7.

9. It may reasonably be assumed that prior to the early 1930s price levels were similar in both areas. If so, the relative price levels afterwards can be judged from the subsequent relative price trends. On that basis, it has been suggested that Northern Ireland enjoyed a price advantage during the 1950s averaging almost 16 per cent — Sheehy et al., *Agriculture in Northern Ireland*, p. 16. The size of the gap estimated in this way is, however, strongly influenced by the year chosen to link the successive price series. Thus, for example, the Northern Ireland official index to base 1927–9 = 100 shows a rise of 7½ per cent from 1954 to 1959, whereas the later but overlapping index to base 1954–6 shows a fall of 6 per cent in the same period. The links we have adopted in Table 5.3 would imply a smaller price advantage in the north than suggested by Sheehy et al.

10. M. Cuddy and M. Doherty, *An analysis of agricultural developments in the north and south of Ireland and of the effects of integrated policy and planning* (New Ireland Forum, Stationery Office, Dublin, May 1984), Tables 2.1 and 2.7.

11. Indeed Sheehy et al. (p. 23) suggest that the gap in terms of value added per labour unit had been closed by the late 1970s. The question is, however, a complex one — see J.M. Whittaker and J.E. Spencer, *The Northern Ireland agricultural industry: its past development and medium-term prospects* (New University of Ulster, Coleraine, 1986), pp. 36–40.

12. D. Johnson, 'The Northern Ireland economy 1914–39' in L. Kennedy and P. Ollerenshaw (eds), *An economic history of Ulster 1820–1939* (Manchester University Press, 1985), p. 200.

13. S. Harvey and D. Rea, *The Northern Ireland economy, with particular reference to industrial development* (Ulster Polytechnic Innovation and Research Centre, Newtownabbey, Co. Antrim, 1982), p. 62.

14. Ibid., p. 67.

15. L.M. Cullen, *An economic history of Ireland since 1660*, 2nd edn (Batsford, London, 1987), p. 174.

16. D. Canning, B. Moore and J. Rhodes, 'Economic growth in Northern Ireland: problems and prospects', paper delivered to Economic and Social Research Council Conference on Economic and Social Research in Northern Ireland, Belfast, January 1987, p. 15.

17. Northern Ireland Economic Council, *Economic strategy: historical growth performance*, Report No.38 (Northern Ireland Economic Development Office, Belfast, 1983), p. 13.

18. Ibid., p. 15.

19. Fair Employment Agency, *Industrial location policy and equality of opportunity* (FEA, Belfast, 1986).

20. J.V. Simpson, 'An investigation into the employment generated by new industry locating in Northern Ireland, 1951–80', *Journal of the Statistical and Social Inquiry Society of Ireland*, vol. xxv, part ii (1984–5), pp. 1–40.

21. Ibid., p. 18.

22. New Ireland Forum, *The cost of violence arising from the Northern Ireland crisis since 1969* (Stationery Office, Dublin, 1983).

23. Canning et al., 'Economic growth in Northern Ireland'.

24. Similar findings are contained in N.J. Gibson, 'The impact of the Northern Ireland crisis on the economy', paper presented to the Conference 'Northern Ireland — the mind of a community in crisis', College of William and Mary, Williamsburg, Virginia, USA, September 1984. This study concluded that 'both unemployment and the growth of the economy as measured by conventionally defined GDP data may in actuality have been little different from what they would have been if there had been no crisis'. Gibson questions, however, whether all of the cost of increased security should be counted as part of GDP. He also argues that the economy was distorted in ways which limit its capacity for future growth.

25. Canning et al., 'Economic growth in Northern Ireland' p. 23.

6

The Economic Growth Record Since Independence

Having described the course of the Irish economy since the 1920s, it is now appropriate to take stock of Ireland's record of economic growth during this period. Comparison with other countries is helpful in providing a context within which to consider Ireland's progress. Since the whole of Ireland was part of the United Kingdom up to 1921, we shall be particularly interested in comparing the growth record in the two parts of Ireland with each other and with the UK. However, British economic growth in that period has been among the slowest in Europe, so that it is important to extend the comparison to other European countries to provide a wider perspective on Ireland's relative progress. The first section of this chapter examines the growth rates of total and *per capita* real product from the 1920s to the 1980s, and for various sub-periods. Section 6.2 then considers how, as a result of the different growth experiences, Ireland's standing has changed *vis-à-vis* other European countries with regard to relative income levels. The final section specifies the key issues that need to be explored further in Part Three in attempting to evaluate the economic performance of the Republic since independence.

6.1 IRELAND'S RELATIVE GROWTH RATE SINCE INDEPENDENCE

In considering Ireland's growth record since independence, it is firstly instructive to compare the position in the Republic, Northern Ireland and the United Kingdom. This is so because of the close association between these areas and the impact of

Table 6.1: Average annual growth rates of total and *per capita* real product in Ireland and the UK, 1926–85 (%)

	Total real product			Population			Real product *per capita*		
	Republic	Northern Ireland	United Kingdom	Republic	Northern Ireland	United Kingdom	Republic	Northern Ireland	United Kingdom
1926–38[a]	1·3	0·7	2·4	−0·1	0·2	0·4	1·4	0·6	2·0
1938–50	1·1	4·0	1·4	0·1	0·5	0·4	1·0	3·5	0·9
1950–60	1·7	2·6	2·5	−0·5	0·4	0·4	2·2	2·2	2·1
1960–73	4·4	3·7	3·1	0·6	0·6	0·5	3·8	3·1	2·6
1973–85	1·7	1·1	1·2	1·2	0·1	0·1	0·5	1·0	1·1
1926–85[a]	2·1	2·4	2·1	0·3	0·4	0·4	1·8	2·0	1·7

Note: [a] For Northern Ireland, the starting year is 1924.

Sources: *Republic of Ireland*. The real product data are linked estimates of GNP at constant prices, derived from the following sources: 1926–50, K.A. Kennedy, *Productivity and industrial growth: the Irish experience* (Clarendon Press, Oxford, 1971), Table 1.2; 1950–70, *National income and expenditure 1960* and *National income and expenditure 1977* (expenditure deflated estimate of GNP at market prices); and 1970–85, A. Punch, 'Real gross national disposable income adjusted for terms of trade 1970–1984: an assessment of technical issues', *Quarterly Economic Commentary (ESRI)*, April (1986), Table 5, and *National income and expenditure 1986* (average estimate of GNP at constant market prices). Population figures from *Report on vital statistics 1982*, and Department of Finance, *Economic review and outlook*.

Northern Ireland. The real product data for 1924–50 were derived by linking the regional income estimates in K.S. Isles and N. Cuthbert, *An economic survey of Northern Ireland* (HMSO, Belfast, 1957) with unpublished estimates by David Johnson, Department of Economic and Social History, Queen's University, Belfast, of Northern Ireland income in 1924, 1930 and 1935. The value figures were deflated by the UK price index of GDP at factor cost in C.H. Feinstein, *National income, expenditure and output of the United Kingdom, 1855–1965* (Cambridge University Press, 1972), Table 61. For 1950–73, data were calculated from the estimates of GDP at constant prices in Northern Ireland Economic Council, *Economic strategy: historical growth performance*, No. 38 (N.I. Economic Development Office, Belfast, 1983). The break in the data for 1962–3 was handled by assuming the growth rate in that year to be the same as the average for the rest of the period 1960–73. For 1973–85, the estimates of GDP at current factor cost in *Regional trends 1984* and *1987* were deflated by the UK price index of GDP at current factor cost in *United Kingdom national accounts*, 1987 edition. Population figures from N.I. *Annual abstract of statistics*, *Digest of statistics*, *Annual report of the Registrar General* and UK *Annual abstract of statistics*, 1987 edition.

United Kingdom. Real product data throughout refer to GNP at constant factor cost derived from the following sources: 1926–63, Feinstein, *National income, expenditure and output of the United Kingdom*; and 1963–85, *United Kingdom national accounts*, 1985 and 1987 editions. An average of the estimates based on expenditure, income and output is used. Population figures are from Feinstein, *National income, expenditure and output of the United Kingdom*, Table 55, and UK *annual abstract of statistics*, 1987 edition.

the much larger entity, Great Britain, on Ireland's progress. In calculating the growth rates in Table 6.1, GNP is the measure of total product used for the Republic and the UK. No GNP figure is available for Northern Ireland, so that GDP is used instead. The full period covered is from the mid-1920s to 1985, since the earliest articulated estimate for the Republic is 1926, and for Northern Ireland 1924.

There were sizeable differences in the growth rates of the three areas in different periods. In the pre-Second World War period, the Republic and Northern Ireland both experienced a slower growth of total and *per capita* real product than the UK,[1] with Northern Ireland in particular having very low growth. During the Second World War, there were boom conditions in Northern Ireland, which gained substantially relative to the UK and the Republic. In the decade 1950–60, the growth of total product in the Republic was well below that in the UK and Northern Ireland, but because population was declining in the Republic, its growth of *per capita* product kept pace with the other two areas. From 1960 to 1973, however, growth in the Republic increased substantially and outpaced that of Northern Ireland and the UK in terms of both total and *per capita* product. Growth slowed enormously in all three areas from 1973 to 1985. Though the Republic maintained the fastest growth of total product, its *per capita* product rose least because its population was now increasing rapidly, whereas there was little population change in either Northern Ireland or the UK.

Despite these significant differences in different time periods, the most remarkable fact emerging from Table 6.1 is that over the full period from the mid-1920s to the mid-1980s, there was little difference between the three areas in terms of the growth of either total or *per capita* real product. On both counts, the figures for the UK and the Republic are almost identical, with Northern Ireland doing somewhat better, but the differences are within the margin of error that must be taken to apply to such comparisons. It should be recalled that the figures for both the UK and the Republic relate to GNP, whereas the Northern Ireland figures relate to GDP. If GDP were used for all three areas, then the Republic and Northern Ireland, with the same growth rate, would both be slightly ahead of the UK.[2] The broad conclusion must be that over the period as a whole since the 1920s, both parts of Ireland experienced much the same rates of growth of total and *per capita* product as the UK. It is also difficult to escape the conclusion that the UK, as the dominant entity, exerted a strong influence on the rates of growth in both the Republic and Northern Ireland. This is supported by the fact that the faster growth in the Republic since 1960 has been accompanied by a progressive reduction in its dependence on the UK economy by diversifying its trading and other international linkages.

Here, however, we are concerned mainly with establishing the facts of Ireland's relative progress and we will return again to its explanation. Given that *per capita* incomes in Ireland, north and south, were well below British levels, then merely keeping pace with British growth rates can hardly be deemed adequate. One might have expected some tendency towards catching up, with a convergence towards British levels rather than British growth. Be that as it may, however, it might still be considered satisfactory to have kept pace with British growth if the latter had been at a high rate. As is well known, however, the British growth record has been poor by European standards, implying that Ireland also fared badly relative to other European countries. This picture is confirmed by the data shown earlier in Table 1.2 of Chapter 1, giving the growth rates of total and *per capita* real product for most of the European countries from 1913 to 1985.

Table 1.2 shows that over the 70 years from 1913 to 1985, Ireland's growth rate of total real product, which refers here to the Republic, was below that of every other European country, apart from the UK, and well below the mean rate for these countries. It also fell far short of the growth rates of total real product in the non-European OECD countries shown in Table 1.2. Furthermore, even though Ireland had a smaller rise in population than any other European country except Austria, its growth of *per capita* product was the lowest apart from the United Kingdom. The Irish figure of 1·6 per cent per annum compares with the European mean of 2·1 per cent. While this difference may not seem large when expressed as an annual rate, over time it accumulates into a substantial difference: taking two countries starting at the same level but experiencing these different growth rates, then after 70 years, *per capita* product in the one with the lower rate would only be 71 per cent of the level in the country with the higher rate.

Examination of growth rates for the countries listed in Table 1.2 for different sub-periods since the 1920s (not shown here) indicates that up to 1960, Ireland's growth rate of total product was below that of most of the countries. Even during the sub-period 1938–50 spanning the Second World War, in which Ireland was not a participant, the growth of total product in Ireland exceeded only that of the countries suffering greatest war damage — West Germany, Austria and Japan. However, it was in the decade of the 1950s above all that Ireland failed most in keeping pace with the rest of Europe. The growth rate of total product in Ireland from 1950 to 1960, at less than 2 per cent per annum, was by far the lowest in Europe and compared with a European mean of 4.8 per cent per annum. In terms of the growth rate of product *per capita* up to 1960, Ireland's performance compared better, because population was declining while still growing rapidly in most of the other countries, but the record was still one of relative decline.

From 1960 to 1973, Ireland's growth rates of total and *per capita* product improved considerably, rising well above the British rates and coming more into line with the general experience of continental Europe. While this improvement was deservedly a cause for satisfaction in Ireland, the extent of the success should nevertheless not be exaggerated. Given that Ireland's progress involved a strong element of catching up on the wealthier countries, it might be more appropriate to compare its growth rate, not with the general experience, but with that of other low income European countries. Viewed in this light, the growth rate of GDP in Ireland from 1960 to 1973 (4·4 per cent per annum) was well below that of the other low-income countries of Western Europe — Finland (5·0), Italy (5·3), Spain (7·3), Greece (7·7), and Portugal (6·9) — and also below most of the Eastern European countries. In the period 1973–85, growth rates declined all round, and Ireland now had one of the fastest rates of growth of total real GDP. However, the impact of this on relative income *per capita* was greatly modified by two factors — the outflow of factor incomes, and the acceleration in population growth at a time of deceleration in Europe. Accordingly, the rise in GNP *per capita* in Ireland was again below the general increase.

It is clear, therefore, that Ireland's achievement since independence in merely keeping pace with Britain in the growth of total and *per capita* product translates into a very mediocre record compared with the generality of European countries. Only after 1960 was there a decisive break towards a better growth rate than in the UK, and it remains to be seen whether an adequate basis has been laid to sustain this improvement. Looking at Table 1.2, the remarkable fact emerges that the growth rate of real product *per capita* in Ireland in the 70 years since the First World War was much the same as in the preceding 70 years or so. Like Britain, but unlike the rest of Europe, therefore, Ireland failed to raise the pace of its improvement in living standards. While Ireland did raise its total growth rate, so also did the rest of Europe (except Britain), and the gap in this respect was not narrowed either.

6.2 IRELAND'S RELATIVE INCOME *PER CAPITA* SINCE 1920

We now turn to the question of how the growth rates outlined in Section 6.1 affected Ireland's level of income *per capita* relative to other countries. As in Section 6.1, we begin by focusing on the comparison between the Republic, Northern Ireland and the United Kingdom. Table 6.2 presents two different comparative measures for selected years from the mid-1920s to the present. Both measures use GDP *per capita*: while we would have preferred to use GNP *per capita*, such data are not available for Northern Ireland. The difference between the two GDP *per capita* measures lies in the method of conversion to a common currency. In the first, the Republic's GDP *per capita* is converted to £sterling using the exchange rate. For most of the period, of course, the Ir£ was linked on a one-for-one parity basis to the £sterling and only from 1979 on, when the Republic joined the EMS, does the rate vary from unity. Although there are serious reservations attached to comparing income levels in different countries on the basis of exchange rates, these reservations are probably less for an Irish/British comparison, given the long-term stability in the exchange rate, the similarity in price movements and price structure, and the many close associations between the two economies.

It is well known, however, that there is a general tendency for domestic prices to be relatively lower in poorer countries than is suggested by the exchange rate.[3] Even when the exchange rate has been stable over time, therefore, its use may still overstate the real gap between a rich and a poor country. Accordingly a second comparison is given in Table 6.2 using the UK/Irish purchasing power parity (PPP) ratio for 1985, deriving the

Table 6.2: Comparative levels of product *per capita* in Ireland and the UK, various years, 1926–85

		1926	1938	1947	1950	1960	1973	1980	1985
GDP/*Capita*, current factor cost (at current exchange rates)									
Republic of Ireland	£stg	48	51	93	112	195	766	2,215	3,609
Northern Ireland[a]	£stg	53	55	134	154	273	849	2,590	3,798
United Kingdom	£stg	86	104	188	225	432	1,169	3,546	5,383
Ratios:[b] Republic/UK	%	55·7	48·6	49·4	50·1	45·0	65·5	62·5	67·0
NI/UK[a]	%	61·8	52·3	71·4	68·7	63·2	72·6	73·0	70·6
GDP/*Capita*, factor cost volume (1985 purchasing power parities)									
Republic of Ireland	£stg	1,016	1,206	1,221	1,361	1,703	2,803	3,297	3,442
Northern Ireland[a]	£stg	1,115	1,207	1,766	1,824	2,279	3,375	3,570	3,798
United Kingdom	£stg	1,855	2,354	2,493	2,697	3,372	4,643	4,903	5,383
Ratios:[b] Republic/UK	%	54·8	51·2	49·0	50·5	50·5	60·3	67·2	63·9
NI/UK[a]	%	60·1	51·3	70·8	67·6	67·6	72·7	72·8	70·6

Notes: [a] The Northern Ireland figures for the first year above relate to 1924 and the ratios have been calculated by reference to the corresponding UK figures for that year.

[b] The ratios have been calculated before the component figures were rounded to the first whole number — hence the slight discrepancies in some cases between the ratios and the value figures given above.

Sources: The basic sources are the same as for Table 6.1 The UK figures include the continental shelf. The data at current exchange rates were derived by converting the Irish figures to £stg at the average exchange rate of each year. There was of course a fixed one-for-one parity up to 1979 when Ireland joined the European Monetary System. Exchange rate data for 1980 and 1985 are taken from OECD *National accounts main aggregates vol. 1, purchasing power parities supplement 1970–85* (Paris, 1987), p. 20. The data at constant (1985) purchasing power parities (PPP) were derived first by converting the Republic GDP data to £stg using the 1985 PPP ratio for GDP from OECD, *National accounts main aggregates*, p. 20. The Northern Ireland figures, like those of the UK, are already in £sterling, and have not been adjusted, the implicit assumption being that the purchasing power of a £stg was the same there as in the UK as a whole. The 1985 figures were then multiplied by a corresponding volume index, derived from the sources given in Table 6.1.

figures for other years by multiplying the 1985 level of GDP *per capita* by the volume index of GDP *per capita*.[4] In fact the PPP ratio suggests that, taking account of the exchange rate difference, the price level of total product in common currency terms was nearly 5 per cent higher in the Republic than in the UK in 1985. Accordingly, whereas the 1985 Republic/UK ratio of GDP *per capita* was 67 per cent in terms of exchange rates, it was only 64 per cent in terms of PPP. A difficulty arises as to how to treat Northern Ireland, for which no separate PPP is available. Since Northern Ireland is part of the United Kingdom, we have assumed that the purchasing power of £1 sterling is the same there as in the UK as a whole.

We now turn to the story emerging from Table 6.2. Looking first at the relationship between the Republic and the UK, both of the indicators used show some improvement in the relative position of the Republic over the period as a whole. It is necessary to emphasise again, however, that the use of GDP *per capita* omits the large negative outflows from the Republic in recent years due to foreign debt interest and repatriation of profits by foreign enterprises. For that reason, the improvement relative to the UK in terms of GNP *per capita* was slight, and was concentrated chiefly in the 1960s and early 1970s. In the 1930s, the position of the Republic deteriorated relative to the UK, and only recovered during the 1960s. Since 1973, the GDP *per capita* indicators suggest that the Republic maintained or even improved its relative position further, but in terms of GNP *per capita*, however, the 1985 level relative to the UK was less than in 1973. Northern Ireland also gained slightly relative to the UK over the full period. The gain came entirely during the Second World War, when conditions were particularly buoyant in the province. Before the war, and especially in the 1930s, product *per capita* was declining relative to the UK, while after the wartime upsurge there has been no further sustained improvement in the relative level. Both in the north and in the south, total product *per capita* remains in the region of 30–5 per cent below the UK level.

In comparing relative living standards in the north and south of Ireland, a further important consideration must be noted. The figures in Table 6.2 do not adequately measure the extent to which Northern Ireland benefits from fiscal transfers as a poorer region in a wealthier country. There is no single indicator that provides an unambiguous measure for this

Table 6.3: Personal disposable income *per capita* in Ireland and the UK, 1985

	Exchange rate conversion £stg	PPP for private consumption £stg
Republic	2,869	2,708
Northern Ireland	3,538	3,538
United Kingdom	4,211	4,211
Ratios:		
Republic/UK	68·1	64·3
NI/UK	84·0	84·0
Republic/NI	81·0	76·5

Sources: Republic data from *National income and expenditure 1986* and Department of Finance, *Economic review and outlook, Summer 1987.* UK data from UK *National accounts*, 1987 edition. Northern Ireland data from Northern Ireland *Annual abstract of statistics 1986.* The exchange rate and PPP ratio are taken from OECD *National accounts, main aggregates vol. 1, purchasing power parities supplement, 1970–85.*

purpose. A useful indicator, however, is the level of personal disposable income *per capita*, which includes government cash transfers, less direct taxes. Comparative data for 1985 are given in Table 6.3 for the Republic, Northern Ireland and the UK. The Republic data have been converted to £sterling using both the exchange rate and the PPP ratio for personal consumption.

The figures suggest that the level of personal disposable income *per capita* in the Republic in 1985 was two-thirds of the UK level. It must again be borne in mind, however, that the Republic's personal income level in 1985 was supported by an unsustainably high level of public foreign borrowing. The relative position of Northern Ireland is decidedly improved and its personal disposable income *per capita* increases to over 80 per cent of the UK level. Furthermore, while personal income includes the current cash transfers and the salaried services, such as health and education, financed from the UK Exchequer, this may not adequately express the full range of economic support from Britain. On the other hand, it is arguable whether expenditure on security should all be treated as output or as an abnormal cost necessary to maintain some kind of stability to enable economic and social life to continue. In terms of conventional national income accounting, however,

127

there can be little doubt that average living standards in 1985 were higher in Northern Ireland than in the Republic, by upwards of 20 per cent.

What of the position of Ireland in relation to other European countries? Earlier, in Chapter 1, we discussed the data in Table 1.1 showing the level of real product *per capita* in European and some other countries relative to the UK at the start of our period. The table also includes similar data for the end of our period. By comparing the 1913 and 1985 figures, we can see how much the differential growth experience discussed in the previous section has altered the relative levels of product *per capita*. The table shows clearly the extent to which Britain's leadership among European countries has been eroded in this regard. Most of the countries which in 1913 were ahead of Ireland, but behind the UK, have now surpassed the UK. Since Ireland had only a slight gain relative to the UK, the gap between these countries and Ireland has widened, relatively and absolutely. Two of the countries that were behind Ireland in 1913 — Norway and Finland — have also pulled ahead of the UK. Several of the others have passed Ireland, while all those that still remain below Ireland have significantly narrowed the gap.

Overall, Ireland's ranking among the 23 European countries in Table 1.1 has dropped to 17th. From a level at, or even somewhat above, the mean of the European countries, Ireland has slipped to a level of about 25 per cent below the mean. While there may be some doubt about whether Ireland was as well off relatively in 1913 as the figures suggest, there can be no doubt that it is now one of the poorest countries of Western Europe,[5] only two other countries — Greece and Portugal — having an inferior position. Ireland's position has also deteriorated relative to the non-European OECD countries shown in Table 1.1, apart from Australia. The contrast with Japan is especially striking. In 1913, real product *per capita* in Ireland was about twice the Japanese level, whereas in 1985 it was little more than half — even though Japan's total product was halved during the Second World War. This, of course, reflects the speed of Japanese growth as much as it does the slowness of Ireland's advance; but it shows the degree to which the relative income levels of countries can change even in a span of time no greater than the lifetime of an individual.

To sum up, then, at the start of our period both the south and the north of Ireland appear to have had an average level of income *per capita* about 40 per cent below that prevailing in Britain. Since then, all three areas have experienced similar rates of growth of total product, population and product *per capita* — though there were considerable divergences in different sub-periods. Ireland has made little progress towards catching up with British levels of product *per capita*, which in both the north and the south remains about 30 per cent below the British level. Due to fiscal transfers, however, living standards, in terms of personal disposable income *per capita*, are closer to the British level in Northern Ireland and upwards of one-fifth higher than in the Republic. Ireland's rate of progress fell far short of what was achieved in the continental European countries. In 1913 Ireland stood at about the mean European level of income *per capita*. This position was attained, however, in an unusual way — through massive population decline, with a very low growth of total output. Since then the population decline has been arrested, and the growth of total output has risen, but not to such an extent as to ensure an acceleration in the growth of *per capita* product. Accordingly, while the Republic is ranked by the *World development report* as an industrial market economy with a higher standard of living than most of the countries of the world, it has become probably one of the poorest countries of Europe.

Systematic studies of the distribution of income in the Republic date only from the 1970s.[6] They suggest that the level of inequality in the Republic, though somewhat greater than in the UK, is only slightly above the median for the range of advanced OECD countries with which comparisons can be made. Since there is some evidence that inequality declines at the higher stages of economic development, this means that the level of income inequality in Ireland is probably no greater than in the generality of OECD countries, and less than in most undeveloped countries. On the other hand, Ireland's secularly high level of unemployment, which was always heavily concentrated in the lower socio-economic classes, together with the fact that these same classes traditionally formed the bulk of Ireland's large-scale emigration, suggests that the degree of inequality of opportunity within Ireland may have been greater than in many other countries. This has been borne out by a study comparing four countries, which showed that social mobility in Dublin was less than in Sweden, Britain or France.[7]

This, then, is the factual record and it is a mediocre one from Ireland's point of view. A poor record, however, is not necessarily the same as a poor performance. The latter depends on the problems and opportunities facing Ireland and how it responded to them. We explore that question further in relation to the Republic in Part Three of this study. Before doing so, it will be helpful to outline briefly in the final section of this chapter the key issues that seem to us to arise in assessing how the Republic fared in exploiting its potential for development.

6.3 ISSUES IN EVALUATING PERFORMANCE

The new Irish state in 1922 consisted of a *small, late-indus-trialising, peripheral* economy with a long-standing *labour surplus*. Each of these features imposed its own constraints and opportunities. A small economy, unless it is to operate at a very low living standard, is inevitably going to depend greatly on international trade. While heavily reliant on international markets, however, a small country has little bargaining power to influence these markets. It must take the external economic environment largely as given, but the measure in which it responds to this environment crucially affects its development path. In the latter regard smallness can have certain advantages: a small country which is sufficiently innovative and flexible may be able, because of its low market share, to find adequate markets abroad even in conditions of stagnant demand.

The only part of the island which could be said to have experienced an industrial revolution, the north-east, remained part of the United Kingdom, and the amount of manufacturing activity in the new state was limited. More than half the labour force was employed in agriculture, many of them on small and low-income holdings; while a significant part of the rest of the labour force was engaged in low-grade service activities. The past history of the country had not been favourable to the emergence of indigenous entrepreneurship, and had left a legacy of attitudes inimical to risk-taking. Artisanship and industrial skills were not well developed. Insecurity was a central feature of nineteenth-century Irish life, and it has been argued that, as a result, 'performance took second place to possession as a criterion of legitimacy'.[8] Yet the retarded development offered the possibility of rapid progress through catching up in the application of technologies already developed abroad. Because of the peripheral location of the economy on the outskirts of Europe, however, such an approach would require a determined effort to overcome tendencies towards insularity — tendencies that were bound to be reinforced by the quest to establish a sense of national identity separate from its nearest neighbour.

The problem of surplus labour was manifest in a long tradition of emigration which, from the middle of the previous century, was on such a scale as to involve substantial population decline. While some other regions of Europe experienced a similar though less extreme problem, none of them, like the new Irish state, constituted a sovereign nation. The loss of population from a depressed region within a country is less damaging to the national psyche when the total population of the nation is expanding, and the depressed region itself can hope to receive transfers from the central Exchequer. For these reasons the social and economic consequences of continuous population decline are more debilitating when they apply to a sovereign state. It could of course be argued that matters would be even worse without emigration, on the grounds that the outflow ensured a higher living standard than would otherwise have been possible both for those who remained and those who left. Even assuming emigration were economically beneficial, however, it was socially undesirable that it should persist on such a scale as to lead to continuing population decline.

The problems and opportunities facing the Irish economy as outlined above were seen in a broadly similar perspective at the foundation of the new state. There was broad agreement that the major economic objectives should be to develop the economy so as to raise living standards, and at least to arrest the decline in population. There was less clarity, however, about potential trade-offs between the objectives; the constraints on meeting the objectives were not always adequately recognised; and there was often outright conflict of opinion about the appropriate strategies and instruments for achieving the objectives. This is hardly surprising given that even today the economic literature does not provide any one generally accepted theory of economic development. Nevertheless, there are a number of central issues that crop up in any consideration of economic development, and these form the subjects of the chapters in Part Three.

Population and labour force, which is dealt with in Chapter 7, is central to any discussion of economic development, since it is both the ultimate object of such development and a chief means of achieving it. Ireland is altogether unique among the countries of Europe during our period of study in that its population was declining while still expanding elsewhere, and then began to rise rapidly when population had virtually ceased to grow, or was declining, in many other European countries. Scarcity of capital is another key factor hampering the development of many poorer countries, yet Ireland was for long classed as a country which exported capital as well as labour. It is important, therefore, to examine the extent to which Ireland operated under a capital constraint, and the use it made of the available capital resources. This is the subject of Chapter 8.

As already stated, the manner in which a small country responds to the external economic environment is central to its development strategy. Free trade is widely held to be advantageous to small countries. Long before it gained independence, however, Ireland had free trade with its dominant trading partner without experiencing satisfactory economic development. Moreover, it would be difficult to cite a single developed country which did not in the earlier phases of its development resort to some form of protection. Ireland proved to be no exception, and in the period we are covering, went from free trade through protection back to free trade again. Chapter 9 examines the effect of these and other developments on Ireland's foreign trade and payments, while the next two chapters consider their impact on the two main internationally traded goods sectors, agriculture and manufacturing.

Agriculture was the dominant traded goods sector at the time of independence. Livestock and livestock products accounted for four-fifths of agricultural output, the greater part of these products was exported, and such exports formed the vast bulk of the country's total merchandise exports. While the country also consumed a substantial amount of imported foodstuffs, these were generally of a kind in which Ireland did not have a comparative advantage, so that the scope for import substitution in agriculture was limited. This situation would seem to provide strong grounds for export-orientated development of agriculture based on the efficient production of those products in which Ireland had a comparative advantage. There were other substantial constraints which posed awkward choices, however. The only export market available to accommodate an expansion in Irish production, Britain, became less profitable due to the agricultural policy adopted there. Besides, Ireland's comparative advantage lay in land-using rather than in labour-using production, and there was already substantial disguised unemployment in agriculture. The acceleration of output growth in accordance with comparative advantage would probably bring about an even faster outflow from agriculture. Unless this outflow was to result in higher emigration and further population decline, rapid industrialisation would have to take up the slack. However, if this industrialisation had to be achieved by tariff and quota protection, such a course could raise costs for agriculture, damage its competitiveness and reduce the real incomes of farmers. Our assessment of Irish agricultural development in Chapter 10 is essentially the story of the varying attempts to resolve these conflicts.

Given the population and employment objectives and the improbability of agriculture being able even to maintain its employment, let alone expand it, the other main traded goods sector, manufacturing, assumes crucial importance. As an increasing returns activity, expansion of manufacturing offered the possibility of raising both incomes and employment. Yet how was rapid industrialisation to be achieved in a small, peripheral country with little industrial tradition? In our evaluation of Irish industrial development in Chapter 11, we examine the results attained by the varying strategies that have been adopted for that purpose. Finally, in Chapter 12, we draw together our conclusions on the performance of the Irish economy since independence.

NOTES

1. UK output in 1926 was depressed by the general strike, but even if we take the average for the years 1925–7, the UK growth rate up to 1938 was, at 2·1 per cent per annum, still much higher than in the Republic or Northern Ireland.

2. The average growth rates of total real GDP for the full period 1926–85 for the Republic, Northern Ireland and the UK are 2·4, 2·4 and 2·2, respectively. The sizeable difference between the GDP and GNP comparison for the Republic arises chiefly because of the much

slower growth of GNP than GDP from 1973 to 1985 — 1·7 per cent per annum as against 2.9 per cent. As already explained in Chapter 4, the difference arises because of the substantial net factor outflows in the form of interest payments on public foreign borrowing and repatriation of profits earned by foreign enterprises in the Republic. Since both of these factors were intimately connected with the rate and character of economic growth in the Republic, we believe that the GNP concept, which includes them, gives a more complete picture than the GDP concept, which excludes their negative impact.

3. T.P. Hill, *Real gross product in OECD countries and associated purchasing power parities*, Working Paper No. 17 (OECD, Paris, 1984).

4. As to the meaning in other years of the figures at 1985 PPPs, they can be interpreted as approximations to the relative levels of product *per capita* at current PPPs. The reason is that the method of multiplying the 1985 levels at comparable PPPs by the volume index of product *per capita* is mathematically equivalent to calculating a PPP ratio for each year using the trend in the (implied) relative product prices, and then using these PPPs to convert the current value figures to a comparable basis. If the trend in relative product prices were an accurate reflection of the trend in relative purchasing power, then the results would be similar to what would be obtained had a full-scale inquiry into price levels been carried out for each of the years. In practice, relative price trends are commonly used over short periods to derive PPPs for years adjoining the benchmark year for which levels are available. It must be recognised, however, that the method is likely to become increasingly inaccurate as a measure of relative purchasing power, the further we depart from the base year: the weighting of products changes, new products enter, old products drop out, and so on. This cautions against laying too much emphasis on small differences in income levels at one point in time, or small differences in growth over time.

5. There is more doubt about where Ireland stands in relation to the East European countries. Figures for Hungary, Poland and Yugoslavia in the World Bank's *World development report 1987* (p. 270), using the UN International Comparison Project purchasing power parities for 1980, indicate rather lower levels in 1985 relative to the UK (and Ireland) than are given in Table 1.2, which are taken from R. Summers and A. Heston 'A new set of international comparisons of real product and prices: estimates for 130 countries, 1950–1985', *Review of Income and Wealth*, series 34, no. 1 (March 1988).

6. B. Nolan, 'The personal distribution of income in the Republic of Ireland', *Journal of the Statistical and Social Inquiry Society of Ireland*, vol. xxiii, part v (1977–8); D.B. Rottman, D. Hannan, N. Hardiman and M.M. Wiley, *The distribution of income in the Republic of Ireland: a study in social class and family-cycle inequalities*, General Research Series no. 109 (Economic and Social Research Institute, Dublin, 1982); T. Stark, *The distribution of income in eight countries*, Background Paper no. 4, Royal Commission on the Distribution of Income and Wealth (HMSO, London, 1977).

7. C.T. Whelan and B.J. Whelan, *Social mobility in the Republic of Ireland: a comparative perspective*, General Research Series no. 116 (Economic and Social Research Institute, Dublin, 1984).

8. J.J. Lee, 'Motivation: an historian's view' in Proceedings of a colloquy *Ireland in the year 2000: towards a national strategy* (An Foras Forbartha, Dublin, 1983).

Part Three

Key Issues in Irish Economic Development

7

Population and Labour Force

In the first 40 years of independence up to 1961, the secular decline in the Irish population continued. Thereafter the population rose, and grew strongly in the 1970s when the rest of Europe was experiencing a sharp deceleration; but in the 1980s the spectre of renewed population decline through emigration looms once more. This altogether unique demographic experience is the subject of this chapter. Section 7.1 sketches the key features of Ireland's population trends since independence. These trends have been dominated by international migration. In turn migration has been strongly influenced by labour market conditions, which are examined in section 7.2. In the third section we consider the consequences for the economy of Ireland's demographic and labour market experience. Finally, section 7.4 discusses some relevant policy issues.

7.1 POPULATION TRENDS

Table 7.1 sets out the population level at ten-year intervals since 1921 and the changes in the key components during these intervals. Changes in the size of a country's population depend on its birth- and death-rates (which together determine the rate of natural increase), and on the level of net external migration. The birth-rate in Ireland in the 1920s, at about 20 per thousand population, was normal by reference to other European countries. However, whereas the Irish birth-rate remained reasonably stable up to the 1980s, birth-rates in Europe fell substantially from the 1950s, so that Ireland's birth-rate diverged increasingly from other European countries after the

Second World War. Only in the last few years has there been a significant decline in the Irish birth-rate, to 17 in 1986, a level that is still well above the EEC average of about 12. The normality of the Irish birth-rate in the 1920s, however, was itself the outcome of two abnormal factors — a low rate of marriage and an unusually high rate of marital fertility. Equally, the stability of the Irish birth-rate was due to opposing trends in the same two variables: while marital fertility fell, the marriage-rate rose, and the proportion of young married women in the total population of married women increased sharply. These changes were particularly marked after 1961. The fall in the birth-rate since 1981 is due to a continued sharp fall in fertility and a reversal of the rising marriage trend.

Table 7.1: Population trends, 1921–86

| | Population (000) | Components of population change in each interval (Average annual rate per 1,000 population) | | | | |
		Births	Deaths	Natural Increase	Net Migration	Change in Population
1921	3,096					
		20·2	14·5	5·7	−11·1	−5·5
1931	2,933					
		19·3	14·2	5·1	−3·1	+2·0
1941	2,993					
		22·1	14·0	8·1	−9·2	−1·1
1951	2,961					
		21·2	12·0	9·2	−14·1	−4·9
1961	2,818					
		21·7	11·5	10·2	−4·7	+5·6
1971	2,978					
		21·7	10·4	11·3	+3·3	+14·6
1981	3,443					
		19·1	9·4	9·7	−4·1	+5·6
1986	3,541					

Sources: *Report on vital statistics* and *Census of Population*. From 1951, the figures relate to April of each year, and previously to June.

The death-rate in Ireland declined continuously after independence and in recent decades has been close to European levels. The rate of infant mortality has fallen dramatically since the Second World War: in 1945, infant deaths in the first year were over 70 per thousand live births, but by the early

1980s the figure had fallen to 10. The decline was due primarily to improved nutrition and health care, especially in the control of infectious diseases. The combination of a stable birth-rate and a declining death-rate resulted in a consistent rise in the rate of natural increase, which was twice as high in the 1970s as in the 1920s.

Nevertheless, the dominant factor in determining variations in the rate of population change in Ireland was net migration. Apart from the 1970s, there was a net outflow in most other years at a level that resulted in an almost continuous decline in population up to 1961. The outflow was particularly marked in the 15 years or so after the Second World War: it has been estimated that two in every five children under 15 in 1946 had emigrated by 1971.[1] The reversal of the population decline after 1961 was primarily due to a substantial decline in the net outflow in the 1960s and the emergence of a net inflow in the 1970s. The inflow has not persisted, however, and by 1986 the net outflow was again on a scale that almost matched the natural increase in population in that year.

The long tradition of emigration from Ireland, and the ease of access to some of the most prosperous countries of the English-speaking world, has made emigration far easier for the Irish than for most. No matter how buoyant the economic conditions in Ireland, some emigration occurs due to considerations such as the desire for wider horizons, the spirit of adventure, the quest for training and experience, and missionary zeal. Even in the 1970s when there was a significant *net inflow*, a *gross outflow* of the order of 10,000 per annum still took place — mainly young adults. Nevertheless, the crucial influence on the scale of net migration is the economic situation in Ireland and in the major immigrant countries. The econometric evidence[2] indicates that emigration was affected by Irish income levels relative to those abroad, by the relative tax and social welfare provisions and by the relative availability of jobs. The overwhelming factor, however, was probably the persistent scarcity of jobs at home, since most emigrants simply did not have the option of a job in Ireland at the going wage rate, or anything like it. Rather, the prospect they faced if they remained was unemployment or dependence on their relatives in agriculture. Equally, the inflow of the 1970s, made up largely of returned migrants and their families, responded mainly to the enhanced employment opportunities for experienced

141

workers. Ireland's employment and unemployment experience is central, therefore, to an understanding of movements in population and external migration.

7.2 EMPLOYMENT AND UNEMPLOYMENT

Table 7.2 gives details of the labour force for the economy as a whole and the major sectors for various census years from 1926 to 1986. The trends in total employment correlate broadly with the trends in emigration. Employment was more or less static from 1926 to 1951 and emigration essentially siphoned off the natural increase that might otherwise have taken place in the labour force. That is not to say, however, that the causation was entirely in a one-way direction. Emigration was restrained during the 1930s and the Second World War because of conditions abroad, and the curtailment of emigration outlets dampened the decline in numbers remaining in agriculture. In the decade 1951–61, when emigration opportunities were abundant, the outflow from agriculture accelerated, but in addition the significant drop in employment in industry and services increased the pressure to emigrate. The decline in net emigration between 1961 and 1981 was associated with a rise in overall employment and a particularly large increase in non-agricultural employment. Since 1981 the drop in total employment has given rise to renewed emigration on an increasing scale. It may be noted that there has also been an unprecedented rise in unemployment since 1971. The main reasons why this was not alleviated by greater emigration were that labour markets abroad were depressed, and unemployment compensation at home was more generous and more widely available. Furthermore, social changes such as the propensity to marry early and increased general education may have reduced the willingness to emigrate as compared with earlier generations, when the bulk of emigrants were young, single and poorly educated.

As may be seen from Table 7.2, total employment in 1986 was less than it was 60 years earlier. While this is a depressing outcome, it should be borne in mind that the structure of employment in the 1920s was not favourable to an expansion of total employment. More than half the total were engaged in agriculture and three-fifths of these were on farms of less than

Table 7.2: Employment and unemployment in Ireland, 1926–86 (thousands)

	Employment				Unemployment	Labour force
	Agriculture	Industry	Services	Total		
1926	653	162	406	1,220	79	1,300
1936	614	206	415	1,235	96	1,331
1946	568	225	432	1,225	64	1,289
1951	496	282	438	1,217	45	1,262
1961	360 (380)	252 (259)	405 (414)	1,018 (1,053)	59 (56)	1,076 (1,108)
1971	272	320	457	1,049	61	1,110
1981	196	363	587	1,146	126	1,272
1986	168	301	606	1,075	227	1,302

Sources: *Census of population*; Department of Finance, *Economic review and outlook*; ESRI *Quarterly Economic Commentary*; D. Conniffe and K.A. Kennedy (eds). *Employment and unemployment policy for Ireland* (Economic and Social Research Institute, Dublin, 1984), Table 1.5; and G. Danaher, P. Frain and J. Sexton, *Manpower policy in Ireland*, Report No. 82 (National Economic and Social Council, Dublin, 1985), Table A.2(i). The figures for 1926–51 have been adjusted to the 1971 *Census of population* classification, while the figures for 1961–86 are on a labour force survey classification. There is therefore a discontinuity in the data at 1961, the size of which can be gauged from the figures in parentheses, which are comparable with earlier years. Because of the difficulties of measuring unemployment on a consistent basis over such a long period, the pre- and post-1961 unemployment figures should not be treated as comparable. Agriculture includes forestry and fishing throughout; industry comprises mining, manufacturing, building and electricity, gas and water; while services embraces all other gainful employment.

30 acres. There was undoubtedly substantial disguised unemployment in agriculture. Two of every five persons engaged in agriculture in 1926 were relatives who were assisting, and their numbers dropped from 262,000 in 1926 to 24,000 in 1981. There was almost an equally large proportionate fall in the numbers of employed workers (mainly farm labourers), from 113,000 to 18,000, whereas the number of farmers fell much less, from 269,000 to 139,000. Given the influence of climate and market conditions on Irish agriculture, no matter what agricultural development had taken place it would have been impossible to avoid a large contraction in employment in the sector that dominated total employment at independence. Equally in sizeable parts of the services sector at that time, employment decline was virtually inevitable. In 1926 there were 85,000 persons, mainly females, engaged in private domestic service. This was a low-paid, low-status occupation which was almost certain to decline with economic and social change, and by 1981 only 6,000 were still engaged in such activity. The distribution sector, which accounted for nearly one-third of services employment in 1926, probably also contained significant

Table 7.3: Average annual growth rates of real product and productivity, 1926–86 (%)

	Volume of GDP	Employment	GDP per worker
1926–38	1·4	0·0	1·4
1938–47	0·2	0·0	0·2
1947–61	2·4	−1·1	3·6
1961–71	4·0	0·3	3·7
1971–81	3·8	0·9	2·9
1981–6	1·7	−1·3	3·0
Full period 1926–86:			
Total	2·3	−0·2	2·5
Agriculture	1·0	−2·2	3·2
Industry	4·0	1·1	2·9
Services	2·0	0·7	1·3

Sources: GDP data from K.A. Kennedy, *Productivity and industrial growth: the Irish experience* (Clarendon Press, Oxford, 1971) and *National income and expenditure*. The data relate to GDP at constant factor cost. Employment sources as in Table 7.2.

under-utilised capacity and disguised unemployment. Without substantial population and income growth in the economy it was unlikely to expand much, particularly given the scope for labour-saving organisational changes, such as the development of self-service outlets.

The high concentration of employment in the 1920s in sectors vulnerable to employment decline meant that massive employment increases would be required in the sectors with employment growth potential, such as manufacturing, if overall employment were to expand. The need for such structural change, of course, was in no way peculiar to Ireland: on the contrary, it is endemic to the process of economic development in all countries. Nevertheless, the structure that existed in the new Irish state, cut off from its industrial arm in the north-east, was particularly daunting from the viewpoint of raising employment. It is true that, given the underdeveloped state of the economy, considerable scope existed for catching up on technological and organisational advances abroad, which, together with improved allocation of resources, would make for a high growth rate of productivity. However, this also meant that unless a sufficiently high growth of output were attained, there would be little impact on employment since most of the growth would take the form of increased output per worker.

The data in Table 7.3 show, in fact, that over the full period 1926-86 and all sub-periods, except 1971-81, the growth of labour productivity in the economy as a whole was about as great as, or greater than, the growth of output. The exception of the 1970s was mainly due to the strong growth in that decade of services, particularly public services, where productivity growth tends to rise slowly — at least as conventionally measured. In agriculture over the period as a whole the growth of labour productivity far exceeded the growth of output, while in both industry and services, about seven-tenths of the growth in output took the form of increased productivity. We shall consider in the next chapter whether the employment content of production was diminished by policy measures favouring undue capital intensity. For reasons already stated, however, a high growth of labour productivity was likely anyway. If so, then the overall growth of output was simply too low to make any great impact in catering for the inevitable outflows from agriculture and other declining occupations as well as the natural increase in the labour force. In subsequent chapters we

145

shall explore the reasons further. Here we take up the question whether the failure to cope with the problem of labour surplus, and the resulting emigration, was itself a factor which damaged the country's capability for development.

7.3 CONSEQUENCES OF DEMOGRAPHIC EXPERIENCE

The impact of population growth on economic development remains an unsettled and controversial issue. The majority of economists has tended to espouse the Malthusian perspective that rapid population growth is unfavourable to improving living standards. A minority, however, has challenged this view on the grounds that it does not give due weight to the potential benefits of a growing population — such as increased markets and economies of scale — and that it understates the extent to which technological progress can keep the 'Malthusian Devil' at bay. The inconclusive state of the issue has, however, been well expressed recently by a former Director of the UN Population Commission when he said that 'Even now, after 40 years of research, our knowledge of the impact of the population factor on development is scanty.'[3]

In Ireland it would be difficult to deny that, in the short run, emigration helped to maintain or increase the incomes of those who remained. However, that much would be conceded by even the most ardent proponents of the economic benefits of population growth, who invariably rely on longer-term considerations.[4] The more crucial issue, therefore, is whether the long-run impact was favourable or unfavourable. Undoubtedly some long-run benefits accrued to the economy in the form of a sizeable stream of emigrants' remittances and income from tourism. Moreover, a proportion of emigrants later returned to work in Ireland with greatly enhanced training and skills. Nevertheless, there were also substantial negative effects.

A major burden on the economy was the high degree of dependency that arose from the combination of emigration and high unemployment. Table 7.4 shows different measures of dependency for various years from 1926 to 1986. The first is the proportion of the population in the active age-groups (i.e. 15–64). Because emigration was overwhelmingly concentrated in the young active age-groups, Ireland has always had a significantly lower share of its population in the active age-groups than other European countries. Moreover, the share of the active age-groups was declining up to the 1960s, though it recovered somewhat thereafter. For much of the period since independence, therefore, emigration resulted in a high and rising level of age dependency. Thus, for example, while in 1966 the population as a whole was much the same as in 1936, the numbers in the active age-groups had declined by 11 per cent, while the numbers in the dependent age-groups had risen by 10½ per cent.

Table 7.4: Demographic dependency indicators for Ireland, selected years, 1926–86

	Pa/P	L/Pa	E/L	E/P
1926	61·7	70·9	93·9	41·1
1951	60·4	70·5	96·4	41·1
1961	57·7	66·2	94·6	36·1
		(68·1)	(95·0)	(37·3)
1971	57·7	64·6	94·5	35·2
1981	59·0	62·6	90·1	33·3
1986	60·2	61·1	82·6	30·4

Symbols: P, total population; Pa, population in the active ages (15–64); L, total labour force; and E, total employment (i·e. labour force minus unemployment).

Sources: See Table 7.2.

This pattern had major social and economic consequences that were adverse to economic development. The heavy loss among persons in their late teens and early twenties tended to make the society conservative and conformist. Debate and dissent, so vital to the life of any community, were dulled by the departure of persons at the very time when their ideas were liveliest and when they might be expected to make their biggest contribution to renewal and regeneration. Those who remained were demoralised by the expectation that many of their children would not have a stake in the community. Some regions became so denuded of young adults that there was little prospect of an active social life for the remainder, so that they also were encouraged to emigrate rather than seek development at home. More directly, a high age-dependency imposes a heavy burden on society for social services — particularly education for the young and health care for the old — relative to its taxable capacity.

147

Of course, not all those in the active age-groups are engaged in, or seeking, gainful employment. The proportion of the active-age population which was economically active (which is known as the participation rate and is the second indicator in Table 7.4) was lower in Ireland in 1981 than the EEC average, though higher than some individual countries like the Netherlands. The low overall participation rate was chiefly due to the low participation rate among married women, which, even though it rose from 7½ per cent in 1971 to over 17 per cent in 1981, remained much below the rate in most Western countries. The overall participation rate in Ireland has fallen substantially since the 1950s, due chiefly to the very marked rise in educational participation. The third indicator in Table 7.4 is the proportion of the labour force in employment, which has always been low in Ireland, the corollary being the high rate of unemployment. The fourth measure, the proportion of the population in gainful employment, is the product of the other three and is the most comprehensive indicator of dependency. In 1986 only 30 per cent of the population was employed, which means that on average, there were 2·3 dependents for every one person at work. If we compare this situation with Denmark, where there was on average little more than one dependent per worker, it implies that even if income per *worker* in Ireland were brought up to the Danish level, income per *head of population* would still be 50 per cent higher in Denmark.

The importance of a buoyant home market in the earlier stages of economic development is well attested. The absence of population growth in Ireland exacerbated the disadvantage of what was in any event a small absolute home market. Moreover, the resulting low density of population gave rise to several economic costs. In 1981 the number of inhabitants per square kilometre was only 49 compared with an EEC average of 175. This pushed up the cost per head of infrastructural requirements (e.g. roads, railways, telecommunications, electricity) which have high fixed costs, and where running expenses are also raised by low utilisation in sparsely populated areas. Furthermore, it is possible for a country with a low population density which is unevenly spread to experience the costs of low density in some areas and the problems of high density (e.g. pollution, congestion) in others. In Ireland population change has long been accompanied by a shift from the west to the east of the country, especially to Dublin and surrounding counties.

This was partly due to high contemporaneous external migration from the west, but it also arose from the much lower rate of natural increase in population in the west because of the low proportion of the population in the reproductive age-groups — the latter being largely a consequence of earlier migration.

Emigration in other countries has aroused concern because of the loss of skills important for economic development, the so-called brain drain. In Ireland, the great majority of the emigrants were unskilled. Side by side with this, however, a high proportion of university graduates in professional courses was forced to emigrate. This was particularly true of medical graduates, and since there was never any great scarcity of doctors at home, the oversupply represented a significant misallocation of resources over a long period. Evidence is also emerging that in recent years the general composition of emigration has been changing so that the outflow now involves 'an inordinately high proportion of qualified people'.[5]

The openness of the Irish labour market imposed considerable constraints on policy measures addressed to domestic labour market conditions. The econometric evidence indicates complex interactions between employment, unemployment, earnings and external migration.[6] While wages were probably not the chief determinant of migration flows, the ease of movement nevertheless placed limits on the degree to which a low-wage strategy might be pursued in the interests of increasing employment at home. Attempts to reduce unemployment by increasing employment were partly frustrated by the fact that the supply of labour was highly sensitive to the demand for labour. Such sensitivity applies in all countries because labour force participation rates tend to increase in response to enhanced job opportunities, but the impact in Ireland was much greater because of variations in emigration. Thus, while emigration served to reduce the overall level of unemployment in the short term, it also created conditions which made it particularly difficult to deal with hard-core unemployment.

In assessing the balance between the costs and benefits of emigration, it is important to stress that most of the damaging consequences listed above can be regarded as genuine economic costs only if Ireland had the capacity to create sufficient employment opportunities at home for those who left. In other words, emigration was economically damaging only if one believes that in its absence the resulting labour force pressures would have forced more radical measures to develop the Irish economy. There can obviously be no certainty after the event about the success of any such possible measures. If, in fact, one took the view that the end result would have been no more favourable on the employment front than what actually happened, then emigration would have to be regarded as a blessing. Since we ourselves do not accept the notion of a rigid ceiling on employment opportunities in Ireland, we cannot look on emigration in that light. However, we must admit that the matter remains one of opinion in which conclusive proof one way or the other is probably unattainable. What can be said with assurance, however, is that Irish experience does not refute the claim made by the French demographer, Sauvy, that 'There is no historical example of a stationary population having achieved appreciable economic progress. Theoretically, it is not impossible, but in practice, in our period especially, it does not happen.'[7]

7.4 POLICY ISSUES

The persistent decline in the population until 1961 struck a heavy blow to the nation's self-confidence. One of the axioms of Irish nationalism was that the country could support a much larger population and it was widely believed that rapid population growth would follow quickly after independence. It was therefore a source of considerable disappointment to find that emigration and population decline not only continued into the era of self-government, but seemed as intractable after the Second World War as at any time in the past. In 1948, the government appointed a commission of inquiry, which came to be known as the Emigration Commission, 'to consider the desirability of formulating a national population policy'. The report of the Commission, which was published in 1954, constitutes the first (and only) serious attempt to appraise the role of the state in the conscious planning and control of population trends.

The report argued that an increase in population was a realistic and desirable aim of policy, and went on to suggest that 'A steadily increasing population should occupy a high place among the criteria by which the success of national policy should be judged.'[8] It accepted that emigration brought static benefits by helping to maintain, or even increase, the standard of living in the short term, but held that this outcome itself was 'responsible for an acquiescence in conditions of under-development which are capable of considerable improvement'.[9] The sole dissenting voice on the Commission that argued for 'a more realistic appreciation of the advantages of emigration' accepted the perspective, though not the objective, of the majority in holding that emigration 'released social tensions which would otherwise explode and made possible a stability of manners and customs which would otherwise be the subject of radical change'.[10]

The Emigration Commission believed that the urgent task facing policy-makers was to break the vicious circle whereby poverty bred emigration and emigration hindered economic development. Despite the perceived urgency of the problem, however, the report advised against direct government inter-vention in the demographic field. It rejected a number of possible policy options, such as the banning or limitation of emigration or the provision of marriage loans and grants, on the grounds that they would constitute an unacceptable infringe-ment of the freedom of the individual. Instead, it proposed that government policy should operate at one remove, aiming to create the economic and social conditions conducive to popula-tion growth. The most important element in Ireland's 'popula-tion policy' would, therefore, be the general effort to develop the economy.

The attitudes embodied in the Emigration Commission's report reflect the approach of successive governments, which have tended to steer clear of the controversial issue of popu-lation planning and control. The number of policy measures which might be regarded as demographic in nature is small and their intent was generally moral or redistributional rather than to influence demographic behaviour. The major economic and social changes in Ireland since the 1960s, however, have brought about considerable changes in attitudes among the public. Contraceptives became widely used despite a legal prohibition on their sale and importation in force from 1935, and the prohibition has been progressively relaxed since the late 1970s. The large rise in unemployment in the 1980s has dented confidence in the belief that population pressure itself would, in the words of the Emigration Commission, 'establish the need for drastic action . . . for full development of our economic resources'.[11]

7.4.1 Education and human capital

As already stated, the main attempt to influence demographic behaviour in Ireland was the general effort to develop the economy. Of course, the latter in turn depended partly on the population. Internationally, it has become increasingly recognised in the past 30 years or so that economic development can be crucially affected by the education and skills of the population, or what has come to be known as human capital. We would like to be able to identify what efforts Ireland has made to raise the level of its human capital and what impact this has had. Unfortunately, these questions have not been the subject of any systematic analysis, and in this volume we can do no more than touch on them briefly.

With regard to education, Ireland had a well-developed primary school system at the time of independence. Although the numbers enrolled in second-level schools rose continuously, it is not clear whether the educational participation rate among teenagers increased much until the 1950s.[12] Between 1951 and 1981, however, there was a very large rise, with the proportion of the population in the 14–19 age-group which was still at school or college increasing from 23 per cent to 62 per cent. The most rapid increase took place between 1966 and 1971, following the introduction of a scheme of state-financed free second-level education. Even before this change, however, the educational participation rates at ages 15 and 16 were considerably higher in the early 1960s than in other parts of the British Isles,[13] and by the second half of the 1960s compared very favourably with the generality of OECD countries up to the age of 18.[14] Above that age, Ireland's position was less favourable, but since then there has been a considerable increase in third-level enrolment, with the numbers more than doubling between 1967 and 1981.

It is improbable, therefore, that the amount of education was a constraint on Ireland's economic development in comparison with other European countries. It is more difficult to pronounce on the central issues of the quality of the education and its relevance to Ireland's economic needs. An examination of Irish post-primary education published in 1981 concluded that at no time since the foundation of the state 'has any sustained assessment and critical analysis been undertaken in regard to the overall purposes and programmes of post-primary education in Ireland'.[15] It is well accepted that, at least up to the 1960s, second-level education had a pronounced academic and literary character. Although the Vocational Education Act of 1930 established a system of technical and vocational education geared to economic and social needs, this stream never attained the prestige and status attached to the secondary stream, which attracted the brighter pupils and controlled access to the universities, the professions and the public service.

Whether this mattered or not from the viewpoint of economic development, however, is open to debate, as is indicated by the outcome of the reforms undertaken in the 1960s. These reforms attempted, *inter alia*, to adapt post-primary education to the needs of the developing economy through a more unified system in which technical and vocational subjects would be more widely available. An assessment[16] of these reforms suggests that they had a mixed success: the secondary stream still dominated; pupils in the senior cycle of second level continued to offer a broad range of subjects for examination rather than to specialise; and the movement towards a more scientific/technical form took place more at third level through the establishment of new types of educational institution. However, the assessment also concludes that the comparative failure to reshape the educational system was not necessarily damaging since, contrary to expectations, most of the extra jobs that became available in the 1970s were in services rather than in manufacturing. It could of course be argued that had the educational reforms gone further, Ireland would be better placed to develop a stronger industrial capability. For that to happen, however, more would be needed than simply to improve educational skills: co-ordinated planning would be necessary to ensure that the skills would be used. Such an integration between education and the labour market would be highly problematic for many reasons,[17] and one cannot be sure that it would produce better results. In the event, it was never attempted in Ireland.

While a full-scale adaptation of education to the labour market might not have been economically beneficial, even ignoring its effects on other objectives of education, neverthe-

153

less the reluctance even to consider the economic consequences of the education system was often taken to extremes. Thus, for example, the Emigration Commission, though recognising that many professional university graduates had to emigrate, nevertheless had 'no hesitation in condemning any proposal to restrict in any way the freedom of individuals to enter universities and the freedom of the university authorities to decide the scope of their own activities'.[18] This view would be unexceptional were it not that the state bore a high proportion of the costs involved, and that the beneficiaries were overwhelmingly drawn from the better-off classes.

To take another example, it scarcely required unusual foresight to recognise that a small open economy heavily dependent on one slowly growing export market (the UK) would need to diversify its trade at some point, and that the acquisition of modern European languages would be helpful for that purpose. Yet the evidence shows that in the first 40 years little was done to further such a development in the schools. In the early 1960s, almost half of pupil hours of boys in the senior cycle of secondary schools were devoted to languages, but only 3 per cent were spent on modern continental languages, while English and Irish accounted for about 15 per cent each and ancient classics 13 per cent.[19] In fact, only 21 per cent of boys studied French to the end of the senior cycle, and only 4 per cent or less studied any other modern European language. The situation was much worse in vocational schools, since modern continental languages were only introduced for the first time in the late 1950s. The position has improved dramatically since then, but the improvement has tended to follow rather than lead other developments, such as the reopening of the economy after protection and the breaking down of the more general cultural isolation that affected many areas of Irish life up to the 1960s.

7.4.2 Public sector employment

Another important policy issue relevant here is the extent to which the government saw itself as having a direct role in job creation through public employment, as distinct from its efforts to develop the rest of the economy (which we consider in later chapters). Employment in the public sector became a major source of increased employment in nearly all Western countries, especially after the Second World War. In Ireland, up to the 1970s little use was made of public sector employment as a means of increasing overall employment. In the first decade of the state, no increase in civil service numbers took place.[20] Although numbers increased thereafter, the rise was brought about by the expansion in the functions by the state, and the increase in public employment was seen as a regrettable corollary of this rather than as something desirable in itself. The overriding view was that state measures should be directed to increasing numbers in the private sector, or failing that, in state-sponsored bodies which it was hoped would become self-financing. Even in the building industry, which was heavily financed by the state, the majority of the workers were employed by private contractors. True, some special employment schemes were operated, mainly through local authorities, but the numbers involved were usually comparatively small. In the 1950s the total number employed in the public domain was cut back. Expansion resumed again in the 1960s and at a rapid rate from the mid-1960s. In the 15-year period between 1967 and 1982, the numbers rose from 138,000 to 226,000.[21] This represented an annual average rate of increase of 3·3 per cent, and was much greater than the overall growth of employment, so that the share of public employees rose from 13·4 per cent in 1967 to 19·6 per cent in 1982. In addition, there were almost 70,000 engaged in state-sponsored bodies, whose numbers, however, did not increase during the 1970s.[22]

This growth in public sector numbers was increasingly seen in official circles during the 1970s as a means of creating employment opportunities — to such an extent that government ministers were known to compliment public sector bodies on raising the staffing levels. This was a far cry from the view of public employment throughout most of the history of the state, and later came in for strong criticism. The National Planning Board argued that 'Increased taxation to pay for new jobs in public services would further reduce taxpayers' incomes (and therefore their expenditures), and the net result would be far fewer jobs than the number newly employed in public services.'[23] This argument is based on a misunderstanding since it neglects the fact that the reduction in the income (and expenditure) of taxpayers would be about equally offset by the increased income (and expenditure) of the extra public servants. The Planning Board was on stronger grounds, however, in going on to argue that the increased taxes could reduce competitiveness and in that way cause offsetting job losses. Econometric modelling carried out at the Economic and Social Research Institute suggests that such job losses would be significant, though they would not be as great as the initial increase in public sector employment, so that the net overall effect would still be positive.

There are clearly severe limitations on the extent to which such a strategy could be pushed, since eventually it could lead to prohibitive tax rates. Nevertheless, in a situation in which output was growing due to high productivity growth while unemployment remained high, and in which a large proportion of the incomes of the employed would be spent on imports, a good case existed for the state absorbing some of the extra resources in order to provide worthwhile public services, which would, *inter alia*, help to increase total employment. The situation in Ireland approximated to these conditions for much of the period from the late 1960s to the early 1980s. Furthermore, neither the level nor the rate of growth of public employment in Ireland were abnormally high by reference to OECD countries.[24] If, however, the beneficial effects on employment of such an approach were to be sustained, two other conditions would have had to be fulfilled: firstly, that a tight rein be held on public sector pay increases, and secondly, that other public expenditures be kept severely in check. Neither of these two conditions was fulfilled, however, and some would even argue that they are incapable of fulfilment when public employment is expanding rapidly.

In the 1980s the stagnation in total output meant that such a strategy was no longer viable without putting further upward pressure on the tax share of GNP. Not surprisingly, therefore, since 1982 strenuous efforts have been made to curb the growth in public sector employment. The basic idea of funding extra employment out of taxation has by no means been abandoned, however. On the contrary, there has been a vast increase in the number of state-supported training and work experience programmes designed to mitigate the worst effects of unemployment.[25] The net effect has been to curb the more expensive forms of public sector employment while trying to provide at least temporary occupation for a greater number of persons at lower rates of pay. While understandable in the light of all the pressures involved, it is doubtful if in the long run the co-existence of two distinct classes of publicly funded employ-ment — one privileged with secure, comparatively well-paid jobs and the other in temporary, low-paid activities — is a viable concept. Certainly, more could have been achieved by reductions in the pay of the privileged groups of public servants, but the political will and capacity to achieve this has been lacking; and not for the first time in its history, the challenge to the *status quo* in Ireland now looks like being relieved once again by emigration.

NOTES

1. D. Garvey, 'The history of migration flows in the Republic of Ireland', *Population Trends*, no. 39, Spring (1985), Table 3.

2. B.M. Walsh, 'Expectation, information and human migration: specifying an econometric model of Irish migration to Britain', *Journal of Regional Science*, vol. 14, no. 1 (1974); P. Honohan, 'The evolution of the rate of unemployment in Ireland 1962–1983', *Quarterly Economic Commentary* (ESRI), May (1984); and P. Geary and C. Ó Gráda, 'Post-war migration between Ireland and the UK: models and estimates', *Working Paper, University College Dublin, Centre for Economic Research*, no. 149 (1987).

3. L. Tabah, 'Interrelationships between population and develop-ment', *Population Bulletin of the United Nations*, nos. 19–20 (1986) p. 97.

4. See, for example, J.I. Simon, 'The present value of population growth in the western world', *Population Studies*, vol. 37, no. 1 (1983), p. 15.

5. J.J. Sexton, 'Recent changes in the Irish population and in the pattern of emigration', *Irish Banking Review*, Autumn (1987) p. 39.

6. J.J. Sexton and B.M. Walsh, 'A study of labour force flows 1961–80', *Quarterly Economic Commentary* (ESRI), May (1982).

7. A. Sauvy, *General theory of population* (Weidenfeld and Nicholson, London, 1969), p. 184.

8. Commission on Emigration and Other Population Problems, 1948–54, *Reports* (Stationery Office, Dublin, 1954), p. 186.

9. Ibid., p. 139.

10. Ibid., Reservation no. 2 by Mr Alexis FitzGerald, p. 222.

11. Ibid., p. 139.

12. The 1926 and 1936 Census of Population gave details by age for those at school only for boys — even though girls have had a higher participation rate in every year since figures became available. The Census figures suggest that the educational participation rate for boys aged 14–19 fell from 27 per cent in 1926 to 21 per cent in 1936 and remained at about the latter level until 1951. The decline between 1926 and 1936 may be more apparent than real, however, since the numbers

described as 'not yet at work' in this age-group rose significantly, and the data may simply reflect differences in the way in which the Census questions were answered. Major incomparabilities can also arise depending on the way in which part-time students are classified, an issue that the early Censuses did not seem to address.

13. Report of Survey Team appointed by the Minister for Education, *Investment in education* (Stationery Office, Dublin, 1965), pp. 19–20.

14. A.D. Tussing, *Irish educational expenditures — past, present and future*, General Research Series no. 92 (Economic and Social Research Institute, Dublin, 1978), p. 90.

15. D.G. Mulcahy, *Curriculum and policy in Irish post-primary education* (Institute of Public Administration, Dublin, 1981), p. 1.

16. R. Breen, 'Irish educational policy: past performance and future prospects' in *Public social expenditure — value for money? Papers presented at ESRI conference, 20 November* (Economic and Social Research Institute, Dublin, 1984).

17. With regard to the demand for labour, the government's control is limited in a highly open, mixed economy. As regards the supply of educated labour, it has been argued that a more vocational type of education might not meet labour markets needs as well as a system producing broadly educated young persons with the capacity and flexibility to be trained later in specific skills — see Breen, 'Irish educational policy'.

18. Commission on Emigration, *Report*, p. 178.

19. Report of Survey Team, *Investment in education*, p. 278.

20. M. Ross, *Employment in the public domain in recent decades*, General Research Series no. 127 (Economic and Social Research Institute, Dublin, 1986), p. 28.

21. Ibid., p. 303.

22. P. Humphreys, *Public service employment: an examination of strategies in Ireland and other European countries* (Institute of Public Administration, Dublin, 1983), p. 88.

23. National Planning Board, *Proposals for Plan 1984–87* (Stationery Office, Dublin, 1984), p. x.4.

24. D. Conniffe and K.A. Kennedy, *Employment and unemployment policy for Ireland* (Economic and Social Research Institute, Dublin, 1984), Chapter 17; and W.K. O'Riordan, 'Public sector myths' in C. Ó Gráda and R. Thom (eds), *Perspectives on economic policy*, no. 1 (Centre for Economic Research, University College, Dublin, 1987).

25. For a review of these measures, see G. Danaher, P. Frain and J. Sexton, *Manpower policy in Ireland*, Report no. 82 (National Economic and Social Council, Dublin, 1985).

8

Capital Resources and Investment

Having considered the development of human capital in the previous chapter, we now turn to the issue of physical capital. We examine in section 8.1 the supply of investible funds and the question whether Irish economic development was retarded by a shortage of resources for capital investment. Section 8.2 outlines the changing volume and structure of investment and discusses how effectively Ireland used its investment resources. Finally, section 8.3 considers the influence of public policy on investment through the level and composition of public capital expenditure and other instruments.

8.1 THE SUPPLY OF CAPITAL

It is widely accepted that Ireland's comparative under-development at the time of independence was not primarily due to scarcity of capital for investment, but that the problem rather was one of insufficient investment opportunities as perceived by investors.[1] In support of this view one may cite the emergence of a considerable outflow of capital from Ireland to Great Britain in the last quarter of the nineteenth century and the large sterling assets held by Irish residents after the First World War. Before considering whether a similar conclusion may be reached with regard to the period since independence, it is useful to examine first the supply and sources of capital.

The supply of capital must come from either domestic or foreign sources. The domestic sources are the savings of persons, companies, and government, together with provisions for depreciation. The total of these items, known as gross

Table 8.1: Consumption, saving and net foreign disinvestment as a proportion of gross national disposable income in current prices, annual averages, various periods, 1938–85 (%)

	1938	1947–51	1952–9	1960–73	1974–9	1980–5
(1) Consumption	89·5	91·6	86·2	81·1	79·8	83·0
Private	77·6	80·0	74·4	68·0	62·8	62·8
Public	11·9	11·6	11·8	13·1	17·0	20·2
(2) Gross national saving	10·5	8·4	13·8	18·9	20·2	17·0
Personal saving	4·0	3·8	6·3	8·9	15·8	14·4
Company saving	2·6	3·3	2·3	3·0	3·7	2·5
Government saving	1·6	−0·5	0·6	0·6	−4·4	−8·0
Stock appreciation adjustment	n.a.	−2·1	−0·3	−1·0	−3·5	−2·2
Depreciation	2·3	3·9	4·9	7·4	8·6	10·3
(3) Gross national disposable income [= (1) + (2)]	100	100	100	100	100	100

(4) Net foreign disinvestment	−1·1	7·8	1·6	2·2	6·8	9·2
Changes in reserves	n.a.	1·4	0·2	−1·3	−1·9	−1·2
Net capital inflow	n.a.	6·4	1·4	3·5	8·7	10·4
Private capital	n.a.	n.a.	n.a.	1·5	2·8	−0·2
Public capital[a]	n.a.	n.a.	n.a.	1·1	5·2	8·9
Other	n.a.	n.a.	n.a.	0·9	0·7	1·7
(5) Gross domestic physical capital formation [= (2)+(4)]	9·4	16·2	15·4	21·1	27·0	26·2

Note: [a] Net foreign borrowing by semi-state bodies is included under net public capital inflow.

Sources: *National income and expenditure*, various years; *Irish statistical survey 1956*; *Irish statistical bulletin*, various years; and D. McAleese, 'Capital inflow and direct foreign investment in Ireland 1952 to 1970', *Journal of the Statistical and Social Inquiry Society of Ireland*, vol. xxii, part iv (1971–2), p. 72.

national savings, is equivalent to the difference between gross national disposable income (GNDI)[2] and total consumption, public and private. The foreign sources of capital may be divided into changes in the country's external reserves and net capital inflows, and the total of these — net foreign disinvestment — is identical to the current balance of payments deficit. The aggregate of the domestic and foreign sources represents the total devoted to physical capital formation at home. Data on these variables are available since 1938 and are presented in Table 8.1 in relation to GNDI for various periods.

Gross saving was comparatively low until the 1960s and was particularly low in the years immediately following the Second World War, when the ratio to GNDI was only 8½ per cent. From 1960 to 1973, however, gross saving increased sufficiently to cover most of the higher investment level attained in that period. There were significant increases in personal saving and provision for depreciation. Company saving also rose, but has never been substantial in Ireland. The improvement in the savings ratio in this period was mainly due to the much higher growth of real incomes, including the effect of favourable terms of trade.[3] Gross national saving rose further in the period 1974–9 to an average of just over 20 per cent of GNDI, despite plummeting temporarily in 1974 under the impact of the first oil crisis. Over these years, however, it was increasingly the product of two contrary factors, high personal saving and large government dissaving. The increase in personal saving to almost 16 per cent of GNDI for 1974–9 from just 9 per cent for 1960–73 is puzzling as real interest rates were strongly negative in the inflationary 1970s, and none of the attempts to explain it has been altogether satisfactory. In contrast with the personal sector the state sector ran substantial current budget deficits after 1974. This latter development intensified in the 1980s and was mainly responsible for a decline in total gross national saving, though with the reduced level of activity and stagnation in real incomes, there was also a decline in both personal and company saving.

National saving was often supplemented in varying degrees in different periods by repatriation of external assets and inflows of foreign capital. Ireland accumulated significant external assets during both world wars due to surpluses in trade and payments. These surpluses could not, however, be used at the time to fund domestic investment, because most capital goods had to be imported and were unobtainable in wartime. The surpluses were instead invested in sterling financial assets. As a result Ireland held external assets equivalent to approximately 1½ times GNP in the 1920s and in 1947.[4] In the 1930s protection raised the return on industrial investment at home and encouraged the repatriation of some sterling assets. The statistics of the time suggest that the inflow amounted to 3 per cent of GNP in 1933 and 1934 but was lower in subsequent years. It seems probable, however, that significant inflows did continue but were not picked up in official statistics.[5]

In the years immediately after the Second World War there was substantial net foreign disinvestment to finance the enlarged level of investment at a time of low current saving. External reserves were drawn on only to a limited extent, and the major inflows were Marshall Aid funds and other, largely private, capital inflows. For the remainder of the 1950s private capital inflows were greatly reduced and the Marshall Aid funds were largely spent. With the state unwilling at this time to undertake foreign borrowing or reduce external reserves, there was little reliance on foreign capital. The position changed somewhat in the 1960s when domestic saving was supplemented by new net inflows of public and private capital. The government broke with its traditional aversion towards foreign borrowing and used external capital in moderate degree to help finance the Public Capital Programme. Private capital inflows also expanded as foreign direct investment in industry grew. Total net capital inflow amounted on average to 3.5 per cent of GNDI in the years 1960–73, more than covering the difference between gross saving and investment, and allowing external reserves to rise.

Throughout the years 1974–9, even though total saving rose, there was an increased short-fall in relation to the greatly expanded level of domestic investment. To fill the gap foreign borrowing by the government and semi-state bodies rose to 5 per cent of GNDI and private capital inflows reached their highest levels at 3 per cent of GNDI. In the 1980s private capital inflows virtually ceased but public foreign borrowing rose even further. However, this level of foreign borrowing left Ireland increasingly vulnerable in its dependence on external capital. From 1981 onwards international real interest rates soared, as did the interest payments that Ireland had to pay on accumulated debts. The unsustainability of the situation engendered a pessimistic sentiment in Irish financial markets, and the very high domestic real interest rates tended to divert funds away from physical capital formation towards investment in government debt and net lending to the banking system.[6] Fears of the fiscal situation, together with uncertainty about the exchange rate, led to large residual capital outflows of 4 per cent of GNDI in 1985 and 9 per cent of GNDI in 1986.

What, then, are we to conclude regarding the question as to whether Ireland suffered from a shortage of capital for investment? For much of the period since independence, it can scarcely be said that Ireland was constrained in this way, at least at the aggregate level. Although total saving was low up to the 1960s, Ireland had accumulated substantial external assets during the two world wars. Moreover, direct foreign investment flows were not wanting whenever there were profitable opportunities for the use of such funds. In the 1960s and 1970s, the country's high credit-rating enabled the government to borrow abroad on favourable terms. Of course, considerable conflict of views existed on the appropriateness of repatriating external assets. In the 1930s the Banking Commission argued that external assets should not be used to fund domestic investment unless it had a net export effect equal to the net inflow. With an apparent lack of such investment opportunities, the low current saving ratio was treated as an absolute shortage of capital. Similar reasoning led to fiscal retrenchment after the sizeable deficits in the balance of payments in 1951 and 1955. These views gave little recognition to the likelihood that, had the resources been used to secure greater economic development, personal and company saving would have responded favourably.

The situation changed in the 1980s with the combination of high domestic investment and substantial government dissaving. True, Ireland still could and did borrow substantially abroad, but only at real interest rates which involved a very heavy burden on the Exchequer and on the economy at large. Such a level of foreign borrowing was clearly unsustainable, and it would be difficult if not impossible to bridge the gap between the rates of domestic capital formation and of saving purely by attempting to raise the saving ratio. It is reasonable to conclude, therefore, that capital had become scarce in relation to the prevailing level of investment. Moreover, even with the prevailing level of investment, unemployment stood at record levels. Thus, capital scarcity was still greater if considered in relation to the additional resources that would be required to equip the total potential labour force with levels of capital intensity comparable to those in employment — even making due allowance for under-utilisation of capacity. It is arguable, of course, that this scarcity of capital sprang not from a shortage of supply but from 'failure to mobilise available capital to optimal effect'.[7] The question of the effectiveness in using capital is taken up in the next two sections.

One further point needs to be considered at this juncture. The fact that in the aggregate the supply of capital was not generally a prime constraint does not rule out the possibility that it may have been a constraint in particular sectors, due to imperfections in the capital market. Certainly, there were strong tendencies to channel funds into financial assets. Moreover, the close inter-linkages between the British and Irish financial markets meant that Irish investors could avail themselves of the secure returns on a wide range of British financial assets, whereas for a long time the Irish financial market remained underdeveloped and the returns to investment seemed less secure. Frequent claims have been made regarding the scarcity of entrepreneurial capital. No doubt these claims were valid to the extent that many prospective entrepreneurial ventures were unable to secure funds to proceed. It is, however, difficult to distinguish the extent to which this happened due to deficiencies in the supply of capital as compared with justified scepticism on the part of lenders about the economic viability of the projects. What is clear is that the state intervened massively, particularly after the Second World War, to influence the scale and direction of investment, as we shall discuss more fully in section 8.3.

8.2 THE USES OF CAPITAL

In the previous section our concern was with the adequacy of the supply of resources available for domestic investment. We now turn to the actual uses of these resources in the form of domestic capital formation. Unfortunately, estimates of the capital stock in Ireland are available only for the industrial sector and these are discussed later in Chapter 11. Here we focus on fixed investment (i.e. investment in plant and buildings) which

Table 8.2: Average annual volume of fixed investment at 1980 constant prices and average ratio of fixed investment to GNP, various periods, 1938–85

	1938	1938–46	1947–51	1952–9	1960–73	1974–9	1980–5
Average annual volume of investment (£ million)	383	205	450	603	1,200	2,174	2,626
Average ratio of fixed investment to GNP at market prices (%)	12·6	n.a.	13·2	16·0	21·4	27·1	29·2

Sources: Data for volume of investment and GNP in 1938 and for 1947 onwards taken from *Irish statistical survey 1956* and *National income and expenditure* (various years). The investment volume data for 1938–47 were constructed by fitting the price and nominal data on investment, given in *National income and expenditure 1938–44*, and *Irish statistical survey 1949–50*, between the revised official figures available for 1938 and 1947.

comprises the vast bulk of total investment. The remainder represents stock building which in all periods averaged less than 2 per cent of GNP. Prior to 1938 there are no comprehensive data on fixed investment. Data on capital goods imports, however, suggest that investment was at a higher level after 1932 than in the 1920s. It appears that by the end of the 1920s the volume of investment was falling after higher earlier expenditures on reconstruction work and on a national electricity generating capacity. In 1932 investment increased again with more state capital spending and the protectionist stimulus to industry. Nevertheless, the level of total fixed investment probably remained low, as indicated by the fact that its ratio to GNP in 1938 was only 12½ per cent (Table 8.2).

The trend of investment since 1938 divides broadly into two periods around the year 1960. In the 22 years between 1938 and 1960, investment grew in volume terms at an annual average rate of 2 per cent, while in the following 22 years, the growth rate was 7 per cent. The extent of the decline in investment during the Second World War may be gauged from the fact that, despite a strong recovery in the early post-war years, the average annual volume of investment for the 18 years 1938–56 was no greater than the 1938 level. The early post-war recovery in investment peaked in 1951, and in the second half of the 1950s the investment ratio fell significantly.

From 1960 investment grew strongly, and the average investment ratio of 21½ per cent for 1960–73 was significantly higher than previous experience but still somewhat lower than many other European countries. By the early 1970s, however, Ireland was investing a comparatively large share of national output and, despite the fall in investment following the first oil crisis, the investment ratio for the 1974–9 period was 27 per cent. The historical peak ratio was reached in 1979 and 1981 at about 32 per cent. Since 1981, however, there has been a sustained decline in the volume of investment which was about 20 per cent lower in 1986 than in 1981. Despite this decline the investment ratio for 1980–5 of 29 per cent remained high. Over the last decade, therefore, Ireland has invested a remarkably large share of total output, with one of the highest investment ratios in Europe. Unfortunately, this has not been sufficient to ensure rapid economic growth.

Table 8.3 shows the structure of investment in terms of its distribution among the major sectors. The two main traded

167

Table 8.3: Investment by sector as a percentage of total fixed investment (1980 constant prices), annual averages, various periods, 1949–84 (%)

	1949–59	1960–73	1974–84
Agriculture	16·2	16·0	11·5
Industry	28·0	28·1	31·8
of which			
Manufacturing	13·2	17·5	19·6
Utilities	11·6	6·7	6·9
Other[a]	3·2	3·8	5·3
Services	29·4	35·5	33·7
of which			
Wholesale and retail	4·5	5·6	5·1
Transport and communications	14·2	14·9	11·9
Community and personal	9·1	12·1	10·7
Finance and insurance	0·4	1·2	3·8
Public administration	1·2	1·7	2·2
Dwellings	26·5	20·4	23·0
Total	100	100	100

Note: [a] This category includes mining, quarrying and building.

Sources: Data supplied by Central Statistics Office for 1949–53 and Department of Finance databank for subsequent years.

goods sectors, agriculture and manufacturing, never accounted together for more than one-third of the total, but that is not unusual among other OECD countries. The combined share of the two sectors has been fairly steady, but with a tendency for the manufacturing share to rise and the agricultural share to fall. While agricultural investment at first grew strongly following EEC entry, the 1980s have witnessed a substantial decline so that the volume in 1984 was over 40 per cent below that of 1981. As in most of the developed countries, the larger proportion of investment in Ireland has been devoted to utilities (electricity, gas and water), services and dwellings, which together have generally accounted for about two-thirds of the total. The share of utilities and of dwellings was relatively high during the 1950s due to the emphasis on infrastructure in the Public Capital Programme. Overall, however, the sectoral shares in investment have remained fairly stable in the face of the substantial rise in the total level since the 1960s.

Table 8.4: Investment ratio, incremental capital/output ratio and investment/labour productivity ratio by sector (at 1980 constant prices), various periods, 1949–84

	1949–61[a]	1962–72	1973–84
Average Gross Fixed Investment Ratio (%)			
Agriculture	9·9	24·0	27·2
Industry	18·7	20·1	25·6
Manufacturing	16·5	23·3	27·4
Services	23·1	25·3	30·9
Total	18·2	24·5	30·3
Gross Incremental Capital/Output Ratio			
Agriculture	11·1	11·9	11·2
Industry	5·2	3·4	6·2
Manufacturing	3·8	4·0	5·0
Services	14·3	6·7	9·4
Total	9·2	6·0	8·8
Gross Investment/Labour Productivity Ratio			
Agriculture	2·7	4·5	5·1
Industry	4·9	5·3	6·4
Manufacturing	6·2	6·0	5·0
Services	11·4	10·7	25·7
Total	5·5	6·5	10·3

Note: [a] Calculated at 1958 constant prices.

Sources: K.A. Kennedy and B.R. Dowling, *Economic growth in Ireland: the experience since 1947* (Gill and Macmillan, Dublin, and Barnes and Noble, New York, 1975), p. 181; and Department of Finance databank. The output concept used is GDP at constant factor cost.

8.2.1 Investment and output

Table 8.4 shows *inter alia* the sectoral investment ratio (i.e. the ratio of gross fixed investment to GDP) for various post-war periods. As stated already, the total investment ratio rose substantially in the 1960s and 1970s and the same was true for the main sectors. The greatest increase was in agriculture, where the ratio rose from an average of less than 10 per cent in the 1950s to 27 per cent for 1973–84, with an historical peak of 41 per cent in 1979. Not only have the investment ratios risen in all sectors but they have also come closer together, so that in the most recent period there was very little variation across sectors.

An important question arises as to what extent the rise in the investment ratio was associated with a higher growth rate. This question can be conveniently considered in terms of changes in the gross incremental capital/output ratio (GICOR) which is calculated by dividing the investment ratio by the growth rate of output. A low GICOR indicates that a high rate of output growth was achieved with a relatively low rate of investment. While this does not necessarily demonstrate that the investment has been effective, the measure does nevertheless provide an empirical framework for exploring further the relation between investment and changes in output. The relevant data are given in Table 8.4.

It may be seen that, with the rise in the investment ratio in the 1960s, the economy-wide GICOR fell considerably from 9·2 for 1949–61 to 6·0 for 1962–72. Ireland's GICOR in the earlier period was high in comparison with most other OECD countries at the same time.[8] The decline in the GICOR in the 1960s was in some degree due to a shift in the share of investment towards assets yielding a larger immediate increase in production, but was mainly due to higher utilisation of the infrastructural capacity developed in the late 1940s and in the 1950s.[9] This is borne out by the fact that the fall in the sectoral GICORs was confined to utilities and services, whereas there was no decline in agriculture and manufacturing. In achieving greater utilisation of capacity, the rise in the investment ratio played a role by helping to sustain a higher level of demand and activity.

In the period 1973–84, the GICOR rose again to a level similar to that prevailing in the 1950s. Despite the superficial similarity between the overall GICORs for the two periods 1949–61 and 1973–84, they differ significantly in the underlying investment ratio. In the earlier period restrictive government spending curtailed public investment and led to a reduction in overall investment and in home demand. In contrast, in the later period Ireland invested to a degree that was exceptional by European standards. However, the response in terms of the growth of GDP was disappointing in the 1980s. Moreover, if GNP were used as the measure of output after 1973, the output growth was even lower, and the GICOR was at the extraordinarily high level of over 15. The high GICOR for the period 1973–84 cannot be explained on the grounds that investment was directed relatively more to raising labour productivity than output. The gross investment/productivity ratio (GIPR), which measures the relation between investment and changes in labour productivity and is also shown in Table 8.4, was much less favourable than in the two preceding periods. Only in manufacturing, perhaps, is there a suggestion that investment in the period 1973–84 was more effective in raising labour productivity than output, as compared with earlier periods.

Ireland was not alone in experiencing a large rise in the GICOR after 1973. The same occurred in most OECD countries, since the sharp fall in the rate of economic growth was not accompanied by a similar decline in the investment ratio. In Ireland the factor mainly responsible for the high GICOR in the 1950s — under-utilisation of new infrastructural capacity — was also operative to some extent in the period 1973–84. There was heavy investment in such areas as electricity and communications, which, because of the depressed output growth, resulted in severe excess capacity in the 1980s. The rise in the GICOR, however, was quite general and applied to all sectors except agriculture, in which there was a slight fall. Another factor operating in this period was the impact of the huge oil price increase in making existing fuel-intensive plant obsolescent, so that a greater proportion of gross investment had to be directed to replacing capacity rather than adding to it. The closure of many of the indigenous firms in the depressed conditions of the 1980s also tended to accelerate the rate of retirement of existing capital stock. While the foregoing factors could explain the large increase in the overall GICOR and GIPR for 1973–84, there are nevertheless also indications that capital was used wastefully in this period.[10] Partly because capital was so readily available in the 1970s at negative real interest rates, there was insufficient stress on the need for the wise use of investment resources, and on the complementary factors required to secure the benefits of investment. This criticism applied particularly to public policy, to which we now turn.

171

8.3 INVESTMENT AND PUBLIC POLICY

As already mentioned, the state has intervened extensively to influence the rate and direction of investment. The most transparent means has been through public investment, both directly and through capital loans and grants to the private sector. In the early years of the state the volume of public investment was relatively small, amounting in 1926 to 3 per cent of GNP. The objectives of this expenditure were limited chiefly to the repairing of war damage, power and housing. In 1932 the new Fianna Fáil administration initiated a more vigorous programme of state investment. A large housing programme was launched and the state also invested in new semi-state industries. As a result, the volume of public capital expenditure was over 50 per cent higher in the years 1933–7 than in 1926 (Table 8.5). The Second World War restricted public capital spending just as it halted investment generally, but when the war ended conditions were ripe for its resumption. The ample supply of capital in the early post-war years facilitated an increase in public capital expenditure of 30 per cent above the level of the 1930s. Public investment accounted for the bulk of the increase in total investment in the early post-war years and amounted to over 11 per cent of GNP in 1951. By then, however, the surfeit of ready capital was diminishing and fears of balance of payments deficits were heightened by a large deficit in that year. The expansion of state investment was checked in 1952, and fell once more with the balance of payments crisis in 1955 and subsequent efforts to restructure public capital spending in 1957.

Notwithstanding the strong and sustained recovery in public investment from the early 1960s, its share in total investment declined and remained at about 45 per cent of the total until the oil crisis of the 1970s. This was because of the buoyancy of non-government investment. In the depressions following the two oil crises, when private investment fell, public capital expenditure was expanded in order to try to maintain demand. Accordingly the public sector share of investment rose substantially to about 60 per cent of the total in the early 1980s, while its ratio to GNP was over 16 per cent. As the depression of the 1980s continued, however, the crisis in the public finances led to cutbacks in the volume of public capital spending. The budgeted Public Capital Programme for 1987 was about one-third lower

Table 8.5: Public capital expenditure (at 1980 constant prices), various periods, 1926–84

	Average annual volume £m	Average share of total investment %	Average annual rate of change %
1926–32	163	n.a.	−2·2
1933–37	251	n.a.	13·3
1949–54	327	56·1	4·1
1955–59	296	50·2	−3·3
1960–64	364	46·9	9·6
1965–69	552	45·7	10·1
1970–74	801	45·5	8·8
1975–79	1,228	55·6	7·1
1980–84	1,510	56·8	0·6

Sources: Current price figures on public capital expenditure for years prior to the Second World War were taken from M. O'Donoghue and A.A. Tait, 'The growth of public revenue and expenditure in Ireland' in J.A. Bristow and A.A. Tait (eds), *Economic policy in Ireland* (Institute of Public Administration, Dublin, 1968), and for post-war years from *National income and expenditure*. The figures are on a national accounts basis and were converted to 1980 prices by the deflator for fixed capital formation used in Table 8.2, and by the consumer price index for pre-war years.

in volume terms than the historical peak. Nevertheless, because of the large fall in private investment, the public sector share remained about half of the total.

The composition of the Public Capital Programme has changed significantly in the post-war period. The traditional areas of involvement were housing and electrical power, and from 1949 to 1954 these accounted for over three-fifths of the total. In the mid-1950s the poor economic performance led to a re-evaluation of the structure of the Public Capital Programme. A policy of switching to more directly productive state investment was adopted, which initially simply reduced the volume of investment in housing. This coincided with a downward revision of projected electricity needs and a fall in the construction of generating stations so that the two categories accounted for an average of only 45 per cent of a reduced Public Capital Programme for the years 1955–9. It took some time before the more directly productive state investment in agriculture, manufacturing and tourism got off the ground, but the seeds of a more effective Public Capital Programme were sown.

The share of the Public Capital Programme devoted to

manufacturing rose from just 1 per cent in the late 1950s to 10 per cent in the late 1960s and 21 per cent in the second half of the 1970s. This investment included the new industry grants which were instrumental in increasing Ireland's share of foreign direct investment. The proportion devoted to agriculture rose from 3 per cent in the 1950s to 10 per cent in the 1960s, while the share of telecommunications also increased to over 10 per cent in the second half of the 1970s. From the mid-1960s, both education and health tended to claim a larger share of public capital but the two together accounted for less than half of public spending on housing, the other main area of social capital expenditure. This last category, which represented one-third of total public investment in the early 1950s, had a falling share up to the early 1960s, but its share increased after a housing crisis was declared in 1963. After that time it remained fairly constant at about one-fifth.

While public capital expenditure was the major means of influencing investment, the rate and direction of investment was also influenced by a great variety of other public measures. Some of these influences were due to measures directly related to investment, such as the tax treatment of depreciation, or the establishment of semi-state institutions (the Agricultural Credit Corporation and the Industrial Credit Company) to improve access to capital; some arose from more general state initiatives to raise the profitability of particular activities, such as the tax relief on manufactured exports; and some were unforeseen consequences of tax avoidance at a time of high inflation.

Although there has been no comprehensive analysis of the impact of state intervention in relation to investment, some broad conclusions can be drawn with reasonable confidence. There can be little doubt but that state initiatives have served to raise the level of investment very considerably, and that this was a necessary though not a sufficient condition for developing the economy. State investment has also influenced the direction of investment in ways that were important for raising living standards. A considerable part of public capital expenditure has always been devoted to providing economic and social infrastructure — power, telecommunications, roads, houses, hospitals and schools. These were quite deficient in Ireland after the Second World War. Subsequently, further major infrastructural needs arose following the increased economic growth of the 1960s and the rapid population growth of the

1970s. Even in much more highly developed economies, various forms of market failure prevent private investment from ensuring an adequate level of many forms of infrastructure, and in Ireland's underdeveloped state the need for state involvement was greater.

However, state measures also had a profound impact on the level of investment in the more directly productive sectors of the economy, such as agriculture, manufacturing and tourism. In the inter-war period there was considerable debate as to whether lack of access to capital was a constraint on productive investment. The Department of Industry and Commerce believed that there was a scarcity in the supply of long-term capital to industry from a banking system which opted for sterling financial assets, whereas the Department of Finance tended to the view that any such problems arose only because the return on the long-term projects was uneconomic. In fact, the direct measures taken at the time, which were confined to improving access to capital in the form of state loans and guarantees, did not at that time have much impact on productive investment. It was only in the post-war period that it became widely accepted that if productive investment were to expand, measures must also be taken to improve the return on investment. This was done directly by outright grants and other measures which lowered the price of capital, as well as by more general steps to enhance profitability.

While state involvement in relation to investment has produced many benefits, however, there is another dimension to the issue. Over the past decade, as the degree of intervention has grown and the supply of capital become more scarce relative to the demand, increasing criticism has been voiced about the ill-effects of state involvement. One line of criticism is that by making capital for investment cheap, over-use has been encouraged. While this criticism is valid enough during the past decade, its application to earlier periods is of doubtful validity, where the problem to be confronted was generally the insufficient use of available capital resources. Even in the last decade the difficulties created by excessive government borrowing sprang not just from high investment, but even more so from the extensive recourse to borrowing by successive governments to finance day-to-day expenditure.

A second line of criticism is that state intervention led to a misuse of capital. A particular dimension of this criticism which has received considerable attention is the argument that, given Ireland's perennial labour surplus, investment should not have been stimulated by measures which lowered the price of capital itself. The latter method, it is argued, favoured products and techniques of production with high capital/labour ratios, making it more difficult to absorb surplus labour. While there can be no doubt that government measures have served to reduce the cost of capital relative to labour,[11] the strength of the criticism depends also on many other factors, such as the degree of choice available in products and technology and the extent to which alternative incentives would overcome barriers in access to capital and attract new enterprise. Certainly, it is curious that the argument has been focused almost exclusively on the manufacturing sector, which accounts for only one-fifth of total investment, and where the choice of capital/labour ratio is probably least open to domestic influence due to the pervasive exposure to foreign competition and technology. Moreover, a high capital/labour ratio is not in itself a barrier to absorbing surplus labour unless there is a shortage of capital, which did not arise until recent years.

Another aspect of the criticism about misuse of capital resources is that the state investment incentives misdirected investment excessively into particular areas at the expense of other areas more crucial to the development of the economy. Property investment, it is claimed, has been favoured unduly relative to tradable goods, and special concern has been expressed at the extent of the incentives to home ownership.[12] Indeed, with the growth of state involvement, the range and diversity of incentives to invest — explicit and implicit — is now such that it is almost impossible to evaluate their impact on the composition of investment. There can be little doubt that the effectiveness of investment in meeting national priorities would gain from a more discriminatory focus in the incentives offered to private investment, and a more explicit quantification of the expected benefits of the government's own capital expenditure. An even more fundamental issue, to which little systematic thought has been given, is the appropriate division of resources between physical investment and other forms of investment — notably in human capital and in immaterial capital in the form of technological knowledge and marketing expertise.

To conclude, this chapter suggests that while Ireland was not constrained by a shortage of capital until recently, for a long time it did not bring these resources fully into use for domestic economic development. The state played a key role in the post-war period in mobilising capital for that purpose — with much success but with increasing distortions as the scale of investment expanded. The experience of the past decade shows all too clearly that investment in fixed assets alone does not ensure growth — an obvious lesson, perhaps, but one that has had to be painfully re-learned.

NOTES

1. See D. McAleese, 'Is there a want of capital in Ireland?', *Administration*, vol. 31, no. 4 (1984).
2. GNDI is the sum of GNP and net current transfer payments from abroad.
3. K.A. Kennedy and B.R. Dowling, *Economic growth in Ireland: the experience since 1947* (Gill and Macmillan, Dublin, and Barnes and Noble, New York, 1975), Chapter 10.
4. L.M. Cullen, *Economic history of Ireland since 1660*, 2nd edn (B.T. Batsford, London, 1987), and T.K. Whitaker, 'Ireland's external assets', *Journal of the Statistical and Social Inquiry Society of Ireland*, vol. xviii, no. 2 (1948–9).
5. Commission of Inquiry into Banking, Currency and Credit, *Reports* (Stationery Office, Dublin, 1938), p. 94.
6. J.D. FitzGerald, *The national debt and economic policy in the medium term*, Policy Research Series no. 7 (Economic and Social Research Institute, Dublin, 1986), pp. 18–19.
7. McAleese, 'Is there a want of capital in Ireland'? p. 406.
8. See, for example, W. Beckerman, 'Britain's comparative growth record', in W. Beckerman and associates, *The British economy in 1975* (Cambridge University Press, 1975).
9. Kennedy and Dowling, *Economic growth in Ireland*, Chapter 11.
10. McAleese, 'Is there a want of capital in Ireland'?
11. F.P. Ruane and A.A. John, 'Government intervention and the cost of capital to Irish manufacturing industry', *Economic and Social Review*, vol. 16, no. 1 (October 1984).
12. Ian J. Irvine, *A study of new house prices in Ireland in the seventies*, General Research Series no. 118 (Economic and Social Research Institute, Dublin, 1984).

9

Foreign Trade

Foreign trade is particularly important for small countries: *ceteris paribus* they tend to participate in international trade to a greater extent than large countries, in order to reap the benefits of specialisation and exchange, which large countries can partly achieve by trading internally. The ratio of exports plus imports of goods and services to GNP in Ireland was about 80 per cent in the 1920s. This was a high figure in comparison with other countries at this time, and arose from the small size of the economy and the fact that Ireland had free trade for a century prior to independence. As described in earlier chapters, Ireland switched to a policy of protection in the 1930s but has gradually returned to free trade in the period since the Second World War. In this chapter we explore this experience in more detail. Section 9.1 outlines developments in merchandise trade; section 9.2 discusses invisibles and the balance of payments; and section 9.3 considers key aspects of Ireland's trade performance and its relation to economic development.

9.1 TRENDS IN MERCHANDISE TRADE

Figure 9.1 shows index numbers of the volume of merchandise exports and imports for each year from 1924 to 1985 to base 1975 = 100, in which year imports exceeded exports by 18 per cent. The data, which are plotted on a logarithmic scale, illustrate the two distinctive phases of Irish trade history since independence. First was the considerable fall in trade during the 1930s and early 1940s, from which recovery was not complete in the case of exports until 1960. Second was the rapid and

Figure 9.1: Annual index numbers of the volume of merchandise imports and exports, 1924–85 (1975 = 100) (log scale)

Source: *Statistical abstract of Ireland* (various years).

steady expansion of both exports and imports which has taken place since then.

The major events influencing the decline in trade in the first phase were the introduction of protection, the Economic War,

179

the world depression and the outbreak of the Second World War in 1939. The country's heavy dependence on imports is illustrated by the fact that they declined far less than exports during the 1930s. Moreover, while imports fell more than exports during the Second World War because supplies were not available, imports recovered to pre-war levels much more quickly. By 1960, when the volume of exports had just surpassed the 1924 level, imports were one-third higher. Over the period 1960–85 export volume has grown faster than import volume, the annual growth rates averaging 8·3 per cent and 6·6 per cent, respectively. The disparity arose in the years since the first oil crisis: from 1973 to 1985 the volume of exports almost trebled while the volume of imports rose by only 60 per cent. The fact that the rapid growth rate of export volume achieved from 1960 was maintained — indeed, slightly increased — in the very disturbed international conditions prevailing since 1973 seems very impressive. As we show later, however, its impact on the economy was greatly diluted by the fact that it was associated with a substantial outflow of profits, etc. through the multinational firms largely responsible for producing the increased exports.

It is essential to view Irish trade performance in an international context in order to identify its distinctive features. Thus, while the fall of 35 per cent in the volume of exports between 1929 and 1934 was substantial, it was not at all unique. In the UK the volume of exports fell by 38 per cent between 1929 and 1932. In the 16 Western countries covered by Maddison,[1] the average peak-to-trough fall in the period 1920–38 was 36.5 per cent, and was about 50 per cent or more in Austria, France, Germany, Italy, Switzerland and the US. During the Second World War, the volume of exports in many Western countries, including the UK, fell much more than in Ireland. The key difference in Ireland's export experience was not that the decline was greater but that the subsequent recovery after the Second World War was slower. By the early 1950s the exports of most Western countries had surpassed the highest level attained at any time prior to the Second World War, which for some countries was the 1913 level. Even in West Germany, where exports had become negligible by 1945, the previous peak was surpassed in 1956. In Ireland, however, the pre-Second World War peak was surpassed only in 1960, by which time the volume of exports of most Western countries — the

Figure 9.2: Index numbers of the terms of trade, 1924–85 (1975 = 100)

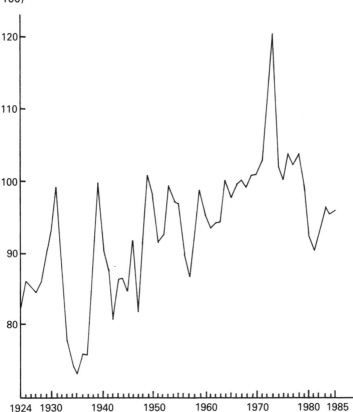

Source: *Statistical abstract of Ireland* (various years).

UK being the notable exception — was at least twice the highest level previously attained prior to the Second World War. Moreover, in the period 1960–73, while the growth of Irish exports was vastly superior to the UK, it lagged somewhat behind many other Western countries.

The economy of a small country is liable to be affected profoundly not only by the volume of its international trade but also by the prices at which it trades. The effect of any given change in the terms of trade (the ratio of the export to the import price index) is greater, the greater is the ratio of trade to GNP, and small countries tend to have high trade ratios. A

181

standard formula for measuring the real volume of the external trading gain (or loss) arising from changes in the terms of trade is $X(1/P_m - 1/P_x)$, where X is the value of exports in the end year of the period in question and P_m and P_x are the price indices of imports and exports, respectively. Thus, for example, where exports amount to 50 per cent of GNP, the percentage gain (or loss) in real GNP will amount to nearly half of the rise (or fall) in the terms of trade.

Figure 9.2 plots the terms of merchandise trade for each year from 1924 to 1985. It is immediately clear just how great were the fluctuations in the terms of trade. Four periods of substantial decline in the terms of trade stand out: 1931–5, 1939–42, 1954–7 and 1973–81. The extent of the decline experienced during these periods was 26 per cent, 19 per cent, 13 per cent and 25 per cent respectively. In all four periods the impact was severe, but it was particularly so in the period 1973–81, given that by 1981 merchandise exports amounted to 44 per cent of GNP at market prices. A major factor underlying the deterioration in this period was, of course, the enormous rise in oil prices. It is true that the terms of trade were at an inordinately favourable level in 1973 by historical standards, having risen fairly steadily by about 40 per cent since 1957. However, the gain, which owed much to favourable prices for agricultural exports and low prices for imports of primary commodities, was taken so much for granted that the adjustment to the sharp deterioration after 1973 was no less painful by reason of the preceding gain.

9.1.1 Trade patterns

The rapid growth in trade since the 1950s was accompanied by considerable changes as regards both area and commodity composition. For the first three decades after independence, the pattern of Irish trade remained firmly rooted in its historical mould. Exports consisted chiefly of food and drink supplied to the UK, which was also the dominant supplier of imports of manufactures. The departure from traditional trade locations has been greatest with regard to exports (Table 9.1). In the 1920s over 90 per cent of merchandise exports went to the UK and the proportion remained at a similar level until the mid-1950s. Since then Ireland's dependence on the British market has fallen progressively. By 1972, the year before EEC entry, the share of exports going to Britain had fallen to 61 per cent, and thereafter the share fell even more rapidly to 33 per cent in 1985.

Table 9.1: Percentage distribution of Irish merchandise trade by geographical area, selected years, 1929–85

	Exports				Imports			
	UK	Rest of EEC 10	US	Other	UK	Rest of EEC 10	US	Other
1929[a]	92	3	2	3	78	6	8	8
1938	93	5	1	2	51	10	11	28
1950	88	7	2	3	53	7	13	27
1960	75	6	8	12	50	14	8	28
1970	62	11	13	14	52	17	7	24
1980	43	32	5	20	51	20	9	20
1985	33	35	10	22	43	22	17	18

Note: [a] Up to 1935 the import data relate to country of consignment, and cannot be taken as comparable with data for subsequent years.

Sources: *Statistical abstract of Ireland* and *Trade statistics of Ireland.*

The falling dependence of Irish exports on the UK market has been accompanied by a major swing towards continental EEC countries and the rest of the world. Diversification to non-EEC markets was greatest in the 1950s and 1960s, the share of exports to such markets rising from 5 per cent in 1950 to 27 per cent in 1970. Subsequently the share rose more slowly, despite the opening up of new export markets in the Middle East and less developed countries. This was because the US share declined in the 1970s, and only partially recovered in the 1980s. By contrast, it is only since the mid-1960s that continental EEC countries have begun to feature as significant markets for Irish exports. Following Ireland's entry into the EEC in 1973 exports to these markets have grown very rapidly and by 1985 accounted for over one-third of the total.

Compared with the vast shift in the direction of Irish exports, the origin of imports has changed little since independence. Changes in the system of classification make it difficult to be precise about the proportion of merchandise imports originating in the UK in the 1920s and early 1930s. The official trade statistics put the UK share at about 80 per cent at that time, but

Table 9.2: Composition of merchandise trade, selected years, 1929–85 (%)

	1929	1938	1950ᵃ	1960	1970	1980	1985
Exports: Commodity composition							
Live animals (0-0)	42	50	38 (42)	30	14	5	3
Other food (0-1–0-9)	33	31	35 (35)	30	33	30	20
Beverages and tobacco (1)	11	10	7 (7)	5	3	2	2
Crude materials, fats and oils (2–4)	12	8	8 (16)	10	10	5	6
Manufactures (5–8)	2	1	7	19	36	54	64
Other (9)			6 (1)	6	4	4	4
	100	100	100 (100)	100	100	100	100

Imports: Main use categories

Finished producers' capital goods	5	7	8	11	17	14	13
Finished consumer goods	45	31	28	21	23	25	25
Materials for further production:							
Agriculture	11	3	3	5	4	4	5
Other	36	57	60	58	55	57	57
Unclassified	3	2	1	5	2	0	0
	100	100	100	100	100	100	100

Note: [a] For imports the figures under this heading relate to 1951.

Sources: *External trade statistics* (formerly *Trade and shipping statistics*), *Trade statistics of Ireland*, *Statistical abstract of Ireland* and *Irish statistical bulletin* (formerly *Irish trade journal and statistical bulletin*). The code numbers after the export categories relate to the SITC sections and divisions. There has been a variety of changes over the years in the coverage and classification of the figures, and the SITC classification is available only since 1950. The export figures in parentheses for 1950 relate to the previous basis of classification. The 1929 figure for imports is taken from K.A. Kennedy, *Productivity and industrial growth: the Irish experience* (Clarendon Press, Oxford, 1971), Table 1.15, p. 36.

the import data were compiled on a country-of-consignment basis up to 1935 and substantially overstate the amount originating in the UK. McAleese has suggested that imports of UK origin probably amounted to 40–50 per cent of the total in the immediate post-independence years.[2] At any rate it is certain that from the late 1930s up to 1980 the share of imports originating in the UK was constant at about half the total. However, this stability in the total UK share masked a very considerable decline in the UK share of manufactured imports from nearly 80 per cent in 1950 to 48 per cent in 1980. That decline was offset, however, by the rising share of manufactures in total merchandise imports from 52 per cent in 1950 to 68 per cent in 1980. Since then the overall UK share has declined every year to 43 per cent in 1985, mainly reflecting the fact that, while the share of manufactured imports has stabilised, the UK share of such imports has continued to decline, and was down to 37 per cent in 1985.

The other half of the merchandise imports, which was of non-UK origin, came from a large number of countries, most of them supplying only a small proportion of the total. Since the commodity composition of a small country's imports tends to be much more diversified than its exports, it is not surprising that the origin of these imports will also generally be more diversified than the destination of exports. The two main countries supplying imports, other than the UK, were the US and West Germany, whose average share of total imports in the 30-year period 1951–80 was 8 per cent and 7 per cent respectively. Between 1980 and 1985, the US share has almost doubled to 17 per cent. This increase owes much to the import of components for the rapidly growing electronics industry in Ireland, which has developed chiefly through attracting foreign firms, mostly of US origin. The gain in the US share since 1980 closely matches the decline in the UK share. Since 1950 there has been a gradual increase in the proportion of imports coming from continental EEC countries and a compensating decline in the share of non-EEC countries (apart from the US). Nevertheless, since 1973 the share of continental EEC countries in total imports has risen far less than their share of Irish exports.

The reorientation of the direction of Irish trade has been associated with major changes in its commodity composition. The historical dependence on primary product exports has given way to a situation in which manufactured exports now account for two-thirds of total merchandise exports (Table 9.2). At independence, the bulk of Irish exports consisted of live animals and food products. The only other substantial individual item was exports of beer, which accounted for 10–15 per cent of the total in the inter-war years. The composition of exports changed little until the 1950s, since when the export-orientated industrial strategy brought about a considerable expansion in manufactured exports. Although food exports continued to grow, their share of the total fell from nearly three-quarters of the total in 1950 to less than a quarter in 1985. Moreover, within food there was a major shift from exports of live animals towards exports of processed agricultural goods.

The commodity composition of imports exhibited a shift in the same direction towards a higher share of manufactures and a lower share of primary products, but the changes were less pronounced and are not shown in Table 9.2. Instead, we show the changing composition of imports in terms of their main uses. This brings out the substantial shift effected by protectionism in the 1930s from finished consumer goods towards imports for further processing in the protected industries. At the same time the protectionist measures for agriculture resulted in import substitution of agricultural raw materials and a decline in the importance of such imports. Even with the demise of protectionism since the Second World War, imports continue to be dominated by materials for further production in the new export-orientated enterprises. There has, however, been a slight upward trend since 1960 in the share of imports of finished consumer goods, while the higher investment ratio has given rise to an increase in the share of imported capital goods.

One noticeable feature of present-day trade flows is their relative stability. This point is brought out clearly in Figure 9.1, which shows that fluctuations in the volume of both exports and imports were quite marked in the period up to 1960 (even ignoring the major dip caused by the Second World War). Since then, growth has been much steadier, and short-term deviations from the trend growth path have been significantly reduced. During the 1950s, the average growth of exports was 6·3 per cent in real terms, with a standard deviation of 10·9 percentage points. By contrast, in the 1970s, when the average growth in the volume of exports was 8·5 per cent, the standard deviation was only 3·7 percentage points. The increasing stability of Irish exports reflects not only the impact of conditions in foreign

187

markets but also the changed commodity composition of those exports. In particular manufactured exports tend to be subject to less volatility than agricultural exports in terms of both supply- and demand-related influences.

9.2 INVISIBLES AND THE BALANCE OF PAYMENTS

Apart from the war years, when import supplies were severely restricted, Ireland always had a large deficit in its balance of trade. Merchandise exports generally accounted for only about one-half to three-quarters of merchandise imports. With the more rapid growth in exports than in imports since the early 1970s, however, the traditional pattern has changed and in 1985 merchandise exports exceeded merchandise imports for the first peacetime year since independence.

The traditional large deficit in merchandise trade was largely offset by a surplus on invisibles. The invisibles account falls into three distinct categories — services, transfers and factor incomes. Traditionally all three categories were in surplus, though that position has changed substantially in recent years. The major component of services was tourism. Data on tourist flows are very limited until the late 1940s, and what evidence there is suggests that tourism probably did not make a major net contribution to the balance of payments prior to the Second World War, though it would probably be going too far to suggest, as the Banking Commission did, that such traffic might represent a net deficit.[3] Tourism experienced a boom in the immediate aftermath of the Second World War due to the plentiful supply of food relative to the UK, the severe currency restrictions on travel to non-sterling areas, and the dislocation in transport and tourist facilities in Europe. In 1948 the net surplus on tourism reached a peak at 10 per cent of GNP at factor cost. The factors responsible for the boom were temporary and after 1948 tourist receipts declined over the next decade. Since Irish tourist spending abroad was increasing, the contribution to the balance of payments fell substantially.

Official measures to develop the potential of Irish tourism were begun in the early 1950s and strengthened during the decade. These measures contributed to a considerable expansion in receipts from the late 1950s to the late 1960s, which was important both for domestic economic activity and for the balance of payments. The outbreak of violence in Northern Ireland in 1969 seriously curtailed expansion, and the real value of receipts fell by one-third between 1968 and 1972. Thereafter, tourist receipts rose but since then have never recovered to the 1968 level. On the other hand, with rising incomes at home, Irish tourist expenditure abroad went on increasing rapidly so that by the early 1980s the traditional net surplus on tourism had turned into a small net deficit. Since then the depression in domestic activity and income has led to a significant real decline in Irish tourist spending abroad, so that in 1985 there was again a net surplus on tourism amounting to just under 1 per cent of GNP.

Traditionally, the largest current transfer received from abroad was emigrants' remittances. During the 1930s they amounted on average to about £3 million per annum, or about 2 per cent of GNP. Though regarded by the Banking Commission as a precarious source of income, they actually expanded after the Second World War, and in 1950 amounted to nearly 3 per cent of GNP. Thereafter they continued to increase in money values but fell as a proportion of GNP, and by 1980, the last year for which figures are given, had fallen to 0·7 per cent of GNP. Since joining the EEC, however, Ireland has benefited from substantially greater foreign transfers from the various EEC funds. As a result, the total of all net foreign transfers, which amounted to 2 per cent of GNP at factor cost in 1972, rose to a peak of 7½ per cent in 1979 and since then has remained in the region of 5–7 per cent of GNP.

The component of invisibles which has changed most radically, however, is net factor income from abroad, where in recent years a traditional surplus has been transformed into a substantial deficit. This item is dominated by the flows of investment income. In the 1930s income received on investment abroad was about two-thirds greater than outgoings, making a net average contribution to the balance of payments of £5–6 million, or about 3–4 per cent of GNP at factor cost. This reflected the fact that Ireland was then a substantial net creditor country. Up to the late 1960s, investment income from abroad kept pace with outgoings, and in 1968 there was still a net surplus equal to over 2 per cent of GNP. This in itself was somewhat surprising, since the accumulation of deficits in the current account of the balance of payments in the post-war period involved significant net foreign disinvestment. The explanation is that while Ireland's assets abroad were pre-dominantly in gilt-edged securities and yielded an annual flow of income, a substantial amount of the external capital in Ireland constituted direct investment, the income from which was not fully repatriated at that time.

The situation began to change from the late 1960s onwards, and by the mid-1970s the surplus on investment income was eliminated. Ten years later, in 1985, the deficit on this item amounted to a staggering figure of £2,000 million, equivalent to 15 per cent of GNP. Two factors in particular accounted for this dramatic change. The first was the large scale of foreign borrowing by the government, semi-state bodies and other agencies. In 1985 national debt interest payments abroad amounted to almost £800 million, while other interest payments abroad were over £600 million.

The other major factor responsible for the change in invest-ment flows was the emergence of a large outflow of what are described as 'profits, dividends, royalties'. They rose from £128 million (2½ per cent of GNP) in 1977 to £1,321 million in 1985 (10 per cent of GNP), and are mainly associated with the rapid development in the last decade of the so-called 'sunrise' industries — notably pharmaceuticals and electronics. These industries are dominated by multinational firms, export nearly all their output, and account for most of the rapid increase in Irish manufacturing exports since 1980. A recent study[4] sug-gests that almost two-fifths of the export earnings leave the country in the form of profits, etc. Although the industries involved earn large surpluses over direct costs,[5] it is however doubtful if the outflow consists in the main of pure profits. More probably, it predominantly represents payment for services undertaken by the parent firm abroad, notably research and development (R & D) and perhaps marketing. These industries are highly knowledge-intensive and in other countries also the share of value added other than direct labour costs is large, and cannot be accounted for by fixed capital intensity.

It is also possible that the phenomenon of transfer-pricing is operating — that is, the practice by which multinationals depress imported input prices and inflate export output prices in foreign branches in order to locate more profits in favourable tax locations. Given Ireland's favourable tax position, it would be to the advantage of the multinationals to allow charges for R & D, etc. to show up as profits in Ireland rather than in the price of imported inputs or as royalty charges. In that case, transfer-pricing would from Ireland's viewpoint affect only the form of the outflow, not its reality, and the repatriated profits would essentially represent an invisible import. We noted earlier that since 1973 imports have risen much less than exports and the disparity was quite marked as regards manufactures, with the volume of manufactured exports rising by 11½ per cent per annum between 1973 and 1985, but manufactured imports rising only by 5 per cent per annum. It seems likely that part of the explanation is that some of the imports for the new industries took the form of invisible rather than visible imports.

The emergence of the substantial 'profit' outflows in the 1980s gave rise to considerable unease about the behaviour of multinationals in Ireland. If the explanation of these outflows advanced here is broadly correct — and it must be said that our knowledge about them remains very inadequate — then the more extreme accusations of exploitation are not well founded. Moreover, foreign Exchequers rather than the Irish Exchequer bear the brunt of the loss of the revenue arising from transfer-pricing. Nevertheless, the existence of these outflows means that a given growth in manufactured exports in the new sunrise industries has much less impact on domestic activity than might appear from the trade and production data, and could therefore distort perceptions. It also raises questions about the depth of industrial development based on huge exports and imports (visible and invisible) with only a comparatively small domestic impact.

The combined outcome of these developments in the components of invisibles was that the overall net surplus ranging from 10 to 20 per cent of GNP up to the early 1970s was transformed into a net deficit of 5 per cent or more by the mid-1980s. Prior to the Second World War the surplus on invisibles was almost sufficient to offset the deficit on visibles, so that taking one year with another the current balance of payments was nearly in balance. During the war, there were sizeable surpluses on the current balance of payments due mainly to the curtailment of visible imports. Since 1947 the current balance of payments has been in deficit in all but two years. The average current account deficit as a percentage of GNP at factor cost was 4 per cent in the 1950s, 2 per cent in the 1960s, 6 per cent in the 1970s, and 10 per cent in the first half of the 1980s. Despite the persistent deficit on the current account of the balance of

191

payments, the general tendency was for external reserves to rise because of capital inflows (which were described in the previous chapter).

9.3 TRADE AND GROWTH

An important question arises as to how far Ireland's poor trade performance up to the 1950s inhibited its economic development, and how much the better trade performance since then has helped to accelerate development. For a small country in particular there are solid theoretical reasons why greater export growth is likely to contribute to faster economic growth. Firstly, exports tend to be an important component of demand in small countries so that their expansion stimulates increased output both directly and indirectly. Secondly, exports enable a high level of activity to be sustained by relaxing the balance of payments constraint. It is true that there were strong self-adjusting mechanisms in the Irish balance of payments arising from the links between exports and production and incomes, and between production and incomes and imports. It does not follow, however, that the balance of payments was not a constraint. The self-adjusting mechanisms worked through deflation of the economy. Moreover, they were not always sufficient for full adjustment, and when discretionary corrective measures were used, as in the 1950s and in the first half of the 1980s, they generally reinforced the deflationary effect. While capital inflows and foreign borrowing could generally be relied upon to finance reasonable current deficits, such a course eventually required an increased stream of exports to service the foreign capital. A third reason why greater export growth contributes to faster economic growth is that strong export growth induces confident business expectations favourable to investment and expansion of capacity. Fourthly, exports can also have favourable effects on efficiency and resource allocation by enabling small countries to specialise and reap economies of scale.

The following figures illustrate the growth rates of volume of Irish exports of goods and services (excluding transfers and net factor income flows) for various periods compared with the growth of GNP volume in the same periods:

	1926–38	1938–50	1950–60	1960–73	1973–85
Exports of goods and services	−1·8	2·0	3·5	7·6	7·9
GNP	1·3	1·1	1·7	4·3	1·7

The data confirm that the slow growth of GNP up to 1960 was associated with slow export growth, and that the high growth of GNP from 1960 to 1973 was associated with higher export growth. However, the poor GNP growth since 1973 in spite of an even greater growth in the volume of exports warns that the relation between exports and GNP is not a simple one. Apart from the overall volume, other factors important in determining the impact of exports on economic growth are the ratio of exports to total GNP, the import content of exports, the amount of value added retained at home, and the prices at which exports are sold.[6] Nevertheless, while a high growth of export volume may not be a sufficient condition of rapid economic growth in a small country, it is probably a necessary one. Certainly, it is hard to see how Ireland could have achieved a much greater rate of economic growth up to the 1950s, given its export performance.

The question then arises as to whether the expansion of exports attained since the 1950s could have been achieved earlier. To answer that question it is important to say what determined the strong export growth since the 1950s. In section 9.1 we showed that this growth was accompanied by considerable diversification in terms of both commodities and export markets. These two forms of diversification were interrelated and were essential to the expansion of exports. This may be seen from Table 9.3, which combines the data on exports by commodity and destination in 1929, 1950 and 1985 for two major groups of exports — food (including drink) and manufactures — which accounted for 90 per cent or more of total merchandise exports in all three years. The export data are given as a percentage of GNP at factor cost. The extreme dependence on exports of one commodity group to one market in 1929 and 1950 is indicated by the fact that over three-quarters of all exports constituted food exports to the UK. This was a doubly unpromising structure on which to base expansion: food exports were not the most buoyant elements in international trade and the UK economy was far from being the most dynamic.

Table 9.3: Irish merchandise exports as a percentage of GNP by major groups and major markets, 1929, 1950 and 1985 (%)

	Food and drink			Manufactures		
	1929	1950	1985	1929	1950	1985
UK	24	15	7	2	1	14
Rest of EEC 10	x	1	5	x	x	18
US	x	x	1	x	x	5
All other countries	x	x	5	x	x	10
Total all destinations	25	16	18	2	1	47

x = Less than 0·5 per cent of GNP

Sources: Trade figures as in Tables 9.1 and 9.2. Exports of tobacco are included with food and drink, but were not of much significance relative to the total. The GNP figures, which are at current factor cost, are taken from Kennedy, *Productivity and industrial growth*, Table 1.2, and *National income and expenditure*.

From 1929 to 1950 the composition of exports by commodity and destination changed little. What did change was the level of exports relative to GNP which fell substantially, chiefly because of the decline in food exports to the UK from 24 per cent of GNP in 1929 to 15 per cent in 1950. This decline was associated with the Economic War and protection in Ireland, agricultural protection in the UK, and the impact of the Great Depression and the Second World War. From 1950 to 1985, food exports grew slightly faster than GNP so that the ratio rose from 16 per cent to 18 per cent. While the absolute level of food exports to the UK increased by improving market access through various trade agreements, of which the most notable was the Anglo-Irish Free Trade Area Agreement of 1965, nevertheless the ratio of such exports to GNP continued to decline. The major expansion in food exports was accomplished by diversification to other markets, mainly as a consequence of EEC entry.[7] Thus, by 1985, three-fifths of food exports went to non-UK markets. Nevertheless, had Ireland's export performance continued to depend heavily on food, the overall growth would have been low. Rapid growth of exports required above all diversification into manufactures.

In 1950 most of Ireland's small amount of manufactured exports went to the UK. The growth of Irish manufactured exports to the UK outpaced the overall growth of UK manufactured imports, and by 1985 such exports had risen from 1 per cent of GNP to 14 per cent. However, it was again chiefly through diversifying markets that manufactured exports expanded so rapidly. By 1985 manufactured exports to non-UK destinations amounted to nearly half of all Irish merchandise exports, and had risen to 33 per cent of GNP as against less than 1 per cent in 1950.

The rapid expansion of manufactured exports was undoubtedly favoured by the buoyant world demand conditions that prevailed for much of the post-war period. Moreover, the free trade agreement with Britain and entry to the EEC improved Ireland's access to these markets. In addition, however, changes in supply conditions were also of major importance, in particular the industrial strategy initiated in the early 1950s favouring manufactured exports, notably through industrial grants and export tax relief. As we will show in Chapter 11, much of the expansion in manufactured exports came from new foreign plants which had been encouraged to locate in Ireland.

It should be stressed that the supply and demand conditions which secured rapid export growth in Ireland since the 1950s were unattainable in many respects in the inter-war period. As regards the demand side, export markets were not buoyant then and, following the Great Depression, the universal drift was towards protection rather than the opening of market access. Ireland might have maintained better access to the UK market, especially for agricultural exports, had it avoided the Economic War, but there was little it could have done to improve access to other markets. On the supply side, Ireland could have chosen to adopt an outward industrial strategy rather than protection. In doing so, however, not only would it have found unpromising demand conditions abroad, but it had a very weak indigenous base from which to start. Furthermore, it should be noted that the post-war industrial strategy has not as yet succeeded in building a strong indigenous export-orientated sector, despite favourable foreign demand conditions: there would have been far less chance that it could have done so in the conditions of the inter-war period. Finally, export-orientated multinational enterprises, on which so much of the post-war expansion has depended, were simply not available on anything like the same scale in the inter-war period.

It therefore seems highly improbable that an outward-looking strategy based on the kind of policies adopted from the 1950s could have achieved comparable results in the inter-war period. It is arguable, however, that such a strategy, while it might not have yielded much in the 1930s, would have left Ireland in a stronger position to take advantage of post-war conditions. As it was, the 1950s in Ireland was a transitional phase during which the protectionist policy began to be reversed and a sounder basis for export growth was established. This process inevitably took time to implement, both in overcoming opposition from the vested interests in protection and in developing new exports to new markets. During this transitional phase, Ireland's export and GNP growth compared very unfavourably with much of the rest of Europe. Had Ireland not followed the protectionist path in the 1930s, the post-war adjustment process might have been foreshortened. Against this, however, must be set the likelihood that Ireland's industrial base in 1950 would have been much smaller in the absence of protection.

9.3.1 Exchange rate, prices and competitiveness

In the preceding discussion we chiefly emphasised the structural factors affecting Ireland's foreign trade. This emphasis reflects our view that these were the dominant influences shaping Ireland's trade performance. Nevertheless, no discussion of the subject would be complete without reference to the issue of price and cost competitiveness.

Exchange rate policy is potentially a major instrument by which an economy can seek to improve its international competitiveness, and the economic literature warns of the damage of maintaining an overvalued exchange rate. In practice, it is not always clear when an exchange rate is overvalued. Besides, devaluation will improve competitiveness only if domestic costs can be prevented from rising in line with the depreciation in the exchange rate. This poses a dilemma with regard to the use of exchange rate policy: unless domestic costs can be controlled, it will not work, whereas if costs can be controlled, there is less need for devaluation. Moreover, exchange rate instability imposes considerable uncertainty and transactions costs, especially for a small economy. For these reasons, therefore, maintenance of a fixed exchange rate with sterling up to 1979 can be defended as a sensible strategy. Whether the link should have initially been fixed at parity is more open to question, however, especially given that sterling itself was overvalued following the return to the gold standard in 1925. For much of the post-Second World War period, sterling was not a strong currency, and the fixed link did not impose an undue discipline on the Irish economy, while the certainty prevailing about the exchange rate with the dominant trading partner lowered the cost of trade and capital flows. Moreover, by joining the EMS when it did, Ireland avoided the severe overvaluation that would have resulted from continuance of the sterling parity link when the latter appreciated as a result of North Sea oil.

It has, however, been argued that Ireland 'is one of the few countries which implemented a far-reaching and comprehensive removal of protection without an accompanying devaluation', and that this placed indigenous industry in an adverse competitive position after the 1950s.[8] In fact it is not quite true that the Irish exchange rate remained constant as protection was removed. While the first explicit unilateral devaluation was the 8 per cent devaluation of July 1986, the Irish trade-weighted exchange rate nevertheless fell considerably in the post-war period as a result of the weakness of sterling and the diversification of Irish trade away from the UK. According to our estimates, although Ireland followed the 1949 sterling devaluation, this still involved a fall of 6 per cent in the Irish trade-weighted exchange rate. Subsequently, the effective rate was constant up to 1967, but it had fallen by 26 per cent in 1978, the year immediately preceding the shift to the EMS link, and it fell by a further 20 per cent up to 1985. Since the process of tariff reduction really began only in the mid-1960s, there was therefore a sizeable fall in the effective *nominal* exchange rate during the removal of protection. It is true that Ireland, with a higher relative level of inflation, did not enjoy a similar fall in the effective *real* exchange rate, but that only illustrates the difficulty of securing a competitive gain through devaluation when domestic costs are not under control. It should also be stressed that the removal of protection in Ireland was preceded by the introduction of substantial industrial incentives, which represent an alternative to protection or devaluation as a means of improving the competitive position of domestic industry.[9]

As regards price trends, economic theory predicts that a small open economy maintaining a fixed exchange rate will have its inflation rate entirely determined abroad. Where the fixed exchange rate is with one dominant trading partner, as in the case of Ireland's relationship with the UK, then theory suggests that the inflation rate in the smaller country will be very similar to that of the larger. Examination of the trends in the Irish and British consumer price indices since 1922 strikingly bears out that prediction. From 1922 to 1978, the year before Ireland broke the link with sterling, Irish consumer prices rose more than ten-fold, but this increase was only 12 per cent greater than the rise in British consumer prices. After the break with sterling, Irish price trends have deviated much more from British in a few years than in the whole of the previous 60 years. From 1978 to 1985, where the Irish consumer price index rose nearly 2½ times, the increase was 25 per cent greater than in Britain. The divergence was somewhat greater than the depreciation of 18 per cent in the Irish pound relative to sterling.

While a close correspondence in the trend of Irish and British prices was to be expected, the very closeness of the trends is nevertheless a little surprising, given that Ireland was not a pure textbook 'small open economy' and that many factors (such as protection) might have been expected to create a wider divergence, at least for short periods. Yet even in the short run the correspondence was generally close. In only two periods was there much divergence. The first was during the Second World War, when in the years 1942–4 the Irish price index rose by 16 per cent more than the British — but it came back into line in the succeeding years. This divergence may have been due to differences in rationing and price control in the two countries. The second significant divergence was in the period 1963–74 when the Irish price index rose by 11 per cent relative to the British, mainly as a result of much larger increases in indirect taxation in Ireland at that time.

There were, however, other forces that might be expected to have led to greater divergence in other periods. In particular, the opponents of protection in the 1930s argued that it would lead to substantial domestic price increases. In the event a subsequent study of the protectionist experience concluded that protection raised the general Irish price level by about 10 per cent.[10] Yet the ratio of the Irish to the British consumer price index was only slightly affected: between 1931 and 1936, the relative rise in the Irish price index was only about ½ per cent.

Nor can the smallness of the divergence at this time be accounted for mainly by differential trends in food prices, which in both countries declined by slightly less than non-food prices. It must be remembered, however, that if Ireland resorted to protection at this time, so also did Britain. Estimates of the average tariff level on a common range of goods in 1937 suggest that while the Irish rate, at 79 per cent, was extremely high, the British rate of 51 per cent in the same year was also substantial.[11] Thus, tariffs must also have tended to raise the British price level significantly during the 1930s. Over the period as a whole during which the sterling link was maintained, it was probably not just the fixed exchange rate and trade relationship alone that kept Irish price trends so near to those of Britain, but also the many other close ties between the two economies — such as the free movement of labour and capital, the broad similarity in consumption patterns, social habits and institutional structures, and the strong tendency for Irish policy-makers to follow British practice.

Even if all prices were determined abroad, Ireland could still in principle improve its cost competitiveness by keeping a tight rein on incomes and other elements of domestic costs. With the reopening of the economy after the Second World War, probably no aspect of competitiveness has been the subject of more exhortation than the need for wage restraint. Several attempts at incomes policies have alternated with periods of decentralised wage bargaining. The subject is a large one and we refer the reader to the key studies.[12] Suffice it to say here that Ireland's attempts at wage control have not been spectacularly successful. Nor is this too surprising, given the strong but fractured trade union movement, the tradition of confrontation rather than co-operation in industrial relations, the sanctity attached to wage differentials, the open nature of the labour market, and the pressure to bring Irish wages up to UK levels. Moreover, in a small open economy vulnerable to many shocks from abroad, it is difficult to offer unions and their workers any tangible assurance that the fruits of wage restraint will emerge in a greater growth of exports, output, investment and employment. The difficulty is all the greater given that the empirical economic studies suggest that an improvement in competitiveness is likely to achieve results only after a considerable time lag.[13] Besides, wages, even when related to productivity, represent only one dimension of competitiveness and may in many cases be less important than other dimensions such as marketing, design, delivery, quality, and so on.

Nevertheless, as the extent of trade dependence increased and wage rates in Ireland have risen closer to, or sometimes above, those in competing countries, the significance of wage trends becomes more crucial. Thus, the acceleration in wage inflation in the late 1960s, the reluctance to accept the cut in real incomes imposed by the oil crises, and the slowness in adjusting wage expectations to those prevailing in EMS partner countries, have all damaged the prospects for expansion of output and employment. In particular, they exacerbated the competitive difficulties of labour-intensive firms in the import-competing sector at a time when protection was being removed, and when those firms had not yet adapted to the other dimensions of competitiveness.[14] The impact on exports was masked by the arrival of new foreign firms, which, because of high technology or capital intensity, were less sensitive to labour costs. The net outcome for employment, however, was undoubtedly adverse.

NOTES

1. A. Maddison, *Phases of capitalist development* (Oxford University Press, Oxford, 1982).
2. D. McAleese, 'The foreign sector' in N.J. Gibson and J.E. Spencer (eds), *Economic activity in Ireland: a study of two open economies* (Gill and Macmillan, Dublin, 1977).
3. Commission of Inquiry into Banking, Currency and Credit, *Reports* (Stationery Office, Dublin, 1938), p. 93.
4. E. O'Malley and S. Scott, 'Profit outflows from Ireland', paper read to the First Annual Conference of the Irish Economics Association, Kilkenny, 8–10 May 1987.
5. The official statistics show that in 1983 wages and salaries as a proportion of net output (i.e. sales less raw materials) amounted to only 8½ per cent in pharmaceuticals and only 12½ per cent in electronics, as compared with 43 per cent in the rest of manufacturing. A survey by the Industrial Development Authority (IDA) found that profit as a percentage of sales in 1983 was 42 per cent in pharmaceuticals and 22 per cent in electronics, as against less than 8 per cent in total manufacturing — Industrial Development Authority, *The Irish economy expenditures of the Irish manufacturing sector: a statistical profile* (IDA, Dublin, Autumn 1985).
6. For more detailed discussion, see D. McHugh, 'Trade, growth

and the role of demand: the experience of Ireland since 1947', *Journal of the Statistical and Social Inquiry Society of Ireland*, vol. xxv, part ii (1984–5).

7. It should be noted that a substantial part of the food exports to non-EEC markets in 1985 depended on the subsidies under the Common Agricultural Policy. Ireland has also gained from a stronger negotiating position as a member of the EEC in concluding bilateral trade agreements with non-EEC countries.

8. D. McAleese, 'European integration and the Irish economy', *Administration*, vol. 35, no. 2 (June 1987).

9. McAleese (ibid.) recognises this point but argues that many indigenous firms were too weak to avail themselves of the industrial incentives. This is true, but the reasons go beyond cost competitiveness, as we shall argue in Chapter 11.

10. W.J.L. Ryan, 'The nature and effects of protective policy in Ireland 1922–39' (Unpublished PhD thesis, Trinity College, Dublin, 1949). A later study of the position in the early 1960s reached a similar result: it concluded that the final price to the consumer of commodities produced in Ireland was on average about 8 per cent higher than in Britain — Edward Nevin, *The Irish price level: a comparative study*, General Research Series no. 9 (Economic and Social Research Institute, Dublin, 1962).

11. Ryan, 'Measurement of tariff levels for Ireland for 1931, 1936 and 1938', *Journal of the Statistical and Social Inquiry Society of Ireland*, vol. xviii, part ii (1948–9), Table II.

12. E. Nevin, *Wages in Ireland, 1946–62*, General Research Series no.12 (Economic and Social Research Institute, Dublin, 1963); W.E.J. McCarthy, J.F. O'Brien and V.G. Dowd, *Wage inflation and wage leadership: a study of the role of key wage bargains in the Irish system of collective bargaining*, General Research Series no. 79 (ESRI, Dublin, 1975); and J.F. O'Brien, *A study of national wage agreements in Ireland*, General Research Series no. 104 (ESRI, Dublin, 1981).

13. Committee on Costs and Competitiveness, *Report* (Stationery Office, Dublin, 1981).

14. K.A. Kennedy and B.R. Dowling, *Economic growth in Ireland: the experience since 1947* (Gill and Macmillan, Dublin, Barnes and Noble, New York, 1975), pp. 272–4 and J. Blackwell, G. Danaher and E. O'Malley, *An analysis of job losses in Irish manufacturing industry*, Report no. 67 (National Economic and Social Council, Dublin, 1983), pp. 117–19.

10

Agriculture

At independence, the agricultural sector accounted for just over half of total employment, about three-quarters of merchandise exports and almost one-third of GDP. The fate of agriculture was therefore of critical importance to the development of the economy as a whole. In this chapter we review first the progress of the sector since independence, from which it emerges that output was stagnant for an extended period. We next consider the major factors which inhibited agricultural development in Ireland, section 10.2 examining the constraints on the demand side and section 10.3 the supply side constraints. Finally, in section 10.4 we assess the effectiveness of government policy in relaxing these constraints.

10.1 GROWTH AND STRUCTURE

Figure 10.1 plots the index numbers of gross agricultural output between 1912 and 1985. The most striking feature is that over a period of nearly half a century, from the eve of the First World War to 1960, there was no sustained increase in the volume of gross output.[1] In 1958, the volume was only 2 per cent higher than in 1912, and while 1958 was admittedly a depressed year for agriculture, even after recovery the 1960 level was still only 12 per cent above that of 1912. Agricultural production was also subject to considerable short-term fluctuations, with a fall of 13 per cent between 1945 and 1947, 7 per cent between 1949 and 1952, and 8 per cent in 1958. From the late 1950s there was considerable expansion in output, averaging 2½ per cent per annum between 1960 and 1985. Moreover,

Figure 10.1: Volume index of gross agricultural output, 1912–85

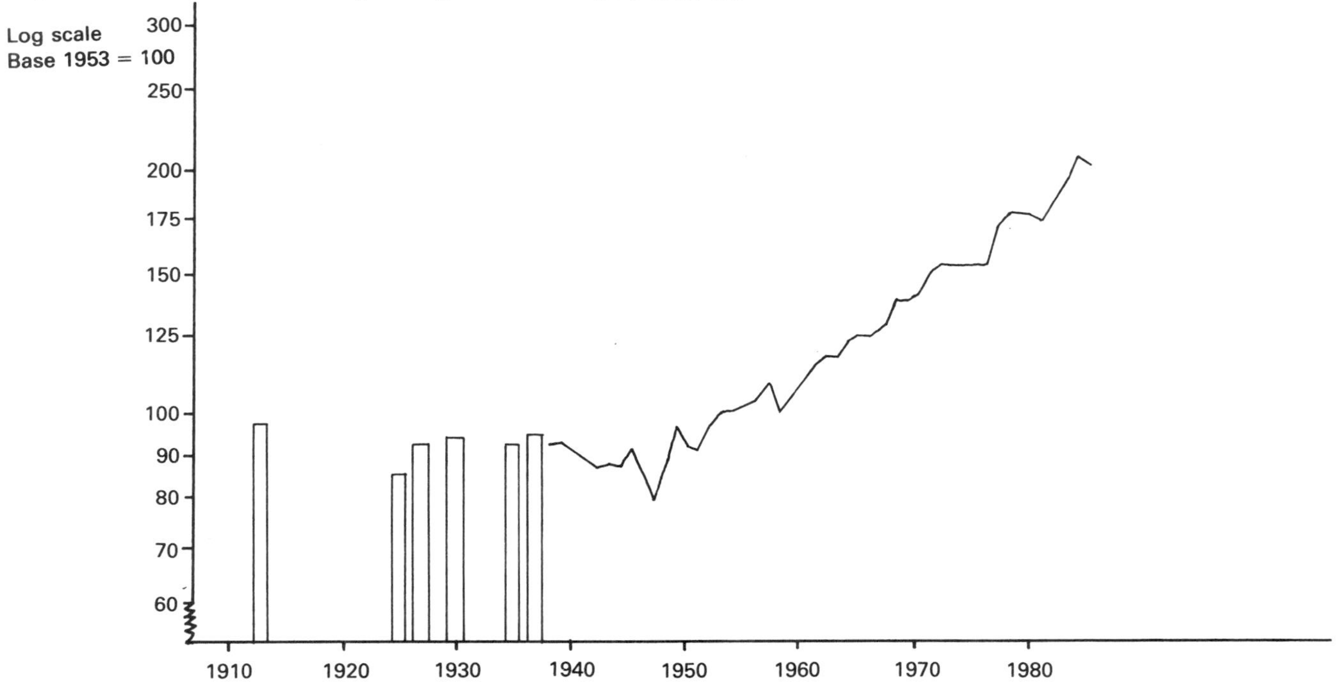

Log scale
Base 1953 = 100

while there were still short-term fluctuations, they tended to be less pronounced than previously.

The long-term trend in the volume of *net* agricultural output, which excludes inputs of feed, seed and fertiliser, was quite similar to that of gross output from 1912 to 1960. There were, however, considerable differences over shorter periods. During the Economic War in the 1930s, and more particularly during the Second World War, the volume of inputs declined so that net output rose more than gross output. After 1960, the sustained rise in volume of gross output was accompanied by an even greater rise in purchased inputs, especially fertilisers, so that the growth in volume of net output between 1960 and 1985 was significantly slower than in gross output — 1·9 per cent per annum as against 2·5 per cent.

The structure of Irish agricultural production had become progressively more pastoral in the second half of the nineteenth century. By 1912/13, livestock and livestock products dominated, accounting for nearly four-fifths of total value of output. The secular decline in the tillage share continued in the first decade of independence and by 1930, crops and turf accounted for only 16 per cent of the value of total output. The switch in agricultural policies towards encouragement of tillage in the early 1930s, and the need to produce as much foodstuffs as possible domestically during the Second World War, raised the share of crops and turf to about one-third of total output by 1944. After the war, however, the relative level of tillage output declined again and by 1985 was down to less than 12 per cent of the total. Not only was the dominance of livestock reasserted, but within this category cattle and milk increased their share, and by 1985 they accounted for nearly three-quarters of the total value of output. On the other hand, pigs, poultry and eggs, which accounted for over one-third of the total value of output in 1930 and in 1950, had declined to less than one-tenth of the total by 1985.

As discussed in Chapter 7, the numbers engaged in agriculture have fallen to about one-quarter of the level prevailing at independence, with most of the decline taking place since the Second World War. The more rapid rate of growth in output in the 1960s and 1970s did not lead to any abatement in the rate of decline of persons engaged: if anything, the decline accelerated, though the absolute reduction in numbers was less as the total diminished. The effect of the decline in employment on the structure of holdings was muted by reason of the fact that it was heavily concentrated on relatives assisting and hired labour rather than on farmers. True, a greater proportion of agricultural production became concentrated in larger farms, more specialised in dairying and beef and more capital-intensive, and this change was most pronounced in the last 25 years of faster output growth. However, the change was also accompanied by a greater polarisation of agriculture. While the number of small farms declined, many remained and became increasingly marginalised, particularly in the poorer western parts of the country. Up to the 1950s these small farms survived on a relatively stable subsistence basis, consuming a significant proportion of their own produce without sale. They worked their land more intensively than on larger farms, with a higher level of output per acre and output per person engaged. Since the mid-1950s, however, the pattern has been reversed and these two measures of productivity are now positively correlated with farm size. Growth was highly concentrated in larger farm sizes. Most of the remaining small farms are no longer viable and their survival is dependent on state social welfare policy, and on the prospect of off-farm employment. With suitable policy measures, however, this increase in part-time farming could play a positive role in agricultural adjustment.

The prosperity of farming is crucially affected by the prices of its outputs and inputs, and how these prices relate to the general price level. The trends in two relative price indices are particularly crucial to the welfare of agriculture. The first is the real output price index, which is the agricultural output price deflated by the consumer price index. The second is the input–output price index, which relates the price of materials purchased for use in agriculture to the agricultural output price. These two relative price indices are plotted in Figure 10.2 for all available years since 1914.

At independence the real output price was falling rapidly from the exceptionally favourable level attained before and during the First World War, which was a time of considerable prosperity for Irish agriculture. The decline continued almost without interruption to the all-time low point in 1935. By then the real output price was only half the 1914 level, which was never again surpassed — though it must be borne in mind that the 1914 level was exceptionally favourable by earlier historical standards. Up to 1930, the fall was similar to that in Britain, but

Figure 10.2: Relative price indices for agriculture, 1914–85

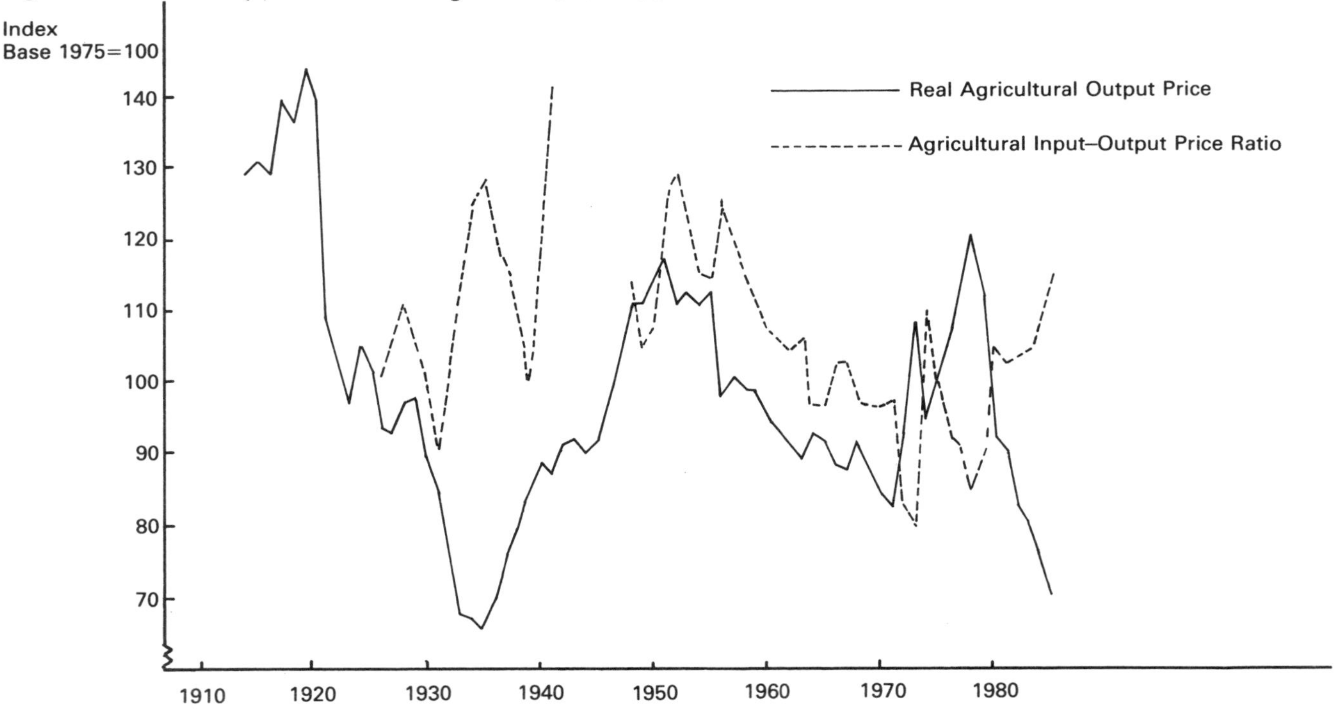

Index
Base 1975=100

the sharp drop in the first half of the 1930s was not matched by a similar decline in Britain. There was a sustained recovery in the Irish real price up to 1951, but even then the level was 10 per cent below that of 1914. During the next 20 years, the real price drifted downwards again and in 1971 was 29 per cent below the 1951 level. Most of the decline, however, was concentrated in the first half of the 1950s when the real price fell by 16 per cent between 1951 and 1956.

The sharp rise in the real output price from 1971 to 1978 more than offset the decline between 1951 and 1971, and raised the index to a new post-independence peak in 1978. A major factor was Ireland's entry into the EEC in 1973 which, over a transitional period of five years, brought Irish agricultural prices up to the levels prevailing in other member states. After 1978, however, the real price fell sharply when, as explained in Chapter 4, the three sources responsible for the rapid increase in Irish agricultural prices in the early years of EEC member-ship — general, transitional and devaluation-based — were largely ended. On the other hand, domestic consumer prices continued to rise rapidly after 1978, so that all of the earlier gains in the real agricultural output price were eliminated, and by 1985 the index had fallen back close to the all-time low point of 1935.

The agricultural input–output price ratio tended to move up-wards in the inter-war period, though the deterioration was not a smooth one, and was concentrated mainly in the period 1931–5. These were the difficult years of the Economic War, which were characterised both by falling real output prices and rising input–output prices so that there was a double squeeze on agricultural incomes. The position was reversed, however, in the second half of the 1930s and the input–output price ratio fell just at the time when the real output price began to improve.

During the war the input–output price ratio rose sharply, but from the early 1950s there was a prolonged decline, so that by 1973 the ratio was nearly 40 per cent below the 1952 level. This improvement led to a significant rise in the use of inputs, such as fertiliser, which contributed to the greater growth in output in the 1960s, despite the fact that the real output price was then trending downwards. Since 1973, the input–output price ratio has become rather less favourable and less stable. The sharp increases in 1974 and 1980 were primarily due to the two oil price shocks. The second of these increases has proved more painful since it coincided with the large decline in the real output price after 1978.

To sum up, then, since independence the trends in the two main price ratios governing agricultural production and incomes have not on the whole been very favourable. Both price ratios have been liable to considerable fluctuation, and only on rare occasions did the two move together in a favourable direction. Perhaps most significant, the real output price never recovered to the level prevailing immediately before independence, and for long periods was very depressed. This unfavourable price experience was closely related to the demand constraints facing Irish agriculture, to which we now turn.

10.2 DEMAND CONSTRAINTS

We have seen that the growth of Irish agricultural production since independence is not impressive. In considering the major factors accounting for this poor record we turn first to demand constraints in the form of limited market availability and low prices. Irish agriculture has always exported a sizeable share of its output, and in the 1920s the proportion amounted to about 50 per cent. If agriculture were to have played a leading role in domestic economic growth, then the proportion exported would probably have had to increase further, at least until the secular decline in the domestic population was reversed. In the event the proportion exported fell to one-third during the 1930s, declined further during the Second World War, and only returned to the levels of the 1920s in the 1960s. The rapid expansion in output during the early phase of EEC membership brought the proportion exported (or placed in intervention storage) up to 60 per cent. Further expansion in the 1980s has been restrained by the EEC measures to cut back on agricultural surpluses.

While supply considerations affected this export performance, demand constraints were of key importance. Agricultural markets have traditionally been highly protected, and strict controls have been placed on the volume and/or price paid for imports. With access to most markets restricted, competition on those markets which did admit imports tended to be intense, and many countries subsidised their agricultural exports in order to dispose of surplus production. In such a situation, prices tended to be pushed down. The difficulties facing Irish farmers were compounded by the fact that, given the size of the agricultural sector relative to the rest of the economy, the scope for government transfers from the rest of the community was limited. Irish farmers, therefore, had to operate for long in the face of highly unattractive profit margins and low incomes.

The problems outlined above were significantly eased by Ireland's entry into the EEC, but for much of the period since independence the only significant export outlet open to Ireland was the British market. For Ireland's two major exports, meat and butter, Britain in the mid-1950s accounted for about 80 per cent of total European imports of both commodities.[2] Imports of Irish agricultural produce by countries other than the UK tended to be sporadic and were usually confined to specific requests for a particular commodity, often to compensate for a temporary fall-off in domestic supply. Such a framework did not provide an attractive basis on which to develop an export trade with these countries. Moreover, following the establishment of the EEC, the possibility of exporting food products to continental markets was much reduced from about 1964 onwards because of the operation of the CAP, which sought to safeguard the Community market for domestic producers.

In understanding the progress of Irish agriculture prior to EEC entry in 1973, it is therefore important to consider how the British market developed and how well Ireland performed in that market. In the following discussion we focus on four main commodity groups which accounted throughout for the vast bulk of Irish agricultural exports: (a) live cattle and beef, (b) dairy produce, (c) poultry and eggs, and (d) pigs and pig meat. Using data from the UK trade statistics, it is possible to derive annual estimates of, firstly, the value of total UK imports of each of these four categories of produce and, secondly, the proportion of these imports supplied by Ireland. These data are available for most years since 1924, and we consider them up to 1972, the year prior to Ireland's entry into the EEC. Attempts to trace changes in the *volume* of British agricultural imports during these years are somewhat more problematic, because of the difficulty of finding suitable price deflators. We used two different price indices to deflate the four value series: the figures on live cattle and beef and on pigs and pig meat were deflated by the UK import price index for meat and meat

Figure 10.3: Volume of UK agricultural imports, 1924–72

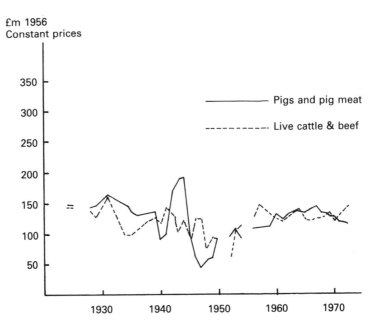

£m 1956
Constant prices

Pigs and pig meat
Live cattle & beef

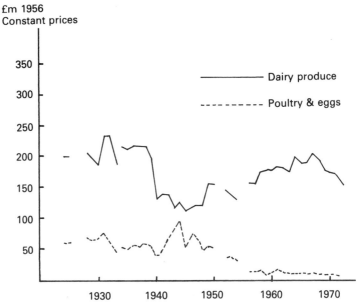

£m 1956
Constant prices

Dairy produce
Poultry & eggs

products, while the data on dairy produce and on poultry and eggs were deflated by the import price index for dairy produce and eggs. The resulting volume indices are plotted in Figure 10.3 for the period 1924–72.

The striking finding which emerges from these data is that there was no sustained growth in the volume of British imports. In the category of most importance for Irish farmers — live cattle and beef — the volume of UK imports fell sharply in the first half of the 1930s. This was partly due to a world-wide rise in protectionism following the Great Depression but was significantly exacerbated by the Economic War between Ireland and the UK, during which Irish agricultural exports to the UK were severely restricted by punitive import duties and by import quotas. These restrictions led to a major slump in Irish cattle exports and, since Ireland supplied over one-quarter of all British cattle and beef imports at this time, the result was a fall in the total quantity imported by Britain. The signing of the coal–cattle pacts in 1935–7 led to a relaxation of the controls on Irish cattle exports and the volume of British imports began to pick up again. The recovery was brought to an abrupt end, however, by the outbreak of the Second World War, and the first half of the 1940s saw a renewed decline in UK cattle and beef imports, this time due to supply scarcities. The downward trend persisted until the early 1950s, when the volume of UK imports had fallen to less than half the level of the 1920s. Cattle and beef imports recovered substantially in the mid- to late 1950s but never again rose much beyond the level of the early 1920s.

As to the other three categories, while the reduction in UK imports in the first half of the 1930s was less pronounced than for cattle and beef, nevertheless the inter-war period can best be described as one of stagnation. The war years brought a sharp fall in imports of dairy produce, but actually saw a temporary increase in imports of both pigs and pig meat and poultry and eggs. In the immediate post-war years there was a steady recovery in dairy produce imports and some further growth was recorded in the latter half of the 1950s and in the mid-1960s. Yet the volume of imports never regained the levels of the pre-war era. British imports of poultry and eggs collapsed in the 1950s, as UK supply expanded to meet domestic requirements: by the end of the decade, imports were less than one-fifth of the pre-war level and the decline continued throughout the 1960s and early 1970s, although at a slower rate. The post-war reorganisation of the British food market also affected the demand for pigs and pig meat. The rapid rise in imports during the war years was more than offset by a dramatic slump in the latter half of the 1940s, which saw British imports falling to only about one-third of their pre-war level. There was a partial recovery in the 1950s, but this growth was not sustained and imports began to fall back again in the late 1960s. The overall picture is thus one of declining export opportunities in a stagnant or contracting market.

Table 10.1: Ireland's share of total UK agricultural imports,[a] selected periods, 1924–72

Commodity group	Average percentage share					
	1924–31	1932–9	1940–9	1950–9	1960–9	1970–2
Live cattle and beef	27·0	19·7	24·4	33·1	37·3	43·0
Dairy produce	6·3	3·3	1·7	1·7	5·7	12·4
Poultry and eggs	17·3	11·3	17·1	17·4	6·9	12·4
Pigs and pig meat	10·9	6·1	1·8	4·4	6·9	8·6

Note: [a] Based on current value data.

Sources: *Annual statement of the trade of the UK with foreign countries and British possessions*, Vol. II, various years; *Annual statement of overseas trade of the UK*, Vol. II, various years.

Faced with this situation, the only way in which Irish farmers could hope to increase their export sales in the UK was by capturing a larger share of the UK market. The difficulty of this task was exacerbated, however, by the fact that other countries were attempting to adopt a similar strategy. Table 10.1 presents details of Ireland's average share of UK imports for each of the four product categories in selected periods since 1924. The most striking feature of the table is the huge fall in Ireland's market shares in the 1930s. This decline, which owed much to the effects of the Economic War, was felt across all categories of agricultural produce and resulted in a serious diminution of Ireland's role as a major supplier of the British food market. Cattle and beef exports recovered best from the effects of the Economic War and by 1939 Ireland had regained a market share of 25 per cent, having risen from a trough of only 14 per cent in 1934. From the early 1950s, there was a significant rise in Ireland's market share, which by 1970–2 was well above the level of the 1920s.

Other classes of agricultural exports, however, took much longer to regain the market shares lost during the 1930s. This was particularly true of dairy produce and pigs and pig meat. Unlike the situation in cattle and beef, where Ireland's absence had led to a reduction in total British imports, in these two markets a number of important suppliers were ready to step into the gap which had been created. These included Denmark and New Zealand in the market for dairy produce, and Denmark again in the market for pigs and pig meat. Although the outbreak of the Second World War might appear to have offered Ireland a golden opportunity to regain market share by displacing some of her main competitors in the UK market, in practice it was very difficult to avail herself of this opportunity — because of wartime shortages of imported feeding-stuffs and fertilisers. The war years thus witnessed a further deterioration in Ireland's market position, with its share of British imports of both dairy produce and pigs and pig meat falling to an average of less than 2 per cent for the period 1940–9.

Irish exports of pigs and pig meat began to recover in the early 1950s and there was subsequently a gradual improvement in market share, though never regaining the level of the 1920s. Butter exports, which constituted by far the most important component of the dairy produce trade, remained negligible until the late 1950s, but rose rapidly in the 1960s, at rates well in excess of the growth in total British butter imports. By the early 1970s, Ireland's share of the huge UK butter market had returned to levels not seen since the 1920s and the proportion of total UK dairy produce imports supplied by Ireland was higher than at any time since independence — though at the cost of substantial subsidies from the Exchequer. The Irish share of the UK market recovered most quickly from the decline in the 1930s in the case of poultry and eggs. Unfortunately, however, this was a rapidly declining market in the post-war period, and these exports were of little significance to Ireland from the 1960s onwards.

Overall, then, Irish farmers faced difficult demand conditions for much of the period from independence until EEC entry. The home market was fairly static and the only export market to which they had significant access was also static. Irish agriculture could have done better had it managed to raise its share of UK imports, which though static were still very large; but it had only limited and long-delayed success in doing so.

Throughout the 1930s and 1940s, the proportion of British agricultural imports supplied by Ireland was well *below* what it had been earlier, and not until the 1950s did Ireland's share of the crucial cattle and beef market begin to increase. In the case of dairy products, the recovery and ultimate growth in market share came even later, in the 1960s, while in the markets for poultry and eggs and pigs and pig meat, Ireland's share of British imports was low by historical standards even in the early 1970s.

The reasons why Ireland failed to improve its market share in Britain were partly due to factors affecting the efficiency of production in Irish farming, which we consider in the next section, but there were also major factors arising from the market situation. Britain combined the continuance of its traditional cheap food policy with domestic agricultural protection by subsidising its own farmers through deficiency payments and improvement grants while leaving market prices to find their own level. Given the intense competition on the relatively open British market, the prices received by Irish farmers were often unattractive.[3] While this helps to explain why Irish producers (as well as others) lost out to British producers on the UK market, it does not account for the failure of Ireland to recover its share of UK *imports* more quickly. Other exporters also faced unattractive prices, though their ability, due to climatic conditions, to grow feed grains more effectively than in Ireland gave them a cost advantage in pig production. It should also be added that when the combination of increased UK production and higher import supplies threatened a collapse in the market price of a particular commodity and an escalation of the Exchequer cost, imports were regulated by the British government. In the case of butter and bacon, quotas were allocated in relation to recent market share, which seriously limited Ireland's prospect of regaining the import share lost earlier on. Only in the case of livestock did Ireland have free access to the British market, but even here on terms less favourable than domestic producers. Moreover, since cattle and milk were partly complementary, restrictions on disposal of milk inhibited expansion of the livestock herd. Thus, in its attempts to recover and expand its market share in Britain after the Second World War, Ireland was still faced by a combination of quantitative restrictions and low prices.

The poor output-price environment contributed to keeping

down Irish farm incomes, thus restricting both the means and the incentive to invest, while the often unfavourable input–output price ratio gave farmers little incentive to move away from the traditional low input–low output system of production, which involved exceptionally low productivity of land in comparison to the generality of European countries.[4] In turn, however, the poor price environment faced by Irish farmers was partly due to inadequate attention to the marketing of Irish agricultural produce. Irish farmers were slower than their European counterparts in combining together to market their output effectively and to secure satisfactory feedback from consumers. No doubt the structure of Irish trade, with its emphasis on live animals and goods with low industrial processing, militated against this. In any event, there was for long a failure to establish a clearly defined image for Irish agricultural products, and Irish farmers acquired the reputation of being erratic suppliers of goods that were sometimes inferior in quality, poorly graded or simply inappropriate to the market in which they were offered.

Most of the initiatives to deal with the marketing problem came from the state, but were often too little and too late. It is true that in the 1920s, the state made a considerable effort to improve the reputation of Irish produce by imposing minimum quality standards. The impetus towards better marketing was not sustained, however, in the protectionist era of the 1930s. It was not until 1961 that a centralised marketing agency for dairy products, Bord Bainne, was set up by the state, and only at the end of the 1960s was a promotional agency, the Irish Livestock and Meat Board, established to encourage the more effective marketing of meat. The marketing boards for pigs and bacon established by the state in the mid-1930s and their successor, the Pigs and Bacon Commission, established in 1939, have been subjected to strong criticism for freezing the structure of the industry, preserving over-capacity, removing market disciplines, impeding new entrants and discouraging the introduction of new products.[5]

While the above problems significantly impeded Ireland's attempts to secure a larger share of the British market, probably the single most important factor behind Ireland's poor performance was the Economic War and the domestic agricultural policies of the 1930s laying greater emphasis on self-sufficiency. As we have seen, the 1930s witnessed a massive deterioration in Ireland's market position and it was several decades before the ground which was lost in these years began to be recovered. In the process of recovery, trade policy also played a considerable role. In the post-war period, various trade agreements with Britain, culminating in the Anglo-Irish Free Trade Area Agreement of 1965, progressively improved the scope and terms of access to the British market. Finally, the most dramatic improvement in the marketing environment for Irish farmers — entry to the EEC in 1973 — was also the outcome of official trade policy.

10.3 SUPPLY CONSTRAINTS

A fundamental dilemma facing Irish agriculture since independence has been that its comparative advantage in land-extensive livestock production requiring little labour was singularly unsuited to the social problem of creating employment. For reasons given in Chapter 1, climatic conditions favoured livestock over tillage and, even within livestock, they favoured land-extensive production. Market demand conditions reinforced this situation. Apart from the 1930s, when special incentives were introduced to encourage tillage, price trends have generally favoured livestock more than livestock products (mainly dairying), and the latter more than tillage. Thus, in the post-war period from 1946 to 1985, the price index for livestock rose fifteen-fold, for livestock products twelve-fold and for crops only seven-fold. Unfortunately, however, given Ireland's employment needs, the ranking of these activities in terms of their comparative advantage was inversely related to their employment intensity. In particular, livestock production required a larger size of farm unit and less labour than the other activities. Given the farm size structure at the time of independence, and the desire to maintain as many holdings as possible, Ireland for long attempted the impossible — to adopt a large-farm style of agriculture on small family holdings.

Historical and cultural factors had combined in Ireland to create an intense sense of attachment to the family holding which militated against any system of tenure other than outright ownership. The settlement of the land struggle of the nineteenth century enabled tenant farmers to purchase their holdings by payment of a land annuity. One of the early agricultural measures implemented by the new government, the Land Purchase Act of 1923, provided for the compulsory purchase of all remaining leasehold land, which was then divided into holdings. Three-quarters of all agricultural holdings in Ireland in 1931 were less than 50 acres in size. While the size-structure of holdings was not abnormal in comparison with continental Europe, the majority of Irish holdings must be considered small in relation to the type of farming practised. Over time there has been a gradual decline in the total number of holdings, the principal decline being in those under 30 acres in size. Nevertheless, the fact remains that the majority of Irish farms still fall below the minimum size of an economically viable holding (i.e. one capable of providing a satisfactory income at prevailing living standards, given the structure of production in Ireland). The reason is that the threshold of viability has itself risen over time: whereas in the 1920s the minimum viable size was about 22 acres, by the 1980s it had risen to at least 50 acres.[6] In 1980, despite the fall in the number of small holdings, two-thirds of all holdings over one acre were below 50 acres in size and accounted for more than one-quarter of total agricultural land.

The rate of adjustment in the farm size-structure of Irish agriculture was therefore slow and less than in other European countries.[7] The reasons lie mainly in the patterns of land tenure and land transfer inherited from the past. Figures for 1975 indicate that 97 per cent of Irish farmers own their land compared with an EEC average of 64 per cent.[8] Moreover, unlike the situation in Denmark, where a significant proportion of owner-occupiers are paying off large mortgages, in Ireland the vast majority of farmers own their land outright. The incidence of renting of land is very low in Ireland, with only about 7 per cent of land being let, most of it for periods of less than 1 year. Several studies have documented the low level of land mobility in Ireland,[9] where by far the most important means of acquiring a farm is by inheritance or gift. Open market purchases are used mainly for adding extra pieces of land to existing farms, rather than for the purchase of new ones.

The rigidities in land tenure and transfer rendered large parts of Irish agriculture comparatively unresponsive to change. One study,[10] for example, showed that in the period 1973–7, approximately half of all farms accounting for over 45 per cent of agricultural land had a stagnant or declining volume of production at the same time as the top 25 per cent of farms recorded dramatic increases in output. Of course, the co-existence of a progressive, dynamic, sector alongside a static or declining group is not unique to Ireland. What is unique is that the progressive sector is so small. One estimate[11] put it as low as 20 per cent of farmers, and while other estimates are more optimistic, few would put it above 50 per cent.

The land tenure and transfer system has contributed to the unfavourable demographic characteristics of many farm operators, such as age, marital status, etc. These are factors which studies have shown to have a crucial bearing on growth performance.[12] The 'ideal' profile of a farm operator would be a young, well-educated, married person with children. Such farmers have always constituted a small minority in Ireland — not surprisingly since the land-transfer system has been charac-terised by aged withdrawals and moderately aged entrants reluctant to marry until in control of the farm. In 1926 more than half of all farmers were aged 55 and over. While the proportion of older farmers has declined since the Second World War, in 1981 44 per cent of farmers were still aged 55 and over. More than two in every five farmers in 1926 were single or widowed, and that proportion has not altered much since then.

Serious deficiencies existed in the educational levels of farmers and these tended to be greater, the smaller the size of farm. The deficiencies were difficult to remedy since the low agricultural incomes were unattractive to those educated. In 1966 only about 10 per cent of farmers had received general education beyond primary level compared with a figure of 37 per cent for the working population as a whole. The educational level of new entrants has risen considerably since then, but because the rate of new entry each year is low, the overall position adapts very slowly: by 1980 three-quarters of all farmers had received only primary education. The numbers taking agricultural training courses, although considerably greater than the very low levels in the 1920s, remained small in relation to the agricultural labour force. Moreover, of those who graduated from these courses only a minority ever returned to work as farmers. The proportion of farmers attending third-level colleges or receiving special training in agriculture is still a tiny minority — 4 per cent in 1980. These low educational levels hindered the progress of good farm management and adaptation to technical change, and made it more difficult for the advisory services to effect improvements. The situation was exacerbated because the late development of the agricultural research infrastructure restricted the flow of profitable technical packages available for application by farmers.

The deficiencies in human capital were matched by deficiencies in physical capital. Compared with other EEC countries, Irish agriculture has always been much less capitalised. In the inter-war period production techniques were virtually unmechanised, and fertiliser inputs declined in the first half of the 1930s and during the Second World War. Indeed, it has been estimated that in the first 50 years of this century, the application of nutrients on Irish farms generally fell short of losses.[13] Immediately after the Second World War, there was a rapid increase in agricultural investment, particularly in the period 1949–54. The rate of mechanisation accelerated sharply, while the volume of fertiliser usage doubled. The growth of agricultural investment petered out in the second half of the 1950s, but after 1961 an upward trend was re-established, and between 1961 and 1973 the volume rose at an average annual rate of 5 per cent, and was much faster than the growth of agricultural output. The year 1973 marked the beginning of a period of great volatility in investment behaviour. Following a temporary setback in 1974–5, investment began to rise at unprecedented rates, growing by an average of 10 per cent per annum between 1976 and 1979. Since 1979, however, there has been an equally severe fall in investment, with major cutbacks in capital development on most farms.

The increase in agricultural investment during the post-war period has resulted in a sharp increase in mechanisation, with a substantial substitution of capital for labour on Irish farms. As well as the rise in fixed investment, the total cattle stock, which had remained relatively stable in the region of 4–4½ million head from 1922 to 1960, rose rapidly to a peak of 7·4 million in 1974, though it fell back again to below 7 million. Alongside these changes, there was a rapid increase in the use of modern production inputs, such as concentrate feed and fertilisers. The latter grew particularly quickly in the 1960s, when the volume of purchases rose by an average of 9 per cent per annum, and strong growth persisted until the late 1970s. Since then, there has been a severe deceleration in the rate of increase of fertiliser application, reflecting the long-established tendency of farmers to cut back on production expenses when faced with falling farm incomes.

The historically low levels of investment in Irish agriculture until the 1960s were to a certain extent a result of the unique structure of Irish agriculture, with its heavy emphasis on livestock production from grass. The structural problems already discussed also played a role, however. The constraint on investment consisted not so much in the absence of funds or unavailability of credit as in the reluctance of farmers to invest. Several aspects of the farm structure — small holdings, age profile, low education, poor management — encouraged a cautious approach to the use of credit. Indeed, the Irish farmer has been noted for financial conservatism, and in rural circles a certain social stigma was attached to being in debt. Even in the depressed 1930s farmers were substantial net creditors to the banking system, with the ratio of agricultural loans to deposits standing at around 30 per cent. In the 1950s various authorities argued that farmers often failed to use credit on projects where it would be commercially justifiable.[14]

Yet in evaluating the significance of supply constraints, it must be borne in mind that for much of the period since independence, farmers were affected by a general pessimism with regard to the availability of remunerative outlets for increased agricultural produce. They simply did not believe that it paid to invest and their pessimism was often justified. On the few occasions when this pessimism lifted — most notably during the boom years of the First World War and in the years succeeding EEC entry in 1973 — Irish farmers were not slow to borrow and invest in their enterprises. They also showed a fair amount of responsiveness in adjusting their output mix to the relative price movements of different products. Furthermore, the fact that, as shown in Table 8.4, the incremental capital/output ratio in agriculture was high whether the investment ratio was high or low, was at least in part a consequence of market restrictions on the expansion of output. Thus, while the adverse supply features undoubtedly constrained the expansion of agricultural production, the more fundamental constraint probably lay in unfavourable market conditions.

10.4 THE IMPACT OF GOVERNMENT POLICY

Public policy towards the agricultural sector has varied considerably over time. In the 1920s, the government took the view that the key to overall economic prosperity lay in the development of a healthy agricultural sector and that this, in turn, could best be achieved by concentrating on the export trade. With the change of administration in 1932 and with changed economic conditions, both parts of this thesis were effectively rejected. In the first place, priority shifted to the industrial sector, with the needs of agriculture being subordinated, where necessary, to those of industry. Secondly, it was argued that the form of agricultural development which had emerged under the policies of the past was inconsistent with Ireland's demographic structure. Instead, there was to be a new emphasis on self-sufficiency with encouragement for labour-intensive tillage farming. Attitudes towards the agricultural sector changed once again in the 1950s and the commitment to exports was reaffirmed. Since then, the emphasis has progressively shifted, though not always explicitly, from employment maintenance towards wealth creation in agriculture.

The different perspectives of agriculture's role as outlined above were reflected in the type of policies adopted by successive governments. In the 1920s, stress was placed on raising the standards of production and presentation of agricultural produce. While these measures met with some success, the extent of policy intervention in these early years was quite limited. This may be attributed partly to an ideological distrust of 'big government', partly to a shortage of resources, and perhaps partly to uncertainty about the areas in which intervention could prove effective.

The policies adopted in the 1930s differed from those of the previous decade, both in terms of their objectives and in terms of the instruments used to achieve those objectives. As described in Chapter 2, the emphasis was on the use of guaranteed prices, subsidies, import restrictions and other protective devices, with a view to restructuring the pattern of domestic production. While these measures undoubtedly helped to sustain agricultural employment at a time when there were few alternative opportunities either at home or abroad, together with the Economic War they also seriously weakened Ireland's position in the UK market. We have already noted the collapse of Ireland's traditional exports during the 1930s, and much of the post-war period was devoted to restoring access to the UK market and regaining market share. This was made more difficult by the fact that the protectionist policies of the 1930s had reduced the momentum towards increased efficiency and improved marketing. They also impaired the competitiveness of agricultural exports by increasing input prices: for example, the maintenance of guaranteed prices for domestically produced barley raised feed prices for pigs and poultry producers. No doubt problems would have arisen anyway because of the evolution of British agricultural policy, but they were certainly exacerbated by the domestic policy stance.

In the post-war period, apart from governmental efforts to improve the extent and terms of access to export markets, already discussed, state expenditure in relation to agriculture rose rapidly, with the twin objectives of supporting farm incomes and raising output and efficiency. Unfortunately, these two objectives were not always compatible and the tension between them was never satisfactorily resolved. The main support for farm incomes was through output price subsidies, particularly butter and milk. These stimulated output, but because of the market situation, the surplus output had to be exported at considerable cost to the Exchequer — until Ireland joined the EEC. In addition, because the subsidy was directly related to output, the larger farmers received the bulk of the subsidies.[15] Another important way in which farm incomes were supported was through the relief of rates on agricultural land first introduced in the 1920s. As with price subsidies, this measure was a costly one, and accounted for about a quarter of total state expenditure on agriculture during the 1950s and 1960s. Moreover, its effects were ambiguous: while it provided a boost to farm incomes, it almost certainly delayed the structural changes necessary for improved farm efficiency. By reducing the cost of holding land, it probably slowed down the rate at which land was transferred into the hands of those who might put it to better use.

Efforts to stimulate higher productivity centred on a variety of investment incentives and input price subsidies. In 1949, a land project was introduced which provided grants of up to two-thirds of the cost of field drainage, land reclamation and similar schemes. This programme was incorporated into a broader farm modernisation scheme following EEC entry in 1973. Fertiliser subsidies were introduced in the late 1950s in a bid to increase the rate of application on Irish farms. Shortly afterwards, the government began to make headage payments for certain categories of livestock with a view to increasing existing stocks. The most important of these schemes was the calved heifer subsidy scheme, introduced in 1964. The state contributed heavily to disease eradication programmes, notably for bovine tuberculosis initiated in 1954, and for brucellosis, initiated in 1969. By 1985 the bovine tuberculosis scheme had cost the state £700 million at 1985 prices, due in part to substantial waste in implementation.[16]

While some of these policies made a worthwhile contribution to the improved growth performances since the 1950s, their impact was hampered by the failure to tackle effectively the problems arising from the structure of land tenure and transfer. Indeed, state measures — such as the Land Purchase Act of 1923, the further land division initiatives of the 1930s, and the remission of rates on agricultural land — served to reinforce the existing structure. It was not until the late 1960s, when the general employment prospects had improved, that the first tentative efforts to alter the direction of land policy were made. A farm retirement scheme was introduced in 1967 in a bid to encourage earlier transfer, but the scheme met with little response, as was the case with subsequent schemes. The most serious defect of the schemes was that, for most farmers, the other state benefits open to them (for example, old age pension, farmer's dole, disadvantaged areas payments and a variety of non-cash benefits) were greater than the pension offered on retirement. Despite an avowed commitment since the 1970s to increasing the rate of land mobility and stimulating more efficient land use, and notwithstanding the strong recommendations of an interdepartmental committee on land structure reform,[17] governments have been slow to adopt effective policy instruments to realise these aims.

The failure to change the pattern of land tenure and transfer significantly impaired the chances of progress in overcoming the other supply constraints. We have already seen that the Irish land system helped to perpetuate the advanced age structure of the farming community and gave rise to a low level of management turnover. On both counts, the scope for effective educational policies was reduced — first, because of the limited capacity and motivation of existing farmers to absorb new ideas; and secondly, because of the restricted inflow of younger farmers, who might ordinarily have been expected to act as a vehicle for educational progress. These problems made it all the more essential that government educational policy be both imaginative and determined, but in fact the opposite was the case. Very little existed by way of educational policy for the agricultural sector prior to the late 1950s. A limited instruction and advice service had been in operation since the 1920s, under the auspices of the county committees of agriculture, but the impact of these schemes was severely restricted, due to shortage of funds.

A major initiative in the field of educational policy came in 1958, with the establishment of a national agricultural institute, An Foras Talúntais (AFT). The institute was set up to undertake, promote and co-ordinate agricultural research and to disseminate information about new practices and techniques. Although its work quickly confirmed the need for urgent improvements in education and training, the government seemed reluctant to grant priority to these areas. The proportion of state expenditure on agriculture devoted to education, research and advisory services remained stable, at only 5–6 per cent, throughout the 1960s, and it was not until the following decade that this figure began to rise significantly. Indeed, it was only in recent years, particularly with the establishment in 1979 of An Chomhairle Oiliúna Talmhaíochta (ACOT), the Council for Development in Agriculture, that an integrated approach was adopted in the organisation of advice, training, and educational programmes for agriculture. Towards the end of 1987, legislation was in preparation to amalgamate AFT and ACOT, but the effectiveness of the new body is likely to be severely hampered by the fact that, due to the public finance constraints, its budget for 1988 has been cut by over 40 per cent.

To sum up, then, the broad sweep of agricultural policy after independence was generally conservative in its thrust and often ambiguous in its impact. In understanding why this was so, it is important to bear in mind two key considerations. Firstly, the intense attachment to the family holding, resulting from the troubled land history, militated against radical changes in the structure of land tenure and transfer, and made any attempt to force the pace of change politically hazardous. Secondly, this political constraint was exacerbated by the fact that developing agriculture in accordance with comparative advantage clashed with the country's demographic problem, which imposed a constant pressure for the retention of jobs wherever possible. Government policy towards agriculture never quite made up its mind how to resolve this dilemma, the persistence of which owed much to the limited success in raising employment in industry, the subject of our next chapter.

NOTES

1. Indeed, the stagnation in the total volume of agricultural output extended over a hundred years, since it is doubtful if there was much growth either in the period from the Great Famine to the First World War — see note 29 of Chapter 1.

2. P. Lamartine Yates, *Food, land and manpower in western Europe* (Macmillan, London, 1960), Table 9.2, pp. 224–5.

3. For example, for a comparison of Irish and Dutch prices, see J.A. Murphy, *A comparative study of output, value-added and growth in Irish and Dutch agriculture*, National Economic and Social Council Report no. 24 (Stationery Office, Dublin, 1976).

4. Data for 1955 show that output per acre of agricultural land in Ireland was lower than in any other Western European country, and was little more than one-fifth that of the Netherlands and one-third that of Denmark — Gavin McCrone, *The economics of subsidising agriculture: a study of British policy* (Allen and Unwin, London, 1962), Table 2, p. 51 and Appendix Table A, p. 179.

5. Survey Team established by the Minister for Agriculture, *Report on the bacon and pigmeat industry* (Stationery Office, Dublin, 1963); K.A. Kennedy, 'Some aspects of the growth of labour productivity in Irish industry' (PhD thesis, Harvard University, 1968), Chapter 5.

6. A. Matthews, 'Agriculture' in J.W. O'Hagan (ed.), *The economy of Ireland: policy and performance*, 4th edn (Irish Management Institute, Dublin, 1984), p. 313, and C. Kelleher and A. O'Mahony, *Marginalisation in Irish agriculture*, Socio-Economic Research Series no. 4 (The Agricultural Institute, Dublin, 1982), p. 6.

7. M.A. Tracy, 'Agricultural policies and the adjustment problem' in I.F. Baillie and S.J. Sheehy (eds), *Irish agriculture in a changing world* (Oliver and Boyd, Edinburgh, 1971), p. 72, and National Planning Board, *Proposals for plan, 1984–87* (Stationery Office, Dublin, 1984), p. 174.

8. *Community survey on structure of agricultural holdings 1975* (Eurostat, Luxembourg, 1978), vol. ii.

9. See, for example, P. Commins and C. Kelleher, *Farm inheritance and succession* (Macra na Feirme, Dublin, 1973); S.J. Sheehy and A. Cotter, *New farm operators, 1971 to 1975*, National Economic and Social Council Report no. 27 (Stationery Office, Dublin, 1977), and P.W. Kelly, *Agricultural land-tenure and transfer*, Socio-Economic Research Series no. 1 (An Foras Talúntais, Dublin, 1982).

10. G.E. Boyle, 'Some agricultural productivity puzzles re-examined', paper delivered at the Sixth Annual Conference of the Economics and Rural Welfare Research Centre, An Foras Talúntais, Dublin, 1982.

11. National Planning Board, *Proposals for plan*, p. 173.

12. See, for example, R. Johnson and A.G. Conway, 'Factors associated with growth in farm output', paper delivered at Agricultural Economics Society of Ireland, June 1976.

13. T. Walsh, P. Ryan and J. Kilroy, 'A half-century of fertiliser and lime use in Ireland', *Journal of the Statistical and Social Inquiry Society of Ireland*, vol. xix, part v (1956–7), pp. 104–36.

14. Department of Finance, *Economic development* (Stationery Office, Dublin, 1958), Pr. 4796; and F.W. Gilmore, *A survey of agricultural credit in Ireland* (Stationery Office, Dublin, 1959) Pr. 5223.

15. R. O'Connor, 'An analysis of recent policies for beef and milk', *Journal of the Statistical and Social Inquiry Society of Ireland*, vol. xxiii, part ii (1969–70).

16. R. O'Connor, *A study of the bovine tuberculosis eradication scheme*, General Research Series no. 133 (Economic and Social Research Institute, Dublin, 1986).

17. Interdepartmental Committee on Land Structure Reform, *Final report* (Stationery Office, Dublin, 1978).

11

Manufacturing

Prior to independence, nationalist sentiment placed great hopes on industrialisation as the means of developing the Irish economy and tackling the long-standing labour surplus. In the event, the period since independence has witnessed a considerable growth in industrial output, but progress in regard to employment has been disappointing. Moreover, the poor performance of indigenous firms once free trade was fully restored in the 1970s, and the fall-off in new foreign enterprise investment from Ireland's major sources in the 1980s, which we discuss later, have raised serious doubts about the solidity of Ireland's industrial achievements.

This chapter examines the development of the largest component of industry, manufacturing, and assesses the strengths and weaknesses of what has been accomplished. Section 11.1 outlines the record of growth in total manufacturing output, employment and productivity and the structural changes within manufacturing. The impact of the different industrial development strategies that were adopted is then considered, section 11.2 being devoted to the protectionist phase and section 11.3 to the outward-looking approach. Finally, the concluding section considers the outlook for the future in the light of past developments.

11.1 GROWTH AND STRUCTURAL CHANGE

Table 11.1 gives the average annual growth rates of volume of output, employment and output per worker in Irish manufacturing over the period 1926–86 and for various sub-periods. In

227

Table 11.1: Growth rates of manufacturing output, employment, and output per head, 1926–86 (%)

	Output	Employment	Productivity
1926–1931	1·6	1·6	0·0
1931–1936	7·2	8·6	−1·3
1936–1946	1·2	1·5	−0·3
1946–1950	10·7	5·9	4·6
1950–1960	3·1	0·8	2·3
1960–1973	6·5	2·3	4·0
1973–1979	5·1	0·8	4·3
1979–1986	4·1	−2·7	7·0
1926–1986	4·5	1·9	2·6
Protectionist phase:			
1931–1960	4·2	3·1	1·1
Outward-looking phase			
1960–1986	5·5	0·6	4·9

Sources: *Census of Industrial Production* and *Industrial inquiries*. Data for 1926–53 relate to transportable goods, which included the comparatively small mining sector in addition to manufacturing. Up to 1973 the data for manufacturing were classified on the United Nations' ISIC basis, but since then the EEC NACE basis is used. Moreover, the coverage of the data has been improved. The above data were linked at 1973, for which data on both bases are available. With regard to the reliability of the pre-war figures, see note 21 to Chapter 2.

the full 60-year period the volume of production has risen over 14-fold, representing an average annual growth rate of 4½ per cent. Growth was slow in the period up to 1931, when protection was used sparingly and the world-wide Great Depression starting in 1929 had begun to have an adverse effect. Protection began in earnest in 1932 and a rapid growth of output was achieved between 1931 and 1936, at an annual rate of over 7 per cent. In the later years of the 1930s, expansion was already tapering off even before the Second World War imposed severe limits on the import of fuel and raw materials on which domestic production was heavily dependent. Growth in the decade 1936–46 averaged only a little over 1 per cent. This was followed by a short post-war boom up to 1950, as imported supplies became available again and home demand increased rapidly.

The 1950s was a decade of transition in economic policy, as it became accepted that the protectionist phase had exhausted its potential for growth. By the end of the 1950s, even though the dismantling of protection had not yet begun, the key elements of a new outward-looking strategy were in place. The strategy, however, had not yet made a major impact on production, which grew slowly in the 1950s. The 1960s and early 1970s were years of steady and significant progress, with an average annual growth rate of 6½ per cent between 1960 and 1973. Ireland attracted a growing stream of foreign direct investment aimed chiefly at export markets, and these markets were buoyant. Some indigenous firms also became export-orientated and many of the others benefited from expanding home demand. The oil crisis of 1973 and the subsequent world depression brought a check to expansion, but this depression was short-lived, and the average annual growth rate in the period 1973–9 was over 5 per cent. The depression following the second oil price shock at the end of 1979 was more severe and lasted longer, and the average growth between 1979 and 1986 was down to a little over 4 per cent per annum.

A major difference existed between the protectionist and outward-looking phases in relation to employment growth. While the choice of any particular year to divide these two phases is somewhat arbitrary, it is reasonable enough to take 1960 as a dividing point. As may be seen from Table 11·1, employment growth was over 3 per cent per annum in the protectionist phase (1931–60), as compared with only ½ per cent per annum in the outward-looking phase (1960–86). This was so despite the fact that output growth was somewhat greater in the outward-looking phase — 5.5 per cent as against 4·2 per cent per annum. The counterpart was that labour productivity grew very much faster in the outward-looking phase. Indeed, in the period when the pace of protection was most rapid, 1931–6, productivity actually fell, whereas in the most recent years of the outward-looking phase, 1979–86, productivity rose by over 7 per cent per annum. Even allowing for the fact that the growth of output and productivity may be overstated in the latter period due to transfer pricing, there is no doubt that in this period the growth of productivity was substantially higher than the growth of output since there was a decline in employment of over 2½ per cent per annum.

These developments have been accompanied, and partly caused, by considerable changes in the structure of manufacturing. Table 11.2 presents the shares of the main industrial

Table 11.2: Shares of main industrial groups in total manufacturing net output and employment, various years, 1926–84

	Net output					Employment				
	1926	1946	1960	1973	1984	1926	1946	1960	1973	1984
% shares										
1. Food	24·2	22·4	23·1	22·6	19·4	32·3	22·9	23·2	22·5	21·4
2. Drink and tobacco	42·0	21·8	13·5	9·6	6·3	15·1	8·9	6·5	4·7	4·3
3. Textiles	3·5	8·3	10·6	7·6	3·0	8·0	11·0	13·6	9·8	5·9
4. Clothing and footwear	3·4	10·7	8·6	7·2	2·8	8·3	16·3	14·2	12·0	8·3
5. Wood	4·4	4·8	3·2	3·6	1·7	7·2	6·3	4·5	4·9	4·4
6. Paper	8·4	9·0	9·9	7·5	4·9	9·5	9·0	9·5	7·7	6·9
7. Chemicals	2·4	3·8	4·7	8·6	17·2	2·9	3·2	3·6	4·5	6·0
8. Minerals	0·8	2·7	4·5	7·5	6·3	1·3	2·7	3·7	6·2	6·6
9. Metals	8·7	11·4	15·2	21·3	34·4	12·8	14·0	16·0	23·4	31·0
10. Miscellaneous	2·2	5·1	6·6	4·4	3·9	2·5	5·7	5·2	4·3	5·2
Total	100	100	100	100	100	100	100	100	100	100
Absolute values		£m (Current Prices)						000s		
Total	16·8	41·3	124·1	727·1	5,274·8	60·1	110·0	150·7	217·6	196·2

Source: *Census of Industrial Production.* The figures for 1973 and 1984 are not strictly comparable with those for earlier years because of the change to the NACE classification and the extension of coverage of the Census. These changes added £31 million to total net output and 14.4 thousand to total employment in 1973, as well as altering somewhat the composition of the industrial groups. The changes are not sufficiently great, however, to invalidate the broad comparisons drawn from the figures, except in the case of the miscellaneous group where the changes reduced the net output share in 1973 from 9.3 per cent on the old basis of classification to 4.4

branches in total manufacturing net output and employment in selected years. In 1926, the food and drink and tobacco groups dominated, accounting for almost two-thirds of total net output. Their share in employment was a good deal less, at under 50 per cent, chiefly due to the very high productivity level in brewing. Protection had the effect of raising the shares of all the other groups, and especially textiles, clothing and footwear and metals (including engineering). By 1960, these three groups had more than doubled their share in total manufacturing net output, from 15½ per cent in 1926 to 34½ per cent in 1960, even though the clothing share had begun to decline again. The food group more or less held its share, so that the bulk of the relative decline was borne by drink and tobacco, the net output share of which was down to 13½ per cent in 1960 from 42 per cent in 1926. In the outward-looking phase since 1960, the share of drink and tobacco has continued to fall, and significant declines have also taken place in the shares of textiles, clothing and footwear, wood and paper. The major gains were recorded in chemicals and in metals, which together accounted for 52 per cent of total net output in 1984, as against 20 per cent in 1960 and only 11 per cent in 1926. The rise in the employment share of chemicals was very small, however, so that even though it accounted for 17 per cent of total net output in 1984, its employment share was only 6 per cent.

One aspect that has not changed as much as might be expected is the size structure of production units (i.e. establishments). Taking small establishments as those with less than 50 persons engaged, their employment share was 33½ per cent in 1929, and while it declined up to the mid-1970s it has recovered somewhat since then, and stood at 28 per cent in 1984. There was a corresponding gain in the share of large establishments (i.e. those with 500 or more persons engaged) up to the late 1960s, but since then their share had tended to fall and stood at 18 per cent in 1984, the same as in 1929. In comparison with other countries, Ireland does not have a high share of manufacturing employment either in small or in large establishments: more so than in most countries its employment is concentrated in middle-sized establishments (from 50 to 500 workers). Moreover, the average size of its large establishments is considerably lower than in the industrialised countries, even those which like Ireland have a small domestic market. No doubt if data were available on trends over time in the size of firms or enterprises, as distinct from establishments or plants, they would probably show a greater tendency towards concentration in larger-sized enterprises. Nevertheless, the EEC Census of Industrial Enterprises for the early 1980s shows that both the share of industrial employment in large enterprises and the average size of the large enterprises are low in Ireland compared with other Community countries.

11.2 THE PROTECTIONIST STRATEGY

We have already outlined in Chapter 2 the major elements in the protectionist strategy launched in 1932, which in the space of about five years moved Irish manufacturing from a position of substantial free trade to one of the most highly protected in Western Europe. Although there was a progressive shift towards an outward-looking strategy from the early 1950s, the high level of protection was maintained well into the 1960s. For 1966, the year in which the Anglo-Irish Free Trade Area Agreement came into operation, the average effective tariff in Ireland has been estimated at 79 per cent as compared with 28 per cent in the United Kingdom and 19 per cent in the EEC Six.[1] The effective tariff, which essentially measures the degree to which value added in Ireland was protected, was much higher than the nominal tariff rates might suggest — because of the low degree of processing in Ireland and the fact that many of the raw materials were imported duty-free.

How well did the strategy succeed? As pointed out already, the aims of the strategy were modest enough. They were partly nationalistic — to keep Irish production in Irish hands — and, more pragmatically, to increase employment and reduce emigration. There was little, if any, stress on other desirable objectives of industrialisation, such as raising living standards, or building up a solid indigenous industrial base eventually capable of competing internationally. As regards the employment objective, there was considerable initial progress, but it was not sustained. By 1950, manufacturing employment covered by the Census of Industrial Production was more than double the level 20 years earlier, but there was little further advance in the 1950s until the new outward-oriented strategy began to take effect. The gain in employment started from such a low base, however, that it was quite insufficient to match the natural increase in the economically active population and the substantial outflow from agriculture that developed after the Second World War. Neither did the industrial drive give rise to sufficient extra jobs in other sectors, such as services. This was partly due to the poor progress in industrial productivity, which limited the rise in living standards of industrial workers, and in turn diminished the induced effects on other sectors that would have come from the spending of higher incomes.

Several factors account for the low overall rate of productivity growth in manufacturing during the protectionist phase. First was the impact of the decline of the brewing industry, as described in Chapter 2. Net output per head in brewing was five times the level in the rest of manufacturing, so that the decline in its share of output and employment would reduce overall productivity even if productivity were unchanged in brewing itself. In addition, however, productivity in brewing declined by over a quarter between 1929 and 1938, and only recovered to the 1929 level again in 1971. The impact of brewing on overall productivity growth was most pronounced in the period 1931–6 when total manufacturing productivity declined by 1.3 per cent per annum, whereas with brewing excluded, there was a rise of 0.6 per cent per annum.

Quite apart from the rather unique experience of brewing, there was a more general tendency for the share of industries with low productivity levels to increase. In particular, the textiles, clothing and footwear and metals industries generally had below-average productivity levels, and these were the groups that expanded most rapidly under the influence of protection. Finally, within individual industries productivity growth was retarded by the fact that the new entrants often had lower levels of productivity than the older and longer-established firms. Much of the initial increase in output under protection came from the setting up of new firms. In 1936, the net output of new establishments less than 5 years old was equivalent to two-thirds of the increase in the total value of net output from 1931 to 1936. The average net output per head in new establishments, however, was about 10 per cent below the overall average (excluding brewing). The impact of the new firms, therefore, was to increase substantially the growth of industrial output and employment, but to pull down the rise in productivity.

The low productivity in new firms was partly a consequence

of the speed and intensity with which protection was introduced, the result being a proliferation of new firms and excess capacity. Firms were forced to try to meet all orders and to produce a wide variety for a small market, so that there was little chance to specialise. Although a significant number of the new establishments were branches of foreign firms, they were set up mainly to cater for a small home market previously supplied from the parent firms abroad, and their scale of operation was therefore likely to be sub-optimal. Indeed, most new firms were making products which previously could not be produced economically at home, whereas the older firms had survived in free trade conditions. Quite a number of the new products were labour-intensive and used a higher proportion of young and unskilled workers than the older firms. In any event new firms would not have found it easy to get skilled labour, since the pool of managers and workers with previous industrial experience was relatively small.

Perhaps an even more important criterion by which the strategy might be judged is the degree to which it laid a solid basis for long-term development. Given the small domestic market in Ireland, this would have required that at least some of the new firms should have been encouraged to think in terms of export markets once a strong base had been established at home. However, this perspective did not really figure much in the thinking of the authorities nor of the firms themselves, and in practice there was no real progress during the protectionist phase in developing exports. Indeed, if anything, the reverse was true. The ratio of exports to gross output in manufacturing (excluding food, drink and tobacco) actually fell from 16 per cent in 1931 to 5 per cent in 1950 — though too much should not be made of the 1931 figure because of the very small extent of manufacturing outside of food, drink and tobacco.

The following figures show the trade ratio (defined as exports less imports as a percentage of total trade) for manufactures (excluding food, drink and tobacco) for selected years from 1931 to 1953:

	1931	1936	1946	1950	1953
Trade ratio (%)	−82	−92	−89	−86	−85

For a country with a balanced trade in manufactures the ratio would be zero, while it would be −100 per cent for a country with no exports. In 1931, Ireland was near to the latter extreme, and in fact moved further in that direction in the 1930s. Even as late as 1953, more than 20 years after the protectionist experiment was launched, the trade ratio remained slightly above the level before protection began. Neither was there much progress in developing exports of processed foodstuffs, while exports of drink fell substantially due to the fate of Guinness, as explained in Chapter 2.

In retrospect, the failure to establish an export capability is hardly surprising. The disturbed conditions of international trade in the 1930s and during the Second World War was scarcely a propitious environment. Besides, there was nothing in the policy to encourage an export orientation, and in fact policy served to work against it in a number of ways. An infant-industry approach to industrialisation that did not encourage the infants to grow up was bound to result in an infantile industrial base. The home market was far too small to enable the generality of firms to produce on an efficient scale and the growth of the home market was retarded by the poor performance of the dominant agricultural sector. The disability arising from the small home market was exacerbated by the speed and scale of protection, which led to the division of the market among an excessive number of firms. Many of the firms engaged themselves in no more than the final assembly stages of production for which a domestic market already existed. This process was encouraged by the indiscrimination of protection and in particular the varying degree of effective protection provided by the same nominal tariff. Later studies uncovered a wide dispersion of effective rates, ranging from less than 50 per cent to over 200 per cent, and firms which merely assembled or packaged final products tended to have as much or more effective protection as those engaged in all stages of the production process.[2] Protection is also estimated to have raised the general price level by about 10 per cent, thereby making exports less competitive given the maintenance of fixed parity with sterling.

The nationalistic aim of keeping production in Irish hands was only partially successful. Since much of the increased output represented the final processing of imported materials, dependence on imports did not greatly diminish. The attempt to keep out foreign enterprise was not fully successful either. Because of the indigenous paucity of the technological, marketing and managerial capabilities needed to run large-scale operations, there was a conflict between 'the twin government policies of maximum self-sufficiency and maximum native ownership'.[3] In the event, a significant number of foreign suppliers were allowed to circumvent the spirit of the Control of Manufactures Acts and establish plants to preserve their Irish sales. However, these foreign subsidiaries were no better equipped than the native enterprises to launch into export production from Ireland: indeed, some of them were explicitly precluded from competing in the overseas markets supplied by their parent firms. Likewise, many native firms produced under restrictive licences from firms abroad, which precluded exports.

The chief benefit of protection in developing an industrial base was that it led to the establishment of many firms that would not have existed without it. Indeed, in the conditions of the 1930s, it is hard to think of any other approach that would have achieved as much. Nevertheless, because the strategy lacked a longer-term vision of the evolution of Irish industry, and because of indiscriminate implementation, the nascent industrial base remained weak and vulnerable. As late as the first half of the 1960s, the detailed reports of the Committee on Industrial Organisation uncovered an extensive catalogue of weaknesses. Among those found to be common to most of the 26 industries surveyed were the small scale of units, short production runs, under-utilisation of plant, lack of specialisation, low quality of design and packaging, inadequate R & D and poor marketing skills.

11.3 THE OUTWARD-LOOKING STRATEGY

The limitations of an introverted manufacturing sector became clear to the authorities during the 1950s and the thrust of policy thereafter was progressively outward-orientated, though the measures only evolved on a piecemeal basis over a long period, as already described in Chapter 3. The new strategy had three main elements: firstly, the use of grants and tax concessions to encourage export-orientated production; secondly, the attraction of foreign manufacturing enterprise; and thirdly, the dismantling of protection in return for greater access to markets abroad. The incentive package involved a considerable and growing cost to the Exchequer: in 1982, for example, the amount of government spending (including tax reliefs) on industry has been estimated at £750 million,[4] which compares with a manufacturing value added in that year of £2,800 million.

We have already shown that the outward-looking strategy led to a higher growth of manufacturing output, especially in the period 1960–73 when demand conditions at home and abroad were buoyant. The strategy was far less successful, however, in achieving what was generally considered to be the key objective of policy — namely, employment creation. Employment in manufacturing itself in 1986 was only 15 per cent above the 1960 level, even though output had risen four-fold. The poor employment performance was mirrored by a strong acceleration in the growth of labour productivity. A number of factors accounted for this. The previous protected environment had led to low productivity levels so that there was enormous scope for increasing efficiency in production. As might be expected those activities which survived in free trade conditions had to raise their productivity substantially, while those that did not survive often had below-average productivity to begin with, so that their disappearance also pushed up the overall average.

In addition, the new foreign enterprises generally had higher levels of productivity than the existing firms, and since they accounted for a large proportion of the growth of output, this also raised average productivity substantially. Indeed, this became a dominant feature in the 1980s when the growth of output was almost entirely concentrated in a few industries — electronics, pharmaceuticals and instrument engineering — dominated by new foreign enterprises with an extremely high level and growth of labour productivity. The average net output per head in the three industries in 1980 was 2½ times the level for the rest of manufacturing, while their average productivity growth between 1980 and 1985 was over 17 per cent per annum, and in electronics alone it was a staggering 29 per cent per annum — though these figures may be exaggerated because of transfer-pricing. The exclusion of these three industries from the total as currently measured is sufficient to reduce the overall rate of growth of productivity from 1980 to 1985 by more than half, from 9 per cent to 4 per cent per annum.

Another factor accounting for the acceleration in labour productivity growth was the increase in capital intensity, though this in turn was linked to the factors already mentioned. The gross fixed capital stock in manufacturing rose in real terms by

6½ per cent per annum on average over the 20-year period 1953–73, and the rate of growth accelerated throughout the period from 4·3 per cent per annum in the quinquennium 1953–8 to 8·9 per cent per annum in the quinquennium 1968–73.[5] These rates were much faster than the growth rates of output or employment, so that capital intensity, whether measured per unit of output or per worker, rose substantially. Although data on capital stock after 1973 have not been published, the investment figures remained high in the 1970s, so that these trends probably continued at least until the early 1980s. It has been shown that the acceleration in the mean growth rate of labour productivity in manufacturing industries in the decade 1963–73 compared with the decade 1953–63 — 4·5 per cent per annum as against 2·7 per cent — could be almost entirely accounted for by the increase in capital intensity.[6] As discussed in Chapter 8, government measures have been blamed for encouraging undue capital intensity by lowering the ratio of capital to labour cost. The fact remains, however, that the effective ceiling on the total of capital grants paid by the Industrial Development Authority was not a shortage of capital, but rather the number of viable projects available — so that the latter must be regarded as the more important constraint on manufacturing employment.

While the direct increase in manufacturing employment was disappointing, the growth in manufacturing output and productivity did contribute to employment growth in other areas, such as services and building. It set up increased demand for banking, transport, communications and a variety of professional services. Although the tax incentives meant that little taxation was raised on manufacturing company profits, the increased labour incomes enlarged the tax base, thereby permitting greater employment in public services, particularly health and education. Because increased production was strongly export-orientated, and repatriation of profits by foreign enterprises did not reach large dimensions until the 1980s, the growth in manufacturing eased the balance of payments constraint and facilitated a more buoyant expansion in home demand than would otherwise be possible.

The growth in manufactured exports was maintained at a very high rate — about 18 per cent per annum in volume terms from 1950 to 1973. Admittedly the initial base was very low; but even after 1973, when the base was larger and world demand conditions less favourable, a growth rate in volume terms of over 11 per cent per annum was maintained. By 1985 manufactured exports amounted to two-thirds of total merchandise exports and to 44 per cent of GNP. While manufactured imports also grew rapidly, the trade ratio, as defined in section 11.2, shows a country moving steadily from being almost a complete net importer towards balance in trade in manufactures:

	1953	1963	1973	1980	1985
Trade ratio (%)	−85	−59	−31	−18	−1

These developments are not, however, conclusive evidence that a vibrant industrial base had been established. To consider that question further, it is helpful to look separately at the foreign and indigenous enterprises.

11.3.1 Foreign enterprise

From 1966, when tariff reductions began in earnest with the coming into operation of the Anglo-Irish Free Trade Area Agreement, most of the increase in manufacturing employment up to 1980 took place in new foreign enterprises. The only other category in which there was significant expansion was in the small-industry sector (i.e. in firms with less than 50 persons employed), while employment fell in the larger indigenous industries. In the 1980s, employment also declined in the foreign enterprise sector. The decline was at a somewhat slower rate than among indigenous industry, however, so that new foreign industry accounted for one-third of total manufacturing employment in 1985 as against only 5 per cent in 1966. The new foreign enterprises were highly export-orientated. In 1983 exports of all foreign firms amounted to 82 per cent of their total sales, compared with 34 per cent in all Irish firms, and the latter figure was much less outside the food sector.[7]

The largest share of new foreign enterprise came from the United States, but there was also a significant flow from the United Kingdom and Germany, and smaller amounts from the Netherlands, Canada, Sweden, France, Japan and other countries. Many of the multinationals which located in Ireland were relatively small and new compared with those locating in other countries. The attraction of Ireland was the availability of a generous package of grants and tax incentives in a country that had free access to the British and other EEC markets, a stable political system and a plentiful supply of labour. These attractions were marketed so well abroad by the Industrial Development Authority that its methods have been copied extensively by promotional bodies in other countries.

The significance of Ireland's locational attractions obviously varied somewhat from one activity to another, and over time. Since independence, three main phases of foreign manufacturing enterprise in Ireland can be distinguished.[8] The first consisted of those firms established under protection to cater for the home market, most of them British firms producing consumer goods. The second phase, from the late 1950s to the late 1960s, consisted largely of firms engaged in the production for export of mature, standardised and relatively labour-intensive products — such as clothing, footwear, textiles, plastics and light engineering. The third phase, that since the late 1960s, consisted of firms producing more sophisticated products, such as machinery, pharmaceuticals, instruments and electronics — again, primarily for export. Although these activities required higher skills than in the earlier phases, they usually involved only those stages of the production process which were least technologically demanding, while the more highly-skilled and innovative processes were performed abroad. All three phases led to increased output and employment for a time, but none as yet has created the basis for lasting expansion. The industries of the first phase declined substantially under free trade conditions. Those of the second phase were vulnerable to competition from low-wage economies, as wages rose in Ireland and competition intensified from the newly industrialising countries. Ireland's main competitors in attracting third-phase foreign enterprises included the advanced European countries, and these have increased their incentives often to match or even exceed those offered by Ireland.

Furthermore, a pronounced life-cycle effect has been observed in the new post-war foreign enterprises, whereby their employment tends to grow rapidly in the initial years while building up to full capacity, but then grows more slowly or declines. For that reason an ever-increasing flow of new first-time foreign enterprise was needed to maintain expansion. Not surprisingly, therefore, with the reduced pool of foreign enterprise from Ireland's major sources — especially the USA, which itself became an important recipient of foreign enterprise in the 1980s — and the intensified competition for that pool, industrial expansion tapered off in Ireland. Underlying this pattern were more deep-seated deficiencies in the contribution of foreign enterprise. The new foreign plants drew their technology from their parent firms and made little use of Irish R & D. By the same token, these plants also relied heavily on their overseas affiliates to provide the market for their products: one study found that 55 per cent of the exports of the new foreign enterprises were sold to affiliates of the same company abroad.[9] The Irish branches were often little more than production platforms which had few linkages with the rest of the economy. They did not therefore go far towards building an indigenous innovative capacity that would be more likely to endure. Finally, as discussed in Chapter 9, the emergence in the 1980s of substantial outflows of profits, etc. in the balance of payments has highlighted the relatively small domestic stimulus arising from the vast increase in the exports of the new 'sunrise' industries.

11.3.2 Indigenous industry

It was recognised that the removal of protection would cause problems for many indigenous firms, but it was hoped that with the new incentive package, supplemented by special measures to help older firms to adapt to foreign competition, many would still expand and prosper by taking advantage of access to larger markets abroad. In the event, the combined effect of free trade and the upheavals caused by the oil crises was far more devastating than most people had imagined.

After 1966, when the dismantling of protection really began, total employment in indigenous industry remained static up to 1980, and fell by one-fifth in the next five years. Allowing for the fact that there was some new indigenous industry, especially in the small industry sector, the picture for the older indigenous firms was much worse. Over the period 1973–80, when employment in indigenous industry as a whole rose by 5 per cent, it fell by 13 per cent in the firms established prior to 1973. Approximately half of the employment of such firms in 1973 was in sectors particularly exposed to foreign competition, consisting of textiles, clothing and footwear, wood, chemicals, metals and miscellaneous. Employment in the firms in these exposed sectors fell by 24½ per cent between 1973 and 1980, whereas there was no change in employment in the firms in the relatively more sheltered sectors, consisting of food, drink and tobacco, paper and printing and minerals. Furthermore, among the firms in the exposed sectors, the decline in employment was very much greater in the larger firms, with a drop of 46 per cent in this period in those with over 500 persons engaged in 1973.[10]

The volume of output in the indigenous sector as a whole expanded more rapidly after 1960 than in the 1950s, at least up to the end of the 1970s. However, the expansion was largely due to the more buoyant growth of home demand, rather than to a dramatic improvement in export performance, and the depression in home demand in the 1980s seriously affected this sector. The percentage of output exported in indigenous manufacturing did indeed rise — from 18 per cent in 1960 to about 31 per cent in 1984[11] — but the latter figure remains far below that of foreign firms and much less than would normally be expected in a small economy under free trade. Moreover, food continued to be the dominant export of indigenous manufacturing firms, and consisted largely in low value-added processing of native agricultural products: there was no real breakthrough in the development of more sophisticated products for export. Towards the end of our period, while indigenous industry still provided about 60 per cent of manufacturing employment, it produced only 30 per cent of total manufactured exports (including food) and less than 20 per cent of non-food exports.

As was only to be expected, import penetration increased: the share of competing imports in home consumption rose from 13½ per cent in 1960 to 25 per cent in 1976. The rise in import penetration applied to all industrial groups, but most of all to clothing and footwear, textiles and chemicals, in which the older indigenous firms suffered the greatest decline in employment. Activities like motor car assembly, which was entirely dependent upon protection, were wiped out. The increase in import penetration was least in minerals, drink and tobacco, food, paper and printing, and the older indigenous firms fared relatively better in these activities up to the mid-1980s. In many parts of the metals and engineering group, indigenous firms did reasonably well up to 1980 despite a considerable increase in import substitution. This was not so much due to the older firms, however, as to the establishment of many new small firms responding to buoyant domestic demand for their output in the 1970s. Thus, while total employment in indigenous metals and engineering firms in 1985 was still 10 per cent higher than in 1973, despite the collapse in home demand after 1980, employment in those which employed over 200 in 1973 had fallen by 74 per cent over the same period.

The employment performance in indigenous industry would have been even worse were it not for the small firms. The Industrial Development Authority introduced a Small Industry Programme (SIP) in 1967 to encourage the creation and expansion of a wide range of small industries, defined as those with less than 50 persons engaged. Over the ten-year period 1973–83 the share of total manufacturing employment in firms receiving SIP grants doubled from 5½ to 11 per cent, though some of this arose from drawing existing small firms into the programme. The SIP firms are heavily concentrated in the metals and engineering, and wood and furniture groups. The bulk of their output is sold at home, with three-fifths of the firms depending totally on the domestic market. While a few have shown the capacity to grow into medium- to large-size firms, they as yet constitute a tiny minority.

The poor performance of the larger indigenous firms emerges as a major factor inhibiting Irish industrialisation. Why did so few of them manage to adapt to the new environment and take advantage of the incentive package and access to foreign markets to expand their businesses? One possible explanation might lie in general competitive deficiencies in the Irish economic environment, such as inadequate infrastructure or excessive labour costs. As against this, foreign firms operating in the same environment were quite successful. The contrast in profitability was very striking: profit as a percentage of sales in native manufacturing firms in 1986 was only 2½ per cent when it was 24 per cent in foreign firms. To some extent this gap arose from the different structural composition of the two sectors, notably the predominance of indigenous firms in the low-margin food-processing activities. Furthermore, the observed profit rate in foreign firms is probably overstated because of transfer pricing. It can also be argued that because of their very different characteristics (for example, highly developed technological and marketing capabilities), the foreign firms were less sensitive to domestic labour cuts. However, this leaves unanswered the question as to why indigenous firms did not manage to develop these desirable characteristics.

Another possible explanation of the poor performance of indigenous industry is that of entrepreneurial deficiency. Such a deficiency need not be ascribed to innate personality characteristics, but could arise from the country's traditions and experience; and it might apply more to specific economic activities, like manufacturing, rather than reflecting a general lack of initiative and organisation capacity. There is certainly much in Irish history that was inimical to evoking the talents needed for successful manufacturing enterprise, and such experience may condition attitudes and skills for a long time after the factors giving rise to them have changed. In opposition to this view, it has been pointed out that the protectionist phase and the Industrial Development Authority (IDA) Small Industry Programme succeeded in bringing forward a large number of new enterprises in a very short period, simply by changing certain elements in the economic environment facing new entrants. While it is true that new-firm formation rates are high in Ireland, it should also be noted that three-quarters of the SIP firms employ only ten persons or less, only 4 per cent employ over 30 persons, and only 1 per cent grow to employ more than 50 persons. Such evidence therefore indicates only that entrepreneurial activity is forthcoming at a small scale and in a sheltered environment: it does not demonstrate that a similar competence exists for the more challenging task of developing large export-orientated enterprises.

Another hypothesis, deriving from the literature on development economics, emphasises the existence of major barriers to entry and expansion facing indigenous firms in late industrialising countries under free-trade conditions. These barriers arise from the superior competitive position of larger and longer-established foreign rivals due to economies of scale in production, technology, finance and marketing. Furthermore, external economies enjoyed by firms in big industrial concentrations — in the form of ready access to specialist supplies and services, pools of skilled labour and large adjacent markets — have been important in enabling firms to take advantage of scale economies. While part of the function of successful new entrepreneurship is to overcome such barriers, the barriers may be so great for a newly industrialising country that they cannot be overcome by the efforts of private enterprise without suitable encouragement from a stronger force, such as the state.

In fact in Ireland, as we have seen, the state did accompany the restoration of free trade with a package of incentives, but while these measures were quite successful in attracting foreign enterprise, it is arguable that they were insufficient to address the barriers facing indigenous enterprise. The capital grants and subsidies certainly went some distance towards reducing the financial constraints, while the various advisory and training services helped to raise the efficiency of production. The export profits tax relief was not, however, adequate to encourage indigenous firms to switch to exports: while it undoubtedly increased the *incentive* to export, it did not improve the *ability* to do so until exporting became a profitable activity. In particular it did not meet the problem facing indigenous firms that, even if they could eventually export profitably, the initial years of building new markets were likely to be characterised by low or even negative profits. The situation was quite different for the foreign subsidiaries, which had the backing of the parent marketing organisation and often had assured markets with their overseas affiliates. The export profits tax relief may also have acted to discourage internal linkages between manufacturing firms: where foreign firms were engaged in transfer-pricing via imported inputs to maximise the tax advantage, this would tend to discourage purchases from domestic producers.

The policy measures also failed to come to grips with the challenge of building an indigenous technological capability. Protection had left a legacy of undersized firms, involved mainly in the final assembly of products for sale on the small home market. These firms did not have the resources needed to engage in innovative R & D, and only in recent years has the IDA shifted the emphasis to R & D, with grants for product and process development rising from 1.5 per cent of total IDA grant approvals in 1978 to 7.3 per cent in 1983. Several studies[12] have documented the low levels of technical innovation in Irish manufacturing and the heavy reliance on foreign technology sources. During the 1970s real R & D expenditure in Irish manufacturing as a whole grew substantially more slowly than the volume of output, and this decline in R & D intensity was superimposed on an already low base, particularly in indigenous industry. Foreign subsidiaries were not penalised by these deficiencies since they could draw directly on the innovative capabilities of their parent firms. However, though the foreign firms were often producing high technology products, this had little spin-off effect in developing an innovative capability in Ireland, since they generally limited manufacturing in Ireland to production activities and kept their innovatory and developmental activities abroad. The Irish economy was deprived not only of the value added in such activities but, even more importantly, of the external economies resulting from the learning experience involved. Ireland continued to export expensively trained scientists, engineers and technicians, who might have been used to build an innovative capacity at home.

The argument that the industrial policy did not address the major barriers facing indigenous industry receives support from the experience of the limited number of relatively successful indigenous enterprises. These progressed mainly in those activities that still remained in some respect sheltered from foreign competition, due to such factors as transport costs (for example, cement) or access to local raw materials (for example, food processing). The remainder which succeeded in the face of foreign competition tended to be in activities in which the technological and marketing requirements were low. A number of indigenous firms have become significant multinationals in their own right; but they have done so largely by acquiring plants abroad to cater for local markets, and their impact in developing a strong Irish industrial base is much less than their global scale would suggest.

Nevertheless, while the entry-barriers hypothesis can provide a convincing explanation of the inter-industry *distribution* of Irish indigenous enterprise, it may not fully account for the inadequate overall *volume* and *performance* of such enterprise even in areas where there seemed to be considerable potential for innovation. In this regard, it is significant that 8 of the 20 largest Irish indigenous manufacturing firms are dairy co-operatives engaged in relatively low value-added food-processing. Since 1960 this industry has changed radically. Total milk supply rose from 280 million gallons in 1960 to 920 million in 1982. There was extensive rationalisation of the processing end, with the number of plants reduced from 160 in 1965 to less than 60 a decade later, and this was accompanied by a vast increase in investment in modern equipment. Despite the large growth in throughput, however, employment rose little, and has been falling since 1979, because the industry failed to upgrade significantly the product mix from the standard bulk commodities. This suggests that other factors besides entry barriers and inappropriate government incentives were at work. The high seasonality of primary production (with a peak/valley ratio of 14:1 compared with the EEC norm of 2:1) undoubtedly operated against high-value-added products with short shelf lives. The vagaries of the CAP regulations have presented other inhibiting factors, and in addition, the dairy co-operatives had little surplus funds for R & D and product innovation because of the determination of the farmers who controlled them to secure the highest possible current price for their milk. The industry is a sizeable one, however, and the difficulties mentioned are of a kind that might have been overcome by greater organisational capacity and more willingness by the parties involved to work together for the long-term interests of the industry. Similar points could be made about meat-processing, where low-value-added products also dominate. It may well be, therefore, that underlying the failure of indigenous manufacturing in Ireland to respond better to the outward-looking strategy lies a more general entrepreneurial deficiency affecting both the public and private sectors — namely, a lack of effectiveness in co-ordinating the resources and devising the instruments needed for the strategic management of large-scale manufacturing enterprises.

11.4 RETROSPECT AND PROSPECT

Independent Ireland came into existence with a tiny manufacturing sector after a century of *laissez-faire*. While the nationalist view that *laissez-faire* itself was responsible for this state of affairs may be exaggerated, it certainly did not provide a strong industrial base. Since independence two interventionist strategies have been tried: both produced quick results but in neither case were the results lasting. The protectionist phase ran out of steam because of the small size of the home market and the inability of the protected enterprises to enter export markets. The impressive initial gains during the outward-looking phase depended heavily on attracting an increasing stream of new foreign enterprises, and when this stream largely declined in the 1980s, there was insufficient impetus to sustain expansion.

Although the two strategies were fundamentally different in orientation — one being inward-looking and the other outward-looking — they nevertheless had important elements in common. Firstly, both strategies involved substantial subsidisation of manufacturing, the cost being borne under protection by consumers and in the outward-looking phase by tax payers. Secondly, neither strategy gave much attention to when this subsidisation should be reduced and eliminated once the infant industries had been given time to grow up. Thirdly, while the strategies reshaped in different ways the environment in which private enterprise operated, they both relied primarily on private enterprise to respond to the new environment rather than on the creation of public manufacturing enterprise. Some state manufacturing companies were established in activities like sugar, steel and fertilisers, but the larger commercial state-sponsored companies were in other activities, notably energy and transport, and the overwhelming bulk of manufacturing enterprises remained private. Fourthly, neither strategy was very selective, and aid was available to any activity that had a chance of being viable. Lastly, while the protectionist strategy gave relatively high employment growth and the outward-looking phase relatively high productivity growth, neither strategy raised output sufficiently from its low initial base to permit a satisfactory expansion of both employment and productivity. The only extended period in which manufacturing came close to that performance was from 1960 to 1973, and only then did its performance approach an adequate contribution to the twin national objectives of raising both employment and living standards in the economy as a whole. That performance, however, did not last following the downturn in the world economy and the elimination of protection.

From the early 1970s several critics drew attention to the shortcomings in industrial strategy,[13] and by the late 1970s it was officially acknowledged that a fundamental review of industrial policy was called for. The most publicised of the resulting series of studies, known as the Telesis Report and published in 1982, documented the limitations arising from the fragility of indigenous industry and the excessive dependence on foreign enterprise. It recommended a modified strategy giving priority to building up a limited number of large Irish companies to serve world markets. For this purpose there should be a high degree of selectivity in regard to the products and firms assisted; the means used should be more *dirigiste*, using sticks as well as carrots to develop suitable corporate entities; and the approach should be comprehensive in addressing the full range of competitive disabilities, particularly in marketing and technology, which were previously neglected. Notwithstanding the merits of the Telesis diagnosis, to which no convincing alternative has been offered, it has to be said that its prescription represents a signpost to the desired destination rather than an itinerary of how to get there. Substantial political, administrative and practical hazards face the implementation of the recommended course of action, which would also be costly and risky.[14] For these reasons, although the government has subscribed in principle to the Telesis proposals, the steps towards implementation have so far been tentative, and it is too early yet to say how far-reaching the change in industrial strategy will be.

While industrial strategy is in a state of flux at present, however, there is a wide consensus about the basic requirements. It is generally accepted that strategy must continue to be outward-looking; that it must concentrate relatively more on indigenous industry; that it must be more selective among sectors and firms; and that greater attention must be paid to management, innovation and marketing. It is also recognised that private enterprise must be supported and/or supplemented by further state initiatives which have yet to be devised and that the task will not be an easy one, particularly if the world economy lacks buoyancy. To end on a more optimistic note, however, while past attempts at industrialisation have not laid a lasting foundation for progress, they have provided much valuable experience that can be turned to good account for the future. The pool of persons with industrial skills has been considerably enlarged. There is a clearer identification of the deficiencies in past approaches. In particular, it is recognised that the task of *developing* indigenous firms is quite different from that of *attracting* foreign enterprise which is already developed, and that quite different measures are likely to be needed. Indeed, for the first time the precise barriers facing indigenous industry are beginning to be addressed systematically. While Ireland therefore has to make a fresh start in its industrial strategy, it is no longer starting from scratch.

NOTES

1. D. McAleese, *Effective tariffs and the structure of industrial protection in Ireland*, General Research Series no. 62 (Economic and Social Research Institute, Dublin, 1971), p. 45.

2. Ibid., p. 46.

3. M. Daly, 'An Irish-Ireland for business? The Control of Manufactures Acts 1932 and 1934', *Irish Historical Studies*, xxiv, no. 94 (November 1984), p. 270.

4. F. Roche, P. Dowling, M. Walsh, A. Hourihan and J. Murray, *The role of the financial system in financing the traded sectors*, Report no. 76 (National Economic and Social Council, Dublin, 1984).

5. R.N. Vaughan, *Measures of the capital stock in the Irish manufacturing sector 1945–73*, General Research Series no. 103 (Economic and Social Research Institute, Dublin, 1980).

6. K.A. Kennedy and A. Foley, 'Industrial development' in B. Dowling and J. Durkan (eds), *Irish economic policy: a review of major issues* (Economic and Social Research Institute, Dublin, 1978).

7. Industrial Development Authority, *The Irish economy expenditures of the Irish manufacturing sector: a statistical profile* (IDA, Dublin, 1985). Figures for 1986, not yet published, indicate a rise in the export ratio for Irish firms to 41½ per cent, with the ratio for foreign firms unchanged at 82 per cent.

8. E. O'Malley, 'Foreign owned industry in Ireland: performance and prospects', *Medium-term Outlook: 1986–1990* (ESRI), no. 1, February (1986).

9. D. McAleese, *A profile of grant-aided industry in Ireland*, Paper no. 5 (Industrial Development Authority, Dublin, 1977), p. 37.

10. E. O'Malley, *Unequal competition: the problem of late development and Irish industry* (forthcoming, 1988).

11. A. Foley, 'Indigenous exports: aspects of firm and sectoral performance', paper presented to the Industrial Studies Association, Dublin, 18 June 1987.

12. For a review of these studies, see K.A. Kennedy and T. Healy, *Small-scale manufacturing industry in Ireland*, General Research Series no. 125 (Economic and Social Research Institute, Dublin, 1985) pp. 38–9.

13. For a review of these studies, see E.J. O'Malley, *Industrial policy and development: a survey of literature from the early 1960s*, NESC Report no. 56 (Stationery Office, Dublin, 1980).

14. K.A. Kennedy, 'The design of a new industrial strategy' (paper read to a Symposium on Industrial Development), *Journal of the Statistical and Social Inquiry Society of Ireland*, vol. xxiv, part v (1982–3).

12

Overall Assessment

In this concluding chapter we attempt to draw together the issues discussed in the previous chapters so as to formulate an overall assessment of Irish economic development since independence. Section 12.1 briefly recapitulates the record of success and failure. We then review the factors inherited from the past or emanating from abroad, which imposed constraints on Irish economic potential during this period. Section 12.3 attempts to identify the chief internal failings during the period which in our view led to a short-fall between actual and potential progress. In the final section we consider how well placed Ireland is now to meet the future.

12.1 THE RECORD OF ECONOMIC PROGRESS

Ireland has achieved a considerable measure of economic development since independence. The volume of manufacturing production is now 14 times greater, exports have risen tenfold, and even in the slowly growing agricultural sector, output has doubled. The structure of the economy now more nearly resembles that of the developed countries, with almost three-fifths of total employment in services, while agriculture's share has fallen from over 50 per cent to just 15 per cent. Whereas agricultural exports dominated in the 1920s, manufactured exports now amount to two-thirds of the total. Such developments have helped to raise living standards, which are about three times higher on average than in the 1920s. This increase in living standards has been accompanied by a substantial improvement in the levels of health, education and housing of

251

the population. Even the secular decline in population itself was arrested in the early 1960s, and the growth since then has raised the level of population to 14 per cent above what it was at independence.

There are darker shades in the picture, however. In particular the problem of labour surplus has never really been solved. Total employment is 12 per cent less than it was in the mid-1920s, while the unemployment rate never even in the best of times went much below 5 per cent of the labour force and is now over 18 per cent. In addition, net emigration since 1922 has amounted to over 1 million persons, and though checked in the 1960s and 1970s, has resumed in the 1980s at a rate close to the natural increase in population. Despite the impressive overall progress of manufacturing production and exports, the indigenous industrial base remains perilously weak, while in agriculture the majority of farms are still below the threshold of viability. Furthermore, Irish economic development has been accompanied by an enormous increase in national debt, which now constitutes a major constraint on further development measures by government.

Indeed, it is striking that many of the areas in which progress has been made have serious negative dimensions. Exports have been raised substantially, but their domestic impact has weakened. Manufacturing production has grown rapidly since 1960 but with a substantial erosion of the indigenous base erected earlier under protection and major reservations about the long-term contribution of overseas firms. The supply potential of agriculture has been enhanced and market access has been widened, but with severe limitations on future price and quantity increases in these markets. Infrastructure has been improved but at a major cost and resultant fiscal problems. Living standards are up but partly at the expense of large population losses through emigration. Population decline has been arrested but threatens to resume again.

Overall, when set in the European context, Ireland's rate of progress emerges as mediocre. The growth of GNP over the period as a whole since the 1920s was about the same as in the UK, so that it was below that of all the continental European countries. Moreover, despite the fact that Ireland's population rose less than in most European countries, the growth of GNP *per capita* was below that of every other European country apart from the UK. At independence average income *per capita* in Ireland was about three-fifths of the UK level. This was a comparatively high level at that time, placing Ireland in the middle rank among European countries. In 1985, Ireland's position had changed little relative to the UK, but this can no longer be regarded as a favourable position given Britain's relative decline. On the contrary, it places Ireland as one of the poorer countries in Europe.

12.2 CONSTRAINTS

As pointed out in Chapter 6, a mediocre rate of progress cannot necessarily be treated as a mediocre performance without reference to the difficulties lying in the way of Irish economic development. The relatively favourable income position (by contemporary European standards) enjoyed by Ireland at independence had not been attained by vigorous economic development but much more by population decline, so that the development of the economy was less advanced than the income level might suggest. While in principle, retarded development offered great potential for catching up, there were major constraints in realising such potential. The inherited structure of land tenure was ill-adapted to rapid progress in agriculture, given the country's comparative advantage in grass-based livestock production. The only part of Ireland which had experienced an industrial revolution, the north-east, remained part of the United Kingdom, and the manufacturing base in the new state was insignificant apart from food and drink. There was therefore no strong tradition of industrial enterprise on which to build.

Ireland was very dependent on foreign trade but its exports were heavily concentrated in agricultural products supplied to the UK. This concentration was to prove doubly unfortunate, given the slow growth of the UK and the strong degree of agricultural protectionism that developed even in the UK. It is surely no accident that Ireland outpaced British growth only when it began to make some progress from the late 1950s in diversifying both the composition and the destination of exports. The scope for expanding employment and reducing emigration was limited by the unpromising structure of employment at independence: well over half the labour force was engaged in activities like agriculture and private domestic service where employment was bound to decline no matter what policies were followed.

In seeking to overcome these obstacles following independence, the Irish people were burdened by a set of preconceptions about the economy which, while potent in mobilising support for the nationalist struggle, were ill-adapted to the task of economic regeneration. The major preconceptions, which Meenan has convincingly identified, were that the economic development of Ireland had been retarded by British misgovernment, that it depended on the policies followed by the state, that self-government would quickly bring about economic recovery, and that the future of the economy would be determined by what happened in Ireland.[1] These preconceptions raised quite unrealistic expectations about the ease with which self-government could bring about economic prosperity, with inevitable disillusionment as the expectations were disappointed. While there was much truth in the view that the British connection in the past had impeded Irish economic development, this connection also had positive features which were overlooked. There was therefore insufficient awareness of the efforts that would be needed in the future to 'reconcile an imperial standard of living with a republican income'.[2] The prevailing preconceptions also fostered an insularity in perspective which hindered creative learning from experience abroad. The tendency to look solely to government to solve all economic ills was not conducive to individual and local community initiatives.

Other attitudes and institutions inherited from the past were inimical to economic dynamism. The insecurity bred by nineteenth-century Irish life carried on into the twentieth century and was evident in the intense attachment to the land, the strong preference for safe jobs in the professions and the public service, and the determined efforts to insulate such activities from changes that would disturb possession. As Meenan aptly put it: 'The Irish community has been profoundly conservative; and the forces which influence it have been preservative rather than innovatory.'[3]

Ireland's administrative system was also shaped profoundly by the events leading up to independence. The dominance of constitutional issues in the preceding decades 'precluded the development of an administrative system within the union which could tackle the central problem of Irish underdevelopment effectively'.[4] This failure was to have lasting repercussions. Irish politicians showed little interest in adapting the administration, as distinct from controlling it, and opted for a highly centralised ministerial system with strong Treasury control — what has been described as Whitehall writ small. This system can be credited with providing high standards of probity and integrity, but its suitability for promoting economic development has been the subject of trenchant criticism.[5] As one writer put it, 'The irony is that the failure of the old system led to the adoption of a new one no more suitable to the country's needs.'[6]

Moreover, the nature of the settlement of the national struggle was not such as to allow economic considerations to take pride of place in either part of partitioned Ireland. In the north there has been a continuous challenge of varying intensity from a substantial minority to the very legitimacy of its constitutional position. In the south the settlement was followed by a civil war. Although the violence was soon ended, the civil war created deep and lasting divisions which for long bedevilled attempts to achieve a unity of purpose in many aspects of life, including economic development. As a result, the prime preoccupation of the government during the first decade of independence was with establishing the legitimacy of the new state. The actions of the new government elected in 1932 were dominated during the 1930s by issues of sovereignty. During the Second World War, the security of the state and economic survival necessarily took precedence. Thus, it was not until 25 years after the achievement of independence that economic development could receive the degree of attention that might otherwise have been expected from the start. Later, since the end of the 1960s, the intensification of the Northern Ireland conflict has absorbed a significant amount of the attention of government as well as involving substantial security and other costs.

Had the international economic environment been more favourable in the inter-war period, perhaps more might have been done to tackle the domestic constraints and structural problems inhibiting economic development — but the international environment was not propitious for that task. In agriculture, the very sharp decline in prices after the First World War persisted during the 1920s and was followed in the 1930s by market restrictions arising from the introduction of agricultural protectionism in the UK. While the latter problem was exacerbated for Ireland by the Economic War, the prosperity of agriculture would in any event have suffered. As regards industry, the Great Depression and the universal resort to industrial protection would have made it difficult for Ireland to build an export-orientated base at that time — even if it had tried to do so. Certainly such an objective could not have been accomplished simply with the type of policies that were used for the purpose from the 1950s onwards, since the success of the latter depended heavily on attracting mobile international export industries — an option that was not widely available in the inter-war period.

As a result Ireland remained structurally unready to take early advantage of the great expansion in Europe after the Second World War. At the end of the war, it still had little experience of exporting to countries other than the UK, its exports remained predominantly agricultural and it had little or no industrial export base. Agriculture did not play a leading role in European economic development after the Second World War, and few other countries had as big a share of total activity located in agriculture. Inevitably, it took time to change Ireland's economic structure and to make improvements in other areas, such as infrastructure, to support the change. Consequently, it was not until the 1960s that Ireland could be lifted on the rising tide of European prosperity.

In adverting to these inhibitions on Irish economic potential — resulting either from the legacy of the past or from external forces beyond Irish control — we in no way wish to deny that other countries also have suffered from similar, or other constraints. Nor, given the often unquantifiable nature of such constraints, is it easy to determine whether they were greater or less in Ireland than in countries that have achieved a better growth record. Nevertheless, in arriving at any judgement about Irish economic performance, it must be recognised that they imposed considerable limitations on Ireland's potential for economic expansion.

12.3 PERFORMANCE

Having recognised the constraints mentioned above it must also be acknowledged that Ireland began its independence with some important advantages. It had no national debt and substantial external capital reserves; population density was low and the level of literacy among the population was high; there was an extensive rail network; the banking system was well developed; and the communications network was satisfactory by contemporary standards. Moreover, it is part and parcel of the challenge of successful economic development in all countries to adapt the legacy of the past and to cope with new external vicissitudes. So much is this so that the effort to overcome constraints often creates new opportunities that might otherwise be overlooked, and in this way what appear first as weaknesses are transformed into strengths by human ingenuity.

Viewed in this perspective there can be little doubt that Ireland's response since independence to its internal and external environment has been far from effective. In previous chapters we have reviewed specific aspects of Irish economic performance, and it has to be conceded that this performance often fell well short of potential — even making due allowance for the constraints. We do not intend to go over the same ground again in any detail: instead, we try to identify some central features that seem to underlie the major shortcomings in different areas.

Before doing so, we should note that several of the explanations put forward at different times for Ireland's poor performance do not stand up when considered in relation to the period as a whole. At present it is widely believed that the country is crippled by high taxation, particularly income taxation, but Ireland's relatively high tax regime is of recent origin. In the 1920s it was a political imperative to reduce taxation because, as Meenan put it, 'it had long been an article of faith that Ireland had been overtaxed under British rule'.[7] The government duly lowered the standard rate of income taxation from 25 per cent to 15 per cent, and while tax rates were raised again in the 1930s and subsequently, Ireland could not be characterised as a highly taxed nation until at least the 1970s. Indeed, until then farm incomes were entirely exempt from income taxation but this alone did not succeed in galvanising that sector.

A related complaint is that government intervention has been excessive, emasculating and crowding out private activity. In fact, however, successive Irish governments have been strongly predisposed to leave economic development to private initiative.

257

Their interventions, though eventually reaching massive proportions, were influenced by the perception — largely justified in our view — that otherwise the rate of development would be even slower. Moreover, many of the interventions — in the form of tariffs, subsidies, grants and tax concessions — were designed to stimulate private activity rather than direct state involvement in production, which in most cases took place only where private initiatives had either failed or were not forthcoming. A constant complaint has been that excessive wage increases have reduced competitiveness. While it is true that greater wage restraint would have helped, it must also be borne in mind that for most of the period since independence, wage levels in Ireland were lower than in most West European countries. To the extent, then, that Ireland was uncompetitive in terms of wage costs, this was due more to low productivity than to high wages, and the former raises much larger questions about Ireland's continued underdevelopment. Neither can the distribution of income — either because it was too wide or too narrow — be considered a significant explanatory factor, since as pointed out in Chapter 6, it was quite normal in Ireland by European standards.

It would be tedious to continue listing factors that are *not* plausible candidates in explaining Ireland's poor performance throughout the period since independence. Instead, we wish to argue that the underlying reasons can be grouped under the three main headings which are discussed below — namely, the failure to grasp the implications of the small size of the country, the lack of any long-term perspective, and inadequate attention to human resources.

12.3.1 The implications of smallness

The general failure to grasp the limitations as well as the opportunities arising from Ireland's position as a very small economy, heavily subject to international influences, showed up in many areas of policy at different times. Successful industrial expansion in a small economy calls for a high degree of specialisation and selectivity. Because of the importance of economies of scale in production, marketing and technology and of external economies arising from the concurrent development of interrelated activities, a small country cannot afford to disperse its limited entrepreneurial and managerial talent over a wide range of activities. Admittedly, there are great risks involved in putting all the eggs in a few baskets, especially if there is insufficient adaptation and restructuring over time — as Northern Ireland's experience shows. Yet these are risks that a small country must take: otherwise, its industrial structure will always be weak and vulnerable. Both of the two major industrial strategies followed since independence, the protectionist and the outward-looking, failed to grasp this imperative.

The neglect of marketing considerations in Ireland is difficult to account for, given that like all small countries, it has always been heavily dependent on trade. We suggested earlier that it might have arisen from the fact that the traditional exports were dominated by live animals and goods with little industrial processing. Whatever the reason, the fact was as evident in the private sector as in government policy. It was not just a case that, as discussed in earlier chapters, the quality of marketing by indigenous firms was poor, or that the state spent little on grants for marketing compared with the amounts devoted to investment. The deeper problem lay in the widely prevailing attitude that development began with production for which markets should then be sought, whereas success is more likely to be attained by starting from a view of what markets exist, or can be created, and determining production accordingly. There has been some progress in remedying this defect, but at a slower pace and later stage than might have been expected.

Small size and openness impose severe limitations on a country's ability to pursue an independent fiscal policy and, in particular, any attempt to boost demand through fiscal expansion at a time when other countries are contracting is bound to be frustrated. Yet such a course was persisted with in the late 1970s and early 1980s, resulting in severe public finance and balance of payments problems, the correction of which is proving to be extremely painful. Ironically, in the 1950s when an expansionary fiscal policy would have been less hazardous — both because the economy was less open and fiscal policy was expansionary abroad — Ireland adopted a contractionary stance.

A small country must be prepared to learn extensively from experience abroad. Only by doing so can it steer a sensible course between the stagnation of complete isolationism and the dangers of cultural subjugation to a dominant foreign model.

While ideally it should weigh the relevance of a variety of such experience, it should above all be concerned with learning from other, more successful, small countries. Ireland did indeed import many ideas, policies and institutions from abroad but it relied almost exclusively on the UK as the model. Apart from the fact that the British model has not been a particularly successful one during the period under consideration, the disparity in its size, economic structure and level of development were unlikely to make it always the most relevant model. The exclusive concentration on Britain was not confined to public policy. Most private economic institutions — such as the banks and the Stock Exchange — took their cue from Britain, while the trade union movement maintained close links, including the continued operation of British unions in Ireland.

In the early years of independence it was only to be expected that a measure of insularity would prevail, given the preconceptions under which the new state began and its peripheral location. Nor is it surprising in the light of proximity, history and common language that it continued to look much to Britain. What is surprising, and undoubtedly damaging, is that it has taken an inordinately long time for Irish awareness of European experience to develop, and that even yet there are few enough systematic attempts to draw on that experience.

12.3.2 Lack of long-term perspective

The major economic problems facing Ireland have generally been such that they could not be solved in a short-term setting. Yet probably more so than in most countries, short-term considerations dominated, and even where longer-term strategies were put in place there was little attempt to form a perspective on their ultimate outcome. Thus, for example, neither of the two strategies of industrial development looked forward to the time when the infant industries were expected to mature, or how that process might be accomplished. Indeed it is only recently that the barriers facing indigenous industry have begun to be investigated systematically with a view to devising appropriate instruments to overcome them. With regard to both state-sponsored and private business, there has been a pronounced tendency to keep lame ducks alive even when there was no possibility of making them economically viable.

In agriculture, there was an unresolved tension between maximising output and the desire to keep as many as possible on the land. This tension might have been resolved more fruitfully had there been a longer-term view of the role of agriculture in relation to the rest of the economy. Thus, for example, a high productivity, low employment, agricultural sector could be made socially acceptable by imposing adequate taxation on agriculture to provide resources for the development of the rest of the economy. The failure to take a long-term view in agriculture was not confined to public policy. The prospect of developing a large food-processing industry was hampered by, among other things, the unwillingness of farmers who controlled the processing co-operatives to forego any short-term advantage on the price of their products, with the result that the co-operatives were starved of development funds.

The same failing has been in evidence in regard to relations with the EEC. Tremendous efforts have gone into lobbying for short-term benefits, often in areas like the Common Agricultural Policy where the gains were unlikely to be held in the long term. On the other hand, little thought and planning have been shown in shaping longer-term arrangements for less favoured areas of the community.[8] It is true that Ireland as a small country has only a small voice; but by building alliances with the other peripheral low-income countries — Spain, Portugal and Greece — it would stand a better chance of influencing the Community to face up to the kind of long-term mechanisms of support needed to reduce income disparities, which are a necessary part of sustaining closer economic union.[9] Instead, however, these countries have been regarded by Ireland, not as potential allies in enlarging the pool of resources for peripheral areas, but as competitors for the existing pool.

It would be easy to multiply examples of the *ad hoc* nature of policies in different areas bearing on economic development. Even where longer-term strategies were put in place on particular aspects of a problem there was a general failure to link together the different aspects. In regional policy, for instance, there was little co-ordination so that the designation of regions for one purpose differed from those established for another purpose. The valiant attempts by a few thoughtful protagonists to develop some clear long-term guidelines on decentralisation and devolution met with little response in practice.

The key benefits of a long-term perspective lie in providing a sense of purpose and direction, forcing the establishment of priorities and helping to ensure more cohesive policies. Long-term economic planning directs attention to questions that have not been faced explicitly, such as the role of the non-traded sector in improving the competitiveness of the traded sector,[10] the balance between export development and the role of the home market as a nursery for new enterprise, and the appropriate degree of devolution and decentralisation of authority and activity. Development policy in Ireland has suffered because the different parts do not fit together so that the instruments have often been implemented on a piecemeal basis, sometimes even working against each other.

Finally, the absence of a long-term perspective was a factor in inducing policy-makers and the community at large to take economic success too readily for granted. The state began with the notion that economic success was virtually automatic once self-government was attained. It was long before the lesson sank home that economic success does not come without much effort and planning. The lesson was no sooner learned, however, than it was forgotten again following the measure of success attained in the 1960s. A sense of historical perspective would have encouraged greater modesty about the achievements of the 1960s by recognising that they depended heavily on a combination of uniquely favourable external and internal circumstances. Ireland of course was not alone in finding it difficult to adjust to the oil shocks and subsequent depressions: every country experienced such difficulties. What was more pronounced in Ireland than in most countries, however, was the slowness in recognising the new realities and adjusting to them, resulting among other things in the exceptionally large and unsustainable build-up of national debt.

12.3.3 Inadequate attention to human resources

Looking at policy statements and planning documents since the foundation of the state, it is striking how little attention was given to the dimension of human capital. Yet this dimension is central to the creation and exploitation of comparative advantage, so much so that the chief impediments to economic development in Ireland have been people-related rather than finance-related. These impediments embrace such factors as ineffective management, poor marketing expertise, low levels of technological competence and inappropriate institutions and structures.

To some extent the deficiency arose from the education system, which went its own way without much serious examination of the purposes of education, and which for long had little connection with the world of work. We suggested in Chapter 7 that, without in any way subordinating education to the needs of economic development, much more might have been done to relate education to economic life. The greater problem, however, lay not just in deficiencies in the education system, but in the failure to make adequate use of the output of the education system. Thus, Ireland continued to export expensively trained scientists, engineers and technicians because Irish firms did not have sufficient resources to engage in innovative R & D and marketing: yet the industrial incentives were not geared to address this dilemma.[11] In agriculture, as shown in Chapter 10, the unwillingness to reform the land tenure and transfer system reinforced the serious deficiencies in the managerial qualities of farmers, which could not be overcome by the advisory services. In the services sector, extensive restrictive practices were tolerated in trades and professions, which limited competition and employment opportunities.

Moreover, despite the continually expressed concern about employment, there has been little evidence of any sustained willingness among the community at large to give priority to this goal in preference to raising living standards in the short-term. It is hard to conceive that this situation would have continued had Ireland been unable to dispose of its labour surplus so readily through emigration. There is of course no certainty that the resulting population pressures would necessarily have had a beneficial outcome: Ireland in that case might have sunk further into poverty. If, however, one takes the view, as we do, that solutions were possible, although difficult, and that the Irish are as capable as other peoples of devising and implementing such solutions if they really have to, then the so-called 'safety valve' of emigration was detrimental to the long-term development of the economy. It served to reinforce what Meenan categorised as the 'profoundly conservative' nature of Irish society. It tempered the urgency of reforming key institutions — such as the public administration, the educational system and the trade union movement — to meet the needs of the Irish situation. Because of the ease of emigration, it was possible for those remaining to enjoy a rising living standard without the disruptions that generally accompany rapid economic progress. The complacency induced by this situation of 'more for less' in the short term was corrosive in its implications for the longer term — most of all, perhaps, in undervaluing the human contribution to economic development and the need to adapt the major institutions through which that contribution is expressed.

12.3.4 Did independence matter?

The weaknesses in performance we have identified basically amount to a failure to overcome the key problems which existed at independence. Although in the course of independence the structure of the economy has been changed substantially for the better, and dependence on the slowly growing UK reduced, many of the major problems still remain unresolved. Indigenous industry is still weak, the potential of the land has not been adequately exploited, the labour surplus problem is as daunting as ever, and living standards have fallen further behind all Western European countries except Britain. It may be asked then if independence made a fundamental difference to the development of the economy. Any answer to this question, of course, is highly speculative because it is impossible to know how the economy would have fared had the Republic remained part of the UK. In particular, since such an arrangement was politically unacceptable, it could only have been maintained by coercion involving an incalculable degree of violence.

Even in the improbable event that the Republic had remained peacefully within the UK, there would undoubtedly have been significant differences in some sub-periods and in some sectors as compared with the actual evolution of the economy. Irish agriculture, for example, would have enjoyed greater prosperity between the 1930s and the 1960s, but there would have been far less indigenous manufacturing activity in the 1930s and fewer multinational enterprises from the 1960s onwards. Over the period as a whole, the differences in many areas would probably be less marked, but with the likelihood that the overall growth of output and employment would have been somewhat lower had Ireland stayed in the UK. Population would probably have fallen even more, but on the other hand, living standards might very well have been higher given that Ireland would have benefited from the UK fiscal transfers and would not have incurred the burden of such a huge national debt. In other words, the pattern might have been very much a continuation of that established in the half century or so before independence. If so, then independence *did* make a difference. It raised the overall economic growth rate sufficient to at least arrest the decline in population, though not enough to absorb fully the perennial labour surplus or to secure a faster growth in average living standards. This achievement is of course much less than was expected at independence, but then, as we have said, such expectations were unrealistically high.

12.4 THE FUTURE OUTLOOK

One critical factor remains to be considered in assessing the economic performance since independence — namely, the extent to which it has placed Ireland in a better position to develop in the future. Even if performance up to now is judged to be mediocre, nevertheless it would emerge in a better light if it had established a solid basis for further progress.

In many important respects Ireland is indeed structurally better adapted to develop economically in the future than it was in the 1920s. No longer is it dependent on one slowly growing market (the UK) and one slowly growing product (food). Instead, as an established member of the EEC, it has free access to a vast market, and its export structure is heavily concentrated in modern manufactures with a good growth record and good growth prospects. Managerial and industrial skills have been improved and are more widely dispersed among the labour force. A much smaller proportion of the labour force is now located in activities subject to inevitable decline.

The fact that from the late 1950s to the late 1970s, the Irish growth rate of GDP matched or exceeded the mean European rate, seemed to hold out the hope that Ireland had already entered a higher growth trajectory. Yet as became abundantly clear in the 1980s, the acceleration in the Irish growth rate of GDP depended too much on factors that were not sustained,

265

and in some cases, were unsustainable. These factors included the buoyant international environment and favourable terms of trade up to 1973, the growing dependence on external debt afterwards, and the initial benefits of the Common Agricultural Policy. The international outlook is now problematic, with little prospect of a resumption of the buoyancy of the quarter century following the Second World War. Irish agriculture again faces market constraints affecting both the quantity and price of output. The inescapable task of slowing down the growth of national debt will inevitably depress home demand. Even more fundamentally, the excessive dependence on foreign enterprise and the weakness of indigenous industry have been exposed. The consequences in the 1980s have been a considerable decline in GDP growth, falling living standards, a vast rise in unemployment and a resumption of heavy emigration.

The completion of the internal market within the EEC, scheduled for 1992, holds out major problems as well as major opportunities for Ireland. The opportunities lie in the fact that, for a small country inescapably committed in an outward-orientated direction, the removal of non-tariff and other barriers offers great scope for increased exports. The problems are mainly those inherent in the impact of closer economic union among areas with widely different living standards where fiscal transfers are inadequate. We noted in Chapter 5 the problems created in the 1920s and 1930s for the Northern Ireland Exchequer until it was accorded similar transfer arrangements to the rest of the UK.

In relation to the EEC, in 1977 the MacDougall Report, following a study of the fiscal transfer arrangements in five existing federations (Germany, USA, Canada, Australia and Switzerland) and three unitary states (France, Italy and the UK), concluded that a Community budget, excluding defence spending, of 5–7 per cent of Community GDP would be the minimum necessary to support a viable monetary union.[12] Even then, they felt that the budget would require to be concentrated much more than at present in reducing geographical disparities in living standards. The report recognised that such a level of funding was unlikely to be forthcoming for the foreseeable future, but even its more modest suggestion for a budget of 2–2½ per cent of Community GDP is not yet under serious consideration.

Moves towards closer economic union, without an accompanying increase in fiscal transfers, is bound to create strong pressures on the Irish Exchequer and to intensify the imbalanced nature of the convergence that has been taking place since 1973. The latter is illustrated by the fact that while there has been considerable convergence in Irish productivity, as measured by GDP per worker (from 69 per cent of the EEC average in 1973 to 81 per cent in 1985), this has not brought about a relative improvement in living standards. GDP per head of population in Ireland over the same period has risen only slightly relative to the EEC average (from 59 per cent to 64 per cent), because of faster growth in population and unemployment; while gross national disposable income per head of population — the most comprehensive measure of living standards — has declined relative to the EEC average.

Notwithstanding these difficulties, there are still some grounds for optimism about Ireland's capacity to develop economically in the future. There is now much greater recognition of the constraints and opportunities facing Ireland, and a considerable body of experience on which to draw in seeking solutions, while the EEC connection forces Ireland to look to other models besides the UK. Past experience suggests that the failure to establish a longer-term perspective was a serious handicap, resulting in strategies that were not fully thought through, and in many *ad hoc* and mutually inconsistent decisions. In our view, future progress in realising Ireland's development potential will depend much on the degree to which this defect can be overcome. Moreover, we also believe that employment creation and the development of human resources should be central to any such long-term perspective — not only because they are desirable objectives in themselves but also because of their potential for motivating the community at large.

Economic growth is obviously a necessary condition for a major assault on unemployment, so that measures to raise the rate of growth are essential instruments. However, while economic growth is a necessary condition of employment growth in Irish conditions, it may not be a sufficient condition. If development were to continue along the path increasingly evident since the 1960s, whereby productivity growth equalled or exceeded the growth of output in the traded-goods sectors, then there is no guarantee that such development on its own would generate adequate employment growth elsewhere in the economy. This is so for several reasons — the tendency for such a pattern of development to push up real wages throughout the economy to a level that restricts employment possibilities, the high proportion of any increase in incomes that is spent abroad on imported goods or foreign holidays, and, where foreign firms are concerned, the repatriation of much of the non-labour surplus. It is not our purpose here to argue how the dilemma is best resolved.[13] Rather, we wish to emphasise that as far as the employment objective is concerned, the *pattern* of development can be as crucial as the *rate* of development, and that only in the context of formulating a longer-term strategy can such issues be constructively addressed.

There can be no certainty that Ireland will take hold of its future in the manner suggested. Neither can there be any certainty as to what kind of world it will have to operate in. Nevertheless, the disappointments as well as the achievements of the past have produced a greater awareness of economic realities. Provided Ireland can recognise its past failings, and begin to learn to overcome them, then its potential for future development is considerable.

NOTES

1. J. Meenan, *The Irish economy since 1922* (Liverpool University Press, 1970), pp. 270–5.
2. P. Lynch, 'The economics of independence: some unsettled questions of Irish economics' in P. Lynch and C.F. Carter, *Planning for economic development*, Pamphlet no. 5 (Tuairim, Dublin, 1959), p. 3.
3. Meenan, *The Irish economy*, p. 276.
4. E. O'Halpin, *The decline of the Union: British government in Ireland 1892–1920* (Gill and Macmillan, Dublin, 1987), p. 217.
5. See, for example, T.J. Barrington, *From big government to local government: the road to decentralisation* (Institute of Public Administration, Dublin, 1975); and J. Lee, 'A third division team?', *Seirbhís Phoiblí*, vol. 6, no. 1 (January 1985).
6. E. O'Halpin, *The decline of the Union*, p. 217.
7. Meenan, *The Irish economy*, p 246.
8. Foremost among the notable exceptions is the work of John Hume, a Northern Irish member of the European Parliament. See, for instance, his report *The regional problems of Ireland*, (Committee on Regional Policy and Regional Planning of the European Parliament, 1987).
9. Commission of the European Communities, *Report of the study*

group on the role of public finance in European integration: vol. 1, General Report (Brussels, 1977) — known as the MacDougall Report.

10. K. O'Rourke, 'The non-traded sector: services, and building and construction' in J.W. O'Hagan (ed.), *The economy of Ireland: policy and performance*, 5th edn (Irish Management Institute, Dublin, 1987).

11. C. Cooper and N. Whelan, *Science, technology and industry in Ireland*, Report to the National Science Council (Stationery Office, Dublin, 1973).

12. Commission of the European Communities, *Report of the study group on the role of public finance.*

13. For a full discussion, see D. Conniffe and K.A. Kennedy (eds), *Employment and unemployment policy for Ireland* (Economic and Social Research Institute, Dublin, 1984); and K.A. Kennedy, *The unemployment crisis*, 1985 Busteed Memorial Lecture (Cork University Press, Cork, 1985).

SELECT BIBLIOGRAPHY

GENERAL

Bristow, J.A. and Tait, A. (eds) (1968) *Economic policy in Ireland*, Institute of Public Administration, Dublin

Gillmor, D.A. (1985) *Economic activities in the Republic of Ireland — a geographical perspective*, Gill and Macmillan, Dublin

Kennedy, K.A. and Bruton, R. (1975) *The Irish economy*, Studies, Economic and Financial Series no. 10, Commission of the European Communities, Brussels

Lyons, F.S.L. (1971) *Ireland since the Famine*, Weidenfeld and Nicolson, London

Meenan, J.F. (1970) *The Irish economy since 1922*, Liverpool University Press, Liverpool

O'Hagan, John (ed.) (1987) *The economy of Ireland: policy and performance*, 5th edn, Irish Management Institute, Dublin

CHAPTER 1

Beckett, J.C. and Glassock, R.E. (1967) *Belfast: the origin and growth of an industrial city*, British Broadcasting Company, London

Cullen, L.M. (1987) *An economic history of Ireland since 1660*, 2nd edn, Batsford, London

Daly, M.E. (1981) *Social and economic history of Ireland since 1800*, Educational Company of Ireland, Dublin

Kennedy, L. and Ollerenshaw, P. (eds) (1985) *An economic history of Ulster 1820–1939*, Manchester University Press

Lee, J.J. (1973) *The modernisation of Irish society 1848–1918*, Gill and Macmillan, Dublin

Lynch, P. and Vaizey, J. (1960) *Guinness's brewery in the Irish economy 1759–1876*, Cambridge University Press

Mokyr, J. (1985) *Why Ireland starved: a quantitative and analytical history of the Irish economy 1800–1850*, 2nd edn, Allen and Unwin, London

Ó Gráda, C. (1984) 'Irish agricultural output before and after the Famine', *Journal of European Economic History*, vol. 13, no. 1, spring

O'Malley, E. (1981) 'The decline of Irish industry in the nineteenth century', *Economic and Social Review*, vol. 13, no. 1, October

Solow, B.L. (1971) *The land question and the Irish economy 1870–1903*, Harvard University Press, Cambridge, Mass.

CHAPTER 2

Commission of Inquiry into Banking, Currency and Credit (1938) *Reports*, Stationery Office, Dublin

Fanning, Ronan, (1978) *The Irish Department of Finance 1922–58*, Institute of Public Administration, Dublin

Geary, R.C. (1951) 'Irish economic development since the Treaty', *Studies*, vol. xl, December

Gwynn, D. (1928) *The Irish Free State 1922–1927*, Macmillan, London

Hobson, B. (ed.) (1932) *Saorstát Éireann Official Handbook*, The Talbot Press, Dublin

Johnson, D. (1985) *The interwar economy in Ireland*, Economic and Social History Society of Ireland, Dublin

Neary, J.P. and Ó Gráda, C. (1986) 'Protection, economic war and structural change: the 1930s in Ireland', *Working Paper, University College Dublin Centre for Economic Research*, no. 40

Nowlan, K.B. and Williams, T.D. (eds) (1969) *Ireland in the war years and after, 1939–51*, Gill and Macmillan, Dublin

Ryan, W.J.L. (1949) 'The nature and effects of protective policy in Ireland 1922–1939', unpublished PhD thesis, Trinity College, Dublin

CHAPTER 3

Department of Finance (1958) *Economic development*, Stationery Office, Dublin

FitzGerald, G. (1968) *Planning in Ireland*, Institute of Public Administration, Dublin, and Political and Economic Planning, London

Gibson, N.J. and Spencer, J.E. (eds) (1977) *Economic activity in Ireland: a study of two open economies*, Gill and Macmillan, Dublin

Kennedy, F. (1975) *Public social expenditure in Ireland*, Broadsheet Series no. 11, Economic and Social Research Institute, Dublin

Kennedy, K.A. and Dowling, B.R. (1975) *Economic growth in Ireland: the experience since 1947*, Gill and Macmillan, Dublin, and Barnes and Noble, New York

Lee, J.J. (ed.) (1979) *Ireland 1945–70*, Gill and Macmillan, Dublin

National Industrial and Economic Council (1967) *Report on full employment*, Stationery Office, Dublin

Norton, D. (1975) *Problems in economic planning and policy formation in Ireland, 1958–1974*, Broadsheet Series No. 12, Economic and Social Research Institute, Dublin

Tait, A.A. and Bristow, J.A. (1972) *Ireland: some problems of a developing economy*, Gill and Macmillan, Dublin, and Barnes and Noble, New York

CHAPTER 4

Bacon, P. (ed.) (1986) *Medium-term outlook 1986–1990*, Economic and Social Research Institute, Dublin, no. 1, February
—— Durkan, J. and O'Leary, J. (1982) *The Irish economy: policy and performance 1972–1981*, Economic and Social Research Institute, Dublin
Bradley, J., Fanning, C.M., Prendergast, C. and Wynne, M. (1985) *Medium-term analysis of fiscal policy in Ireland: a macroeconometric study of the period 1973–1980*, General Research Series no. 122, Economic and Social Research Institute, Dublin
Dowling, B.R. and Durkan, J. (eds) (1978) *Irish economic policy: a review of major issues*, Economic and Social Research Institute, Dublin
FitzGerald, J.D. (1986) *The national debt and economic policy in the medium term*, Policy Research Series no. 7, Economic and Social Research Institute, Dublin
Kennedy, K.A. (1982) 'Poverty and changes in the socio-economic environment in Ireland 1971–1981' in P. Berwick and M. Burns (eds), *Conference on Poverty 1981*, Council for Social Welfare, Dublin
National Economic and Social Council (1986) *A strategy for development 1986–1990: growth, employment and fiscal balance*, Report no. 83, NESC, Dublin
National Planning Board (1984) *Proposals for plan 1984–87*, Stationery Office, Dublin
Ó Gráda, C. and Thom, R. (eds) (1987) *Perspectives on economic policy*, Centre for Economic Research, University College, Dublin, no. 1

CHAPTER 5

Bradley, J.F. and Dowling, B. (1983) *Industrial development in Northern Ireland and in the Republic of Ireland*, Report no. 9, Co-operation North, Belfast and Dublin
Gibson, N.J. (1984) 'The impact of the Northern Ireland crisis on the economy', paper presented to the Conference, 'Northern Ireland — the mind of a community in crisis', College of William and Mary, Williamsburg, Virginia, USA, September
Government of Northern Ireland (1965) *Economic development in Northern Ireland, including the report of the economic consultant* (Professor T. Wilson), HMSO, Belfast
Harvey, S. and Rea, D. (1982) *The Northern Ireland economy, with particular reference to industrial development*, Ulster Polytechnic Innovation and Research Centre, Newtownabbey, Co. Antrim
Isles, K.S. and Cuthbert, N. (1957) *An economic survey of Northern Ireland*, HMSO, Belfast

Northern Ireland Economic Council (1981) *Employment patterns in Northern Ireland 1950–80*, Report no. 23, Northern Ireland Economic Development Office, Belfast

Rowthorn, R. (1981) 'Northern Ireland: an economy in crisis', *Cambridge Journal of Economics*, vol. 5, no. 1, March

Sheehy, S.J., O'Brien, J.T. and McClelland, S.D. (1981) *Agriculture in Northern Ireland and the Republic of Ireland*, Paper III, Co-operation North, Dublin and Belfast

Simpson, J. (1983) 'Economic development: cause or effect in the Northern Irish conflict' in J. Darby (ed.), *Northern Ireland — the background to the conflict*, Appletree Press, Belfast

Wilson, T. (ed.) (1955) *Ulster under home rule: a study of the problems of Northern Ireland*, Oxford University Press, London

CHAPTER 6

Foley, A. and Walbridge, P. (1981) *The socio-economic position of Ireland within the European Economic Community*, National Economic and Social Council Report no. 58, Stationery Office, Dublin

Maddison, A. (1982) *Phases of capitalist development*, Oxford University Press, Oxford

Matthews, R.C.O., Feinstein, C.H. and Odling-Smee, J.C. (1982) *British economic growth 1856–1973*, Clarendon Press, Oxford

New Ireland Forum (1983) *A comparative description of the economic structure and situation, North and South*, Stationery Office, Dublin

Northern Ireland Economic Council (1983) *Economic strategy: historical growth performance*, no. 38, Northern Ireland Economic Development Office, Belfast

CHAPTER 7

Cogan, D.J. (1978) *The Irish services sector: a study of productive efficiency*, Stationery Office, Dublin

Commission on Emigration and Other Population Problems, 1948–1954 (1954) *Reports*, Stationery Office, Dublin

Conniffe, D. and Kennedy, K.A. (eds) (1984) *Employment and unemployment policy for Ireland*, Economic and Social Research Institute, Dublin

Danaher, G., Frain, P. and Sexton, J. (1985) *Manpower policy in Ireland*, Report no. 82, National Economic and Social Council, Dublin

Drudy, P.J. (1985) 'Irish population change and emigration since independence' in P.J. Drudy (ed.), *Irish studies 4: the Irish in America*, Cambridge University Press, Cambridge

Geary, R.C. and Hughes, J.G. (1970) *Certain aspects of non-agricultural unemployment in Ireland*, General Research Series no. 52, Economic and Social Research Institute, Dublin

Kennedy, R.E. (1973) *The Irish: emigration, marriage and fertility*, University of California Press, Berkeley

Ross, M. (1986) *Employment in the public domain in recent decades*, General Research Series no. 127, Economic and Social Research Institute, Dublin

Survey Team appointed by Minister for Education (1965) *Investment in education*, Stationery Office, Dublin

Tussing, A.D. (1978) *Irish educational expenditures — past, present and future*, General Research Series no. 92, Economic and Social Research Institute, Dublin

Walsh, B.M. (1968) *Some Irish population problems reconsidered*, General Research Series no. 42, Economic and Social Research Institute, Dublin

—— (1974) 'Population policy in developed countries: Ireland' in B. Berelson (ed.), *Population policy in developed countries*, McGraw-Hill Inc., New York, and ESRI Reprint no. 40

CHAPTER 8

Capital Investment Advisory Committee (1958) *Third report*, Stationery Office, Dublin

Daly, M.E. (1984) 'Government finance for industry in the Irish Free State: the Trade Loans (Guarantee) Acts', *Irish Economic and Social History*, vol. xi

McAleese, D. (1971–2) 'Capital inflow and direct foreign investment in Ireland 1952 to 1970', *Journal of the Statistical and Social Inquiry Society of Ireland*, vol. xxii, part iv

—— (1984) 'Is there a want of capital in Ireland'?, *Administration*, vol. 31, no. 4

O'Connell, T. (1985–6) 'The flow of funds 1960–1985', *Journal of the Statistical and Social Inquiry Society of Ireland*, vol. xxv, part iii

Roche, F., Dowling, P., Walsh, M., Hourihan, A., Murray, J. (1984) *The role of the financial system in financing the traded sectors*, Report no. 76, National Economic and Social Council, Dublin

Vaughan, R.N. (1980) *Measures of the capital stock in the Irish manufacturing sector, 1945–1973*, General Research Series no. 103, Economic and Social Research Institute, Dublin

Whitaker, T.K. (1948–9) 'Ireland's external assets', *Journal of the Statistical and Social Inquiry Society of Ireland*, vol. xviii, part ii

—— (1955–6) 'Capital formation, savings and economic progress', *Journal of the Statistical and Social Inquiry Society of Ireland*, vol. xix, part iv

CHAPTER 9

Committee on Costs and Competitiveness (1981) *Report*, Stationery Office, Dublin

Coombes, D. (ed.) (1983) *Ireland and the European Communities: ten years of membership*, Gill and Macmillan, Dublin

Dowling, B.R. (1970) 'Post-war tourism in Ireland and western Europe', unpublished MA thesis, University College, Dublin

Drudy, P.J. and McAleese D. (eds) (1984) *Irish studies 3: Ireland and the European Community*, Cambridge University Press, Cambridge

FitzGerald, J.D. (1987) *The determinants of Irish imports*, General Research Series no. 135, Economic and Social Research Institute, Dublin

Geary, P.T. (1976) 'Lags in the transmission of inflation: some preliminary estimates', *Economic and Social Review*, vol. 7, no. 4, July

McAleese, D. (1971) *Effective tariffs and the structure of industrial protection in Ireland*, General Research Series no. 62, Economic and Social Research Institute, Dublin

—— (1987) 'European integration and the Irish economy', *Administration*, June

McHugh, D. (1984–5) 'Trade, growth and the role of demand: the experience of Ireland since 1947', *Journal of the Statistical and Social Inquiry Society of Ireland*, vol. xxv, part ii

O'Hagan, J.W. and Harrison, M.J. (1984) 'UK and US visitor expenditure in Ireland: some econometric findings', *Economic and Social Review*, vol. 15, no. 3, April

Whitaker, T.K. (1973) 'From protection to free trade — the Irish experience', *Administration*, vol. 21, no. 4

CHAPTER 10

Baillie, I.F. and Sheehy, S.J. (1971) *Irish agriculture in a changing world*, Oliver and Boyd, Edinburgh

Boyle, G.E. (1987) *How technically efficient is Irish agriculture? — methods and measurement*, An Foras Talúntais, Dublin

Breen, R. and Hannan, D.F. (1987) 'Family farming in Ireland' in Boguslaw Galeski and Eugene Wilkening (eds), *Family farming in Europe and America*, Westview Press, Boulder, Colorado

Conway, A.G. and O'Hara, P. (1986) 'Education of farm children', *Economic and Social Review*, vol. 17, no. 4, July

Crotty, R. (1966) *Irish agricultural production: its volume and structure*, Cork University Press, Cork

Drudy, P.J. (ed.) (1982) *Irish studies 2: Ireland: land, politics and people*, Cambridge University Press, Cambridge

Interdepartmental Committee on Land Structure Reform (1978) *Final Report*, Stationery Office, Dublin

Murphy, J.A. (1976) *A comparative study of output, value-added and growth in Irish and Dutch agriculture*, National Economic and Social Council Report no. 24, Stationery Office, Dublin
—— O'Connell, J.J. and Sheehy, S.J. (1977) *Alternative growth rates in Irish agriculture*, National Economic and Social Council Report no. 34, Stationery Office, Dublin
O'Connor, R. (1961) *The world meat situation with special reference to Ireland*, Central Statistics Office, Dublin, Technical Series no. 2, supplement to *Irish Trade Journal and Statistical Bulletin*, June
Sheehy, S.J. and O'Connor, R. (1985) *Economics of Irish agriculture*, Institute of Public Administration, Dublin

CHAPTER 11

Cooper, C. and Whelan, N. (1973) *Science, technology and industry in Ireland*, Report to the National Science Council, Stationery Office, Dublin
Fitzpatrick, J. and Kelly, J.H. (eds) (1985) *Perspectives on Irish industry*, Irish Management Institute, Dublin
Kennedy, K.A. (1971) *Productivity and industrial growth: the Irish experience*, Clarendon Press, Oxford
—— and Healy, T. (1985) *Small-scale manufacturing industry in Ireland*, General Research Series no. 125, Economic and Social Research Institute, Dublin
McAleese, D. (1977) *A profile of grant-aided industry in Ireland*, Industrial Development Authority, Dublin
O'Farrell, P.N. (1986) *Entrepreneurs and industrial change: the process of change in Irish manufacturing*, Irish Management Institute, Dublin
O'Malley, E.J. (1980) *Industrial policy and development: a survey of literature from the early 1960s*, National Economic and Social Council Report no. 56, Stationery Office, Dublin
—— (forthcoming, 1988) *Unequal competition: the problem of late development and Irish industry*
O'Neill, H. (1971) *Spatial planning in the small economy: a case study of Ireland*, Praeger, New York and London
Survey Team (1967) *Survey of grant-aided industry*, Stationery Office, Dublin
Telesis Consultancy Group (1982) *A review of industrial policy*, Report no. 64, National Economic and Social Council, Dublin

CHAPTER 12

Barrington, T.J. (1975) *From big government to local government: the road to decentralisation*, Institute of Public Administration, Dublin

Barry, Frank, (1987) 'Between tradition and modernity: cultural values and the problems of Irish society', *Centre for Economic Research Policy Paper, University College, Dublin*, no. 23

Kennedy, K.A (ed.) (1986) *Ireland in transition: economic and social change since 1960*, Mercier Press, Cork and Dublin

Lee, J.J. (ed.) (1985)*Ireland: towards a sense of place*, Cork University Press, Cork

Litton, F. (ed.) (1982) *Unequal achievement*, Institute of Public Administration, Dublin

Lynch, P. (1959) 'The economics of independence: some unsettled questions of Irish economics' in P. Lynch and C.F. Carter, *Planning for economic development*, Tuairim Pamphlet no. 5, Dublin

McAleese, D. (1978) 'Political independence and economic performance: Ireland outside the United Kingdom' in E. Nevin (ed.), *The economics of devolution*, University of Wales Press, Cardiff

Meenan, J.F., Fogarty, M.P., Kavanagh, J. and Ryan, W.J.L. (1982) *The economic and social state of the nation*, Economic and Social Research Institute, Dublin

Plunkett, Horace (1982) *Ireland in the new century*, Irish Academic Press, Dublin (first published 1904)

Vaizey, J. (ed.) (1975) *Economic sovereignty and regional policy: a symposium on regional problems in Britain and Ireland*, Gill and Macmillan, Dublin

Whitaker, T.K. (1986) 'Ireland — land of change', Presidential Address to Royal Irish Academy, Dublin, 15 December

Index